DOSTOEVSKY'S RUSSIANS

JANE SHUTTLEWORTH

Copyright © 2012 Jane Shuttleworth

The author thanks D.M. Thomas for permission to use his translation of
Pushkin's poet *The Prophet* on p229

Cover photograph: Sennaya Ploshchad, St Petersburg
© Oleg Mirabo. Used with permission
Author photograph: © Edmund Smith

Typeset using Georg Duffner's EB Garamond

Author contact: janeshuttleworth@gmail.com

All rights reserved.
ISBN-10: 1479292338
ISBN-13: 978-1479292332

For Liz

Thank you for keeping me company on
this strange and wonderful journey

Let it not be held against me, therefore, if I record only that which made an impression upon me personally and which has particularly stuck in my memory. I may well have confused the essential with the irrelevant and even totally omitted the most important aspects... Still, I realise it is better not to make any excuses. I shall do my level best, and the readers themselves will understand that that was all I could do.

(The Karamazov Brothers)

Contents

Preface i

Biographical Note v

One: The Russians 1

Two: Raskolnikov 24

Three: Prince Myshkin 47

Four: Nastasya Filippovna 70

Five: Nikolai Stavrogin 92

Six: Razumikhin and Dunya 114

Seven: Father Zossima 137

Eight: Dmitry Karamazov 160

Nine: Lizaveta Prokofyevna 183

Ten: Kolya 207

Eleven: Pyotr Verkhovensky 230

Twelve: Ivan Karamazov 251

Epilogue 273

Appendix 1: Russian Names 277

Appendix 2: Character Glossary 278

Appendix 3: Reading List 280

Preface

I met him when I was seventeen – a dangerous age for such encounters – and I remember it as vividly as my first kiss. I was chatting to my mother about books late one Sunday evening, and she was suggesting things I ought to read. I was flirting with the idea of applying for Russian at university so she suggested that I try some Dostoevsky. She fussed around a bit, looking for her old copy of *Crime and Punishment,* and when she finally produced it, I thought I'd better have a quick look. I opened the first page, and began to read. Several hours later, I was still reading, absolutely absorbed, unable to tear myself away from the hypnotic attractions of Raskolnikov, and my life would never be quite the same. A few months later, I found myself sitting in an office on the banks of the River Wear, with a hideous hangover, prattling happily away about Dostoevsky, mixing up character names, probably not saying anything particularly clever, but obviously showing enough enthusiasm to get myself a place studying Russian at Durham.

Over the years, my love of Dostoevsky has stayed with me, often dormant as I got stuck into the business of building a life, a career, a family, but never leaving me. From time to time, I would pick up one of his novels, and plunge myself again into Dostoevsky's frenzied, chaotic world, where life is lived with the volume turned right up. Then one day, a couple of years ago, I had dinner with an old friend, now a lecturer in Russian, and he made an incredible suggestion. We were talking about a recent book by a certain well-known cleric, and lamenting that so much that of what is written about Dostoevsky tends to get bogged down either in technical literary criticism, or intense theological discussion – what was needed, we agreed, was a straightforward, down-to-earth introductory guide to Dostoevsky's novels. Why don't you write one, said Philip. Why not? I said. My career was in the doldrums; my brain was atrophying; Dostoevsky tempted me and I took a huge bite.

So, the aim of this book is not to add anything to the shelves of scholarly literature, but to share with others the pleasures of reading Dostoevsky, and to allow his Russians to guide us together, writer and readers, through the cultural, religious, historical and biographical context of his novels. What I hope is that you, the readers of this book, will be inspired to return to Dostoevsky, or to try a novel you haven't read, or to explore new lines of thought, and with this in mind, I have done my very best to avoid giving away the delicious twists and turns of Dostoevsky's plots. (I have still not forgiven the Penguin editor of *Anna Karenina* for revealing Anna's fate in the first paragraph of the introduction, perhaps forgetting that there is always a first time for reading the great classics).

Dostoevsky's genius lies in his astute identification of universal traits of human behaviour and psychology, and he sets them in such a way that successive readers, generation after generation, are seduced into thinking that he is somehow writing about them and their own time. Within his pages, we encounter terrorism and the fear of aimless, angry young men. There's a murder case where it is clear that justice cannot be done because everyone has heard and read too much about the case to guarantee a fair trial. We can read about cases of manic depression, suicide, crises of faith, and ecstatic high-spirits. There are headstrong young girls, hopelessly in love with lost causes, and destructive, passionate men and women, determined to destroy themselves and everyone around them. Nothing changes. He has the intellectual courage to subject his own deeply held beliefs, and those of his enemies, to rigorous tests, stretching them to breaking point to see what happens to them, and in the course of this gives us human life in all its messy, confused reality.

Finally, a brief note on translations. My own favourite translator of Dostoevsky is David Magarshack, whose words tumble off the page and convey the spirit and energy of Dostoevsky's Russian. His translations for Penguin Classics are now out of print, replaced by others that are perhaps more technically accurate, but which lack Magarshack's vivaciousness. The best modern editions by far are Ignat Avsey's translations of *Humiliated and Insulted, The Idiot* and *The Karamazov Brothers*[1] because, like Magarshack, Avsey captures the heady excitement of Dostoevsky's story telling, with a mischievous sense of fun. A list of the translations that I have used here can be found in the bibliography, and I have noted chapter numbers on quotations, so that they can be found in other editions.

I am indebted to friends old and new for their support and help in writing this book. After putting the initial idea into my head, Philip Bullock has given me endless encouragement and advice, and I'm very grateful for his insightful comments, from the first hesitant drafts, to finished manuscript. Long late-night kitchen table conversations with Elizabeth Roberts have given me the chance to thrash out my thoughts and I owe her a huge debt of gratitude for her stimulating ideas, and for her help with editing the manuscript. Thanks also go to Elizabeth Owen, Ignat Avsey, Rosamund Bartlett, Steve and Svetlana le Fleming, Mark

---

[1] The first translator, Constance Garnett, used *The Brothers Karamazov*, in keeping with the Russian word order, and it has stuck that way, even though it makes little sense in English. The distorted word order grabs the attention unnecessarily, making the title seem exotic, when it's supposed to be plain and understated, giving no clue as to the earth-shattering drama within. Ignat Avsey and other modern translators, have reverted to the natural English word order.

Roberts, Alison and Eamon McManus, Claire Llewelyn, Jo Setchell, Rosie Hopkins Felicity Morgan and Ted Shuttleworth for all their varied contributions and conversations, to Oleg Mirabo for generously allowing me to use his stunning photo of Sennaya Square for the cover, and to my dear friends in Moscow, Ira, Oleg and Nastya.

Finally, but most importantly of all, I thank my mother for telling me to read *Crime and Punishment* and setting me off on this great adventure, and Russell and Ned for their love, support and for putting up with piles of books in the kitchen.

BIOGRAPHICAL NOTE

Fyodor Mikhailovich Dostoevsky was born in Moscow, on 30 October 1821,[1] the second son of a military doctor. His father was strict, but loving, and Dostoevsky spent an uneventful childhood in Moscow, and at the family's small country estate at Darovoe in Tula Province. At his father's wishes, Dostoevsky studied at the Academy of Military Engineers in St Petersburg, but by the time he graduated, his father had died and he left the army in 1844 to pursue his literary interests.

The 1840s were years of potentially exciting political developments, in Russia and Europe, characterised by the growth of liberal ideas, and early socialism. In this climate, Dostoevsky's debut novel, *Poor People* (1846) was ecstatically received but his more experimental follow-ups were less successful, and largely forgotten, with the exception of *The Double* – a fascinating psychological study that is perhaps more comprehensible to later readers than it was in the 1840s.

---

[1] Old style date – Russia was, at this point, still using the Julian calendar, which was 12 days behind the Gregorian calendar already adopted in Western Europe. Therefore, in our modern calendar, his birthday falls pleasingly on 11 November, the same day as mine.

The failed European revolutions of 1848 terrified the Russian authorities, and the political atmosphere became increasingly repressive. Dostoevsky had become a member of the Petrashevksy Society, a clandestine political group, and although their activities were mostly confined to discussion, they were all arrested in 1849. After several months imprisoned in the Peter Paul Fortress in St Petersburg, the men were led out onto Semenovsky Square, whereupon the death sentence was pronounced, and they were prepared for the firing squad. This was, however, a sadistic joke on the part of the authorities, for a pardon was immediately announced, and sentences were changed to hard labour in Siberia .

Dostoevsky spent four years in prison, in Omsk, an experience he later fictionalised in *Notes from the House of the Dead* (published 1861). He was released from prison in 1854, but had to remain in exile in Siberia for another five years, until, in 1859 he was finally granted permission to return to European Russia. Dostoevsky had written several novellas and articles during his exile, including *The Village of Stepanchikovo,* and on returning to St Petersburg, he plunged himself back into literary activity and political debate, and made his first visits to Europe. He and his older brother, Mikhail, published two journals, first *Time* and then *Epoch,* and his first major novels were serialised in these journals: *Humiliated and Insulted* (1861) and *Notes from Underground* (1864) prepared the way and then, in 1866, came *Crime and Punishment,* the first of his four great novels.

Whilst exiled in Siberia, Dostoevsky fell in love with Maria Isaeva, the wife of a poor schoolmaster, and they married shortly after her husband's death. The marriage did not get off to a good start when Dostoevsky suffered the horrors of his first major epileptic fit on their wedding night – he had already had a few minor attacks, but this fateful night confirmed Dostoevsky's suspicion about his condition. The marriage was not particularly happy and Maria died in 1864. A few years later, Dostoevsky married his second wife, Anna Snitkina who had been employed as his stenographer.

His second honeymoon was, in some ways, as unlucky as his first, but his new wife was made of much tougher material than Maria and the marriage was long and happy. The newly-weds intended to travel to Europe for a few months, but Dostoevsky had accrued such terrible debts in Russia that they had to remain abroad so that he could avoid debtors' prison. The couple lived an itinerant life, Dostoevsky was possessed by a gambling addiction that continued to destroy their fragile finances, and their adored first child died at the age of just three months, but somehow he managed to write his second masterpiece, *The Idiot* (1868), which, unsurprisingly, is one of his darkest works.

By 1871, the Dostoevskys' financial position had stabilised enough that they were able to return to St Petersburg, and in 1872 Dostoevsky completed his political novel *The Devils*, the first part of which had been published while he was still abroad. Anna took a firm hand on the family finances, managing negotiations with creditors and publishers, and eventually running the business of publishing Dostoevsky's books herself. In the 1870s, Dostoevsky was at last able to enjoy a comfortable family life, dividing his time between St Petersburg and a summer cottage in the small town of Staraya Russa, and taking great delight in bringing up his two children, Lyubov and Fyodor (although a second son, Alexey, tragically died of epilepsy, in 1878, aged just three). His wildly popular one-man journal, *Diary of a Writer*, which was published by the Dostoevskys in 1876-77 established his reputation as one of the country's foremost writers and commentators, but he had to stop publication so that he could concentrate on his last, and greatest novel, *The Karamazov Brothers*.

The first installation of *The Karamazov Brothers* appeared in February 1879, and held Russia transfixed until its completion in November 1880, just a couple of months before Dostoevsky's death. In 1880 Dostoevsky was invited to give a speech during the festivities marking the unveiling of a statue to Russia's greatest poet, Alexander Pushkin, and if there was any doubt about the esteem in which he was held, it was confirmed by the rapturous reception his speech received. When he died of emphysema in January 1881, the crowds of mourners at his funeral stretched back for almost a mile behind his coffin, bringing St Petersburg to a halt, and for a brief moment, the growing political turmoil in Russia came to a standstill, as the country united in grief at the loss of one its greatest writers.

Russians, in general, are men of large, expansive natures, as large and wide as their own vast country, and they are extraordinarily disposed to the fantastic, the chaotic. But it is a great misfortune to possess such a large expansive nature without at the same time possessing a spark of genius.

(Svidrigaylov, Crime and Punishment)

ONE: THE RUSSIANS

The journey that led me to Russia began with an atlas, sometime in the late 1970s. *The Hamlyn Boys' and Girls' Picture Atlas* contained delightfully simple pictures of people in traditional costumes, and the picture for the USSR showed a girl wearing a full-length red kaftan trimmed with gold brocade, with a head-dress to match. As a child, I was fascinated by that picture. I spent ages gazing at it, or copying it and imagining stories for that mysterious princess. I came across a copy of that atlas on a friend's bookshelf not long ago, and turned straight to that page to find this icon of my childhood, looking just as I remembered her. (I'm sure it's no coincidence that my friend, another Russian graduate, has similar memories of that picture).

As I grew up, those initials, USSR, began to hint at something more mysterious and shadowy, for Russia was, of course, the Soviet Union, a dangerous place, where the Bad Guys lived. The fear of annihilation by nuclear bombs hung over us, and the Russians were the stock enemies in fiction, fact and children's games. We were fed tales of the evil communists who suppressed freedom and religion: I particularly remember reading a worthy Scripture Union storybook about Christian children doing brave deeds in Moscow, and thinking that Katya was an incredibly pretty name. The music of Russia began to work its magic on me too: at middle-school we learnt to sing *Kalinka,* that best known of Russian folk songs, and there was Sting's sentimental pop song about the Russians loving their children too, with its haunting pseudo-Slavic tune. The best stories in the Andrew Lang fairy-tale collections were the Russian ones, with their dark forests, bears and (again) the beautiful princesses with pretty names. Even the country's own name mesmerised me, like the name of a beloved person – Russia, that long sssshhh tempting me with the promise of mysterious secrets to be told. It all dripped into my subconscious, creating memories which lay in the depths, waiting for their chance to be useful.[1] Of course this is all too complicated to explain when a Russian asks me why I chose to study their language, so instead, I give them the simple answer: I read too much Dostoevsky as a teenager.

Growing up in a quiet, respectable west-country market town, where the deadening gloom of Thomas Hardy was celebrated at every turn, I found myself attracted like a moth to flame by the passion and exuberance that seemed to explode out of any form of Russian art. The heart-breaking melodies and rich orchestrations of symphonies by Rachmaninov and Tchaikovsky, and the dazzling playfulness of Stravinsky's ballets conjured up big, raw emotions, without any sense of restraint. This was what life should be about, I felt; no messing around with a stiff upper lip, but letting everything out, whether it's utter jubilation, or the depths of despair. I was also beginning to discover Soviet-era poets, particularly Yevtushenko, and even in translation the beauty and anguish of their writing, with so much emotion packed into deceptively simple phrases, was unlike anything I had come across before. Then of course there was Dostoevsky; the big, raw emotions again; the dramatic confrontations; the soul laid bare. If this was what Russia was all about, I wanted it.

---

[1] In *Dostoevsky's Unfinished Journey*, Robin Feuer Miller writes about the importance of submerged childhood memories in Dostoevsky's fiction.

When I started writing this book, I had quixotic ideas about searching for Dostoevsky's Russians in the real world and relating his characters to my own experiences of living in Russia, but I quickly realised that this was very naïve, for I led a very straightforward, un-Dostoevskian existence during the few years that I spent living in Moscow, and I had little to draw upon in the way of real-life examples, although once, on a Siberian train, I was convinced that I was sitting opposite Raskolnikov. As work developed, one theme that particularly caught my imagination was that of Dostoevsky's relationship with the Russian people. As I read about how Dostoevsky endeavoured to reconcile his intense love for the Russian people with the harsh realities that he experienced, particularly during the time he spent in prison in Siberia, I wondered whether he might have something useful to say for those times when we have to confront the worst of what happens in Russia. It's a country with a consistently brutal history; where extravagant, flamboyant wealth comes at the cost of terrible suffering; where a callous and corrupt bureaucracy sucks the soul out of civic life; where poverty, boredom and alcohol drive people to do terrible things; whose leaders think nothing of flaunting their disdain for international opinion and where the elite is utterly indifferent to the needs of anyone else.

There must be times when people think I'm a little deranged for loving Russia so much at a time when the general image of the country is overwhelmingly negative, but still I cheer for their ice-hockey team in the winter Olympics (to the disgust of my Canadian-born son), and I also sometimes ask myself why. Dostoevsky may not recognise the Starbucks coffee shops or the glitzy designer boutiques on Tverskaya Street, but if he were to visit Moscow or St Petersburg today, he would still see the same Russia underneath it all. It seemed therefore that by looking at Dostoevsky's creations, his own Russians, through the prism of his writing, I could add something to the spectrum of views on how Russia has got to where it is today, and remind myself why I love Russia and its people. This, at least, was where I started, but

Dostoevsky and his Russians led me on an entirely different, and surprising, journey, to a destination I never imagined.

Dostoevsky was writing during a time of feverish debate about Russia's relationship with Western Europe; it was a debate that affected literature, art, philosophy and politics, but at the root of it all was the question of how Russia should be governed. It's sometimes characterised as a clash between the dual European and Asiatic natures of this vast country that sprawls across both continents, and it can be traced back to the very origins of Russian national consciousness. Consider, for example, the story told about St Vladimir, Prince of Kiev, the man who brought Christianity to Russia. According to a Byzantine chronicler, St Vladimir had decided that his people needed to adopt one of the great monotheistic faiths, and he carefully considered Islam, Judaism and Western Catholicism before he plumped for Greek Orthodox Christianity – it may be just an embellished legend, but all those faiths are represented in Russia today, and any one of them could plausibly have taken root. Just imagine how much history hinged on that decision.

Having adopted the Greek faith, and acquired its own alphabet, Russian culture largely developed in its own way for the next seven centuries, isolated not only by geography, but also by the Mongol occupation, and then by civil strife and general barbarism, until the 17th century, when Peter the Great dragged his noblemen kicking and screaming into Western Europe, forcing them to abandon their kaftans in favour of European fashions and insisting that they shaved off their beards. He instigated a series of far more important reforms too, modernising the bureaucracy, the church and the military, and he built himself a magnificent new capital, modelled on the great European cities and designed by an Italian architect: St Petersburg, his 'Window on the West'. Slavic Moscow, with its ancient citadel, onion-domed cathedrals and ramshackle narrow streets, was definitely not the place for Peter.

Peter's reforms initiated the great Westerniser-Slavophile battles, and this duality remains part of Russia's identity today. In his notebooks for *The Devils,* in a draft of Stavrogin's late-night conversation with Shatov, Dostoevsky sums it up thus:

A full two hundred yeas of unsteadiness. The entire reform begun by Peter has amounted to as much as taking a rock which had been resting firmly on the ground and standing it up precariously on one end. And so we are standing there, trying to keep our balance. A wind will blow, and we'll be hurled down.[2]

In the 19th century, the Westernisers, as the name suggests, wanted to follow Europe along the path to liberal democracy, whilst according to the Slavophiles, Russia's unique geographical, social and historical circumstances meant that she had to draw upon her own traditions to find a suitable way of governing herself. The question of whether Russia can be governed under a Western democratic model, or whether there is truth in the myth that this vast and unwieldy country needs a strong leader, still remains unresolved; it's a contest that remains sadly academic for as long as the strongmen remain in charge and prevent the democratic alternative from ever having a chance to flourish. The debate remains more open in the field of literature. I recently heard two Russian writers explaining to a British audience how they both thought Russian literature should develop, and whether Russian writers should continue to draw on their own great narrative traditions, or whether, in fact, this is a stale dead end that needs to be refreshed by looking instead to the Western post-modern emphasis on words and meanings. Again, little has changed: the writer who put the case for a Western approach has emigrated to Switzerland, whilst the one who advocated the importance of Russian narrative still lives in St Petersburg.

---

[2] *The Notebooks for The Possessed* ed Edward Wasiolek, University of Chicago Press 1968, p214

Following Peter the Great's reforms, the Russian intelligentsia gradually polarised into Westernising and Slavophile camps, not just in politics, but culturally too. The Slavophiles idolised the Russian peasantry, glorifying the people and their faith, believing, (as, in fact many European socialists did about their own working classes), that the common people were morally superior to their upper-class oppressors, and that the key to building a better society was to draw exclusively on the traditions of the native Russian people. The Westernisers, of whom the best known is the novelist Ivan Turgenev, sought inspiration from the political, social and cultural developments of Western Europe, and were often scornful of anything their own country had to offer, believing that Russia was simply a bit behind and needed to catch up. Slavophiles, on the other hand, were determined that Russia was different and should find her own way, based on her own history and institutions.

The battles between the Westernisers and Slavophiles dominated the cultural life of the 19th century, and occupied considerable literary energy as both sides slugged it out in the pages of their journals and novels. Dostoevsky tends towards the Slavophile end of the spectrum, but in his own way, and with qualifications. He detested the corruption and moral emptiness that he saw in Western European society, and which he mostly blamed on the Catholic church, but neither did he seek to roll back the clock to an imaginary golden age of rural bliss like some of the more naïve Slavophiles. He had a deep-rooted faith in the Russian people, but that love was so deep that it gave him the confidence to think about what could be improved, to see where he thought Russia could learn from the West, and where her own people should take the lead in building a better society that, he believed, would provide a shining light to guide all the world.

To understand more of this all-encompassing Slavophile versus Westerniser debate, it is helpful to look briefly at the way Russian society was organised, and the forces that held it together. It's usual to begin a survey of Russian history with a review of the country's formidable geography: the immense size and the extremes of climate speak for themselves, and we all have our own anecdotes to illustrate the point. Mine comes from my first visit to Russia, in the autumn of 1993, when I spent some time in the Siberian city of Krasnoyarsk for part of my university year abroad. The flight from Moscow to Krasnoyarsk was longer than the London-Moscow leg of the journey, and so, a few weeks after our arrival, when worried relatives heard about tanks on the streets of Moscow and rang to see if we were safe, we all took great delight in pointing out that we were further from Moscow than they were.

Before the modern age, most of the country, even in the European heartland, was almost inaccessible for much of the year. Villages and small towns were cut off by snow in the winter and by equally impassable mud during the spring and autumn, and of course this meant that it was impossible to keep the roads properly maintained, so they were little better even in the summer. Gogol's great novel *Dead Souls* paints a vivid picture of ordinary life in the Russian countryside as his hero Chichikov struggles along the terrible roads from one country estate to another, frequently losing his way, or getting bogged down in mud. Only the great rivers, and later the thin threads of the railway network provided any sort of reliable long-distance transport. With such appalling communication links, the authorities needed some strong buttresses to prop up the whole fragile edifice of the state. Those buttresses were the peasant village, the Tsar and the Orthodox faith.

One important consequence of Russia's geographical circumstances was that, as a proportion of the whole, the population was predominantly rural, and remained so whilst Western Europe was undergoing the upheavals of the industrial revolution and the growth of vast cities. The continuance, well into the 19th century, of the institution of serfdom hindered mobility, not only of the peasants who were tied to their villages, but of the landowning classes too, as they relied on the slave labour on their vast estates to maintain their wealth. The Tsarist authorities perpetually feared the potential for revolt from this vast peasant population, but serfdom usefully allowed them to outsource control and monitoring of the peasantry to the landowners, and movement restrictions on serfs were gradually tightened throughout the 17th and 18th centuries. In return, the landowners benefited from cheap labour and the freedom to (mis)treat their serfs as they saw fit. A massive standing army backed up the landowners, and mopped up surplus manpower, but the rulers feared that this was still not enough, so to support the physical control of the countryside, the Tsars called on divine authority too, encouraging the myth of the ruler anointed by God, the father of his people; a belief inherited, with the Orthodox faith itself, from the Byzantine Empire. Dostoevsky describes how he thinks the relationship between Tsar and people should work, in a speech given at the Slavic Benevolent Society to mark the 25th anniversary of Alexander II's reign:

The ancient truth, which from time immemorial has penetrated into the soul of the Russian people: that their Tsar is also their father, and that children always will come to their father without fear so that he hears from them, with love, of their needs and wishes.[3]

This kind, loving, paternal Tsar was the ideal of which Dostoevsky and others dreamed, even though the reality had never really matched up to the vision, and so these remarks can be seen as a very careful criticism directed at the Tsar but also at those who desired his replacement with constitutional rule. Dostoevsky was passionately moved by the misery and cruelty inflicted on the Russian peasantry and by the sufferings of the urban poor, but in his view, it was ultimately the Tsar's job, as a father to his people, to take steps to improve the lives of ordinary citizens, so

---

[3] *Collected Works* Vol 30 bk 2 p48 / translation Frank p 806

whenever Dostoevsky is critical of the Russian state, he is advocating change from above, not revolution.

Underpinning the power of the Tsar, and helping to keep the people in check, was the national myth of Russian greatness. Russia has never been a single nation state, but a fluctuating empire encompassing many nationalities, religions and languages, including, among others: a large Jewish population; Muslim Tartars and Caucasians; Georgians and Armenians with their own ancient Christian traditions; and northern tribes with animistic and shamanic religions. Russian nationalism has always been strongly promoted as a unifying force and as a means for those in power to assert their authority: time after time, non-Russian ethnic groups are used as scapegoats whenever the stability of the empire comes under threat. Meanwhile, wars against foreign powers can be billed as a spiritual battle to defend the nation's beloved Orthodox Church – something that even Stalin understood when he allowed the church greater freedom during World War II, knowing its power to boost Russian morale.

Orthodox Christianity in the abstract has always played a strong symbolic role in this national myth, but the organised church itself has been, on the whole, an ineffectual body, captured by the government from the time of Peter I onwards, and staffed by what became an increasingly closed caste of poorly-educated priests.[4] The power of the church lay not in its official institutional form, but in the deeply held beliefs of the ordinary people, and the richness of the folk tradition that accompanied it. Thus, when the Russian people needed spiritual comfort or guidance, they tended to turn not to their parish priest, but to the monasteries, particularly those where holy men, known as elders, (*starets,* plural *startsy* in Russian) were in residence. The *startsy* sought God through a doctrine of stillness and contem-

---

[4] Dostoevsky himself was only a couple of generations away from the priestly caste. His paternal grandfather was a priest, and his father was supposed to follow the same career, but escaped his destiny by running off to Moscow to train as a doctor.

plation, and shared their wisdom with the crowds of visitors who came in search of spiritual help. Dostoevsky visited one such holy man, Father Ambrose, at the hermitage of Optina Pustyn after the terrible death of his three-year old son, and the words of consolation he received eventually found their way into the mouth of Father Zossima, the *starets* who guides Alyosha in *The Karamazov Brothers,* as he offers consolation to a mother who has lost her own small child.

The story of the Russian peasantry is a tale of misery. Life in such a hostile climate can never be easy, and the struggle for survival was made worse by the brutalities inflicted on the peasants by Mongol invaders and later by the violent excesses of their own rulers. The endless suffering of the peasantry at the hands of the climate and of men gave rise to strong village institutions, and an ingrained sense of collective responsibility. Two Russian words, *obshchina* and *mir,* describe the structures that governed peasant life: *obshchina* derives from the word for society, and is often translated as 'commune', whilst *mir,* meaning both 'world' and 'peace' was the name given to the village council that governed daily life. The land accorded to the peasants was jointly controlled by the members of the *obshchina* and the community was collectively responsible for the payment of taxes, the provision of men for military service and the administration of justice for minor crimes – a collectivist principle known as *sobornost'*. The *obshchina* also acted as a social welfare system, with richer peasants being expected to support the poor in times of hardship. Unsurprisingly, this system, along with the parallel *artel*, or artisans' cooperative, was looked on as a potential model for the society of the future by some socialists in Russia and Europe, who thought that this communal peasant land ownership would enable Russia to bypass the painful capitalist phase of social development, and head straight for full communism.[5]

---

[5] Engels admitted that the Russian communal system could be useful, but only if it survived the ravages of the bourgeois capitalism that he and Marx considered to be an essential step on the road to communism.

The contract between the Tsar and the landowners was broken with the emancipation of the serfs in 1861 and the social structures of Russia showed signs of moving towards a Western European model. The peasants were able, to some extent, to buy and sell property or leave the land altogether, and the landowners themselves found it increasingly easy to sell their estates to entrepreneurial, wealthy peasants and take up new professions or found new businesses in the cities. The justice system had to be overhauled to cater for the new arrangements, and jury trials and open courtrooms were introduced – something Dostoevsky took great advantage of in his fiction and journalism.

These three buttresses of Russian society that I've briefly outlined – the Tsar, Orthodoxy and peasant life – all come together in Dostoevsky's novels and in his own idiosyncratic vision of Russia's future. He fused the three into his particular brand of Russian nationalism which was known as *pochvennichestvo*, meaning 'of the soil', and in the early 1860s, he and his brother Mikhail set out their agenda through the pages of their journals, first *Time* and later, *Epoch*. *Pochvennichestvo* was different from the naïve idealism of the Slavophiles, for it did not deny the possibility of learning from the West. The Dostoevskys wanted to fuse the knowledge and culture of the educated upper-classes with the quintessentially Russian virtues of the ordinary people. This fusion would be brought about by the *return* of the intelligentsia to their native soil, bringing with them the best of what they had acquired from other cultures. Later, in *Diary of a Writer*, in a passage titled *On the Love of the People. The Necessary Contract with the People* Dostoevsky sums it up thus:

"Who is better – we or the people? Do the people have to follow us, or do we have to follow the people?" – This is what everybody says ... I shall candidly reply: it is we who have to bow before the people and await from them everything – both thought and expression; it is we who must bow before the people's truth and recognise it as such ... however, we must bow on one condition only ...

that the people accept from us those numerous things which we have brought with us.[6]

A similar idea emerged later in the Populist movement of the 1870s and 1880s. Many wealthy young people, feeling that their riches and comforts had come at the expense of the peasantry, actively went out to the countryside to live among the people, to learn from them and to teach them, although the peasants themselves were often confused and baffled by their attempts. The ethos was similar to that which inspires armies of privileged youngsters today to seek fulfilment by doing good works in the developing world, and its effectiveness was just as patchy. This unprecedented contact with the peasantry and first-hand experience of their misery then drove many young people towards more extreme political positions, and it was the Populists who were responsible for a frighteningly familiar spate of terrorist attacks on leading officials, culminating in the assassination of Tsar Alexander II.

Dostoevsky, who, as we will see, had spent most of his literary career probing and exposing what he saw as the weaknesses of the radicals suddenly found himself, in the last decade of his life, in extraordinary sympathy with the generation who were their immediate successors, although the terrorism appalled him.[7] In turn, the younger generation hung on his every word, and it was his search for salvation in the soul of the Russian people, as well as his own personal history, that inspired their devotion. Dostoevsky was excited to see that his own ideas were now being put into action; he was eager to maintain contact with the younger generation; and, as we will see in more detail in Chapter Ten, his fiction responded with thoughtful concern to the Populist movement.

---

[6] *Diary of a Writer* p 204 (Feb 1876, Chapter 1, section 2).

[7] Alexander II was assassinated just a few weeks after Dostoevsky's death. Anna Dostoevskaya remarks in her *Reminiscences* (p346) that had her husband survived that long, the shock of the Tsar's death would probably have killed him.

The affection felt for Dostoevsky by the younger generation, and by the Russian public in general, was never more visible during his life than at the unveiling of the statue in Moscow to Russia's greatest poet, Alexander Pushkin, an event that was accompanied by a week of celebrations, speeches and poetry readings, and which culminated in a truly triumphant speech given by Dostoevsky. The Pushkin festivities also marked the climax of one particular skirmish in the on-going Westerniser-Slavophile war, for the other key speaker was the novelist Ivan Turgenev. Turgenev was the polar opposite of Dostoevsky: aristocratic, cosmopolitan, and brought up as an atheist, he was a passionate Westerniser who spent long periods living abroad, and who frequently upset his fellow countrymen by sharply criticising Russia. Dostoevsky and Turgenev lurched from initial friendship and literary comradeship to vicious and, at times, very personal confrontation as they faced each other across ideological barricades. Turgenev, as we will see, provided Dostoevsky with the seeds that sprouted into the complexities of Raskolnikov, and he himself was brutally satirised as the pompous writer Karmazinov in *The Devils*.

In their speeches, both writers used Pushkin's legacy as a peg on which to hang their own beliefs. Turgenev spoke about how truly great poets transcended national boundaries, and cited Shakespeare, Molière and Goethe as examples. He hesitated to raise Pushkin to this level, leaving the question of his global legacy unanswered, and spoke instead about the poet's great contribution to the Russian language and his role as the founder of modern Russian literature. Dostoevsky had no such doubts. He used examples from Pushkin's work to express his own particular message about Russian society through the prism of Pushkin's artistic development, and he described Pushkin as having already prophesised the same role for the Russian people that Dostoevsky now identified. He discusses first how Pushkin imitated European poets before finding his own distinctive Russian voice, and how Pushkin's early works dealt with 'wanderers' – educated Russians whose European ways alienated them from the Russian people, and who thus found themselves lost and rootless in their own land. Aleko, hero of *The Gypsies* attempts to find a place for himself by living with a roving band of gypsies, and Pushkin's greatest hero, Eugene Onegin, is so detached from his native soil that he is unable to see the true Russian virtues in Tatyana, the simple young girl who is in love with him. Dostoevsky calls Tatyana the 'perfect Russian woman' and suggests that Pushkin should have named his poem after her, not Onegin.

In direct contradiction to Turgenev, Dostoevsky then goes on to assert that Pushkin in fact surpasses other great European writers, because he is able to understand other nations to such an extent that he can embody their own characteristics in his works: for example, he claims that Shakespeare's Italians are indubitably English, whereas you could never guess that Pushkin's *Don Juan* had not been written by a Spaniard. He ascribes this not to a mere talent for mimicry but to a superior Russian understanding of other nations – and he alludes to this too, on occasions, in his fiction, in *The Gambler* and *The Idiot* for example. Other peoples cannot understand Russia, he says, but Russians are 'universal men' who are destined to lead a great brotherhood of nations. Dostoevsky claimed that Pushkin understood this and that he prophetically revealed in his poetry Russia's destiny as a god-bearing nation who would lead the rest of the world to salvation. Had Pushkin lived longer, says Dostoevsky, he might have been able to convince the rest of Europe:

Perhaps he might have explained to [our European brethren] *the whole truth of our aspirations, and thus they would comprehend us better than at present and might foresee our destiny; they would cease to look upon us as suspiciously and haughtily as they still do.*[8]

---

[8] *Diary of a Writer* p980 (August 1880, Chapter 2)

At best it's hysterical nonsense, and at worst it's highly inflammatory and dangerous, and it is sad, but not at all surprising, that Dostoevsky should be championed by the nasty right-wing of Russia today. It goes without saying that the crowds in Moscow loved it, and the speech received a rapturous reception. What Pushkin himself might have made of it is quite a different matter and, personally, I think Turgenev was closer to the mark in choosing to emphasise Pushkin's incalculable contributions to the literary Russian language.

Dostoevsky's unpleasant nationalism dominates his non-fiction, particularly towards the end of his life. He set out many of his ideas in *Diary of a Writer* which was an idiosyncratic combination of journalism, commentary and fiction, put together each month by Dostoevsky and issued as a one-man journal.[9] Some of his statements, particularly about the Jews, are deeply offensive, and a brief war in Southern Europe against Turkey, in which Russia aided the various Southern Slav peoples in their struggle for freedom from the Ottoman Empire gave him the opportunity to wallow in allegations of atrocities committed by the heathen Turks, to glorify the exploits of the Russian soldiers, and to paint the war in apocalyptic terms as Russia's first step on the road to fulfilling her destiny. Whilst nothing at all can justify what he says, his opinions were not unique, and *Diary of a Writer* was wildly popular. Dostoevsky's messianic vision of Russia's future has been seized upon by the crazier elements of the Russian racial supremacist movements today, and garners many sympathetic nods amongst ordinary Russians.

It makes for uncomfortable reading, but fortunately the nasty extremes of Dostoevsky's xenophobia and racism are mostly absent from his fiction, bar a few vicious caricatures of Germans (in *Crime and Punishment*) and Poles (in *The Karamazov Brothers*)

---

[9] I've heard it described as being the world's first blog, and there is some justification in the comparison.

and an impassioned anti-Catholic rant in *The Idiot.* Like Richard Wagner's anti-Semitism, it's important to remember what Dostoevsky thought, but his opinions don't intrude to the point that we cannot enjoy his novels. His metaphysical ideas about Russia's supreme destiny to save mankind are harder to ignore, but it's also easier to deal with them. His idea of the Russians as a god-bearing people is strange and unearthly, and from it we can extract whatever degree of metaphor we choose, according to our own spiritual tastes. Rather than thinking about his vision in terms of the Russian nation state, it is more helpful to look at those virtues that Dostoevsky has identified as residing in the Russian people, with the understanding that there are people throughout the world who possess those particular spiritual qualities and who will all take a part in leading the rest of us towards salvation. It is Dostoevsky the nationalist, the Slavophile, who projects these saving qualities onto the Russian people, but it is Dostoevsky the great spiritual psychologist who has identified them in the first place.

We'll be returning to Dostoevsky's thoughts about Russia and her destiny frequently, as we examine the Russians that he imagined. He uses his characters to take ideas to their extreme, and in so doing, he subjects his own deeply held beliefs, and those of his enemies, to rigorous tests, stretching them to breaking point to see what happens to them. In the course of this, he gives us human thought and emotion in all its messy, confused reality. His incredible gift for psychological insight means that however distorted the views of his characters, however bizarre their behaviour, they always remain entirely convincing human beings, they are never one-dimensional caricatures.

To complete this introduction to Dostoevsky's Russians, we will consider three of the characters that illustrate his more straightforward nationalist ideas: Alexey, narrator of *The Gambler;* Ivan Shatov, the Slavophile portrayed in *The Devils;* and the Peasant Marey, from a short story of the same title.

The Gambler is unique among Dostoevsky's novels in that it is the only one which is set outside Russia. In the other novels, all of the narrated action takes place exclusively within Russia with an almost entirely Russian cast of characters and events which happen in Europe are only referred to obliquely. Set in a fictitious German spa town, Roulettenberg, with a cast of Russian, French, German and English characters, *The Gambler* is a sharp, light-hearted satire, affording Dostoevsky the opportunity to take pot-shots at commonly perceived national characteristics. The story hinges around three men: Alexey, the Russian narrator; a French aristocrat – de Grieux; and Mr Astley – a rich Englishman, all of whom are competing for the hand of Polina, a beautiful and potentially rich young Russian girl. De Grieux and the other French characters are polished and charming but superficial and mercenary; De Grieux is revealed to have seduced Polina already, and Alexey himself allows himself to be swept off to Paris by the dubious Mlle de Blanche, in full knowledge that she's going to help herself to all of his roulette winnings. Mr Astley is a rich industrialist, taciturn, cool and restrained, and always quietly on-hand to help with practical problems. On the periphery of the story are the Germans of the spa town, who are mocked by Alexey for their hard-working petit-bourgeois lifestyle. There are also cheap, nasty jibes against Poles and Jews: a sign of the xenophobia to come.

Alexey mocks the Europeans, but is also blisteringly honest about the Russians: according to him, Russians want the wealth of the Germans, but they don't want to work for it, and they immediately squander what they do acquire. The architecture of Moscow and Petersburg stands as testimony to the great talent of Russians to spend vast sums of money, from the baroque excesses of the Romanov palaces, to the ghastly mansions that circle modern Moscow. This is why, says Alexey (although we cannot help but hear Fyodor Mikhailovich Dostoevsky justifying his own gambling addiction here), roulette with its quick-win mentality is eminently suited to the Russian character.

The point that Alexey and Dostoevsky make is that what distinguishes the Europeans is a sense that they know exactly how they should behave, perhaps even to the point of dutifully conforming to their national stereotypes, whereas working out how to manage that big, complex Russian personality is too much for most people. The result is that the polished Europeans don't understand the Russians and look down upon them for their apparently undignified ways:

All Russians are too richly gifted and too many-sided to be able to find an acceptable form immediately ... finding our proper form needs genius. Well, but the genius usually doesn't exist, because it is rare anywhere. It is only the French and perhaps a few other Europeans who have such a well-defined form that they can look extremely worthy and yet be utterly unworthy. That is why formality means so much to them.[10]

This is the first sense we get of that idea to be spelt out later in gruesome detail during the Pushkin speech that Russians can understand the West and Western culture but that the Europeans cannot even hope to understand Russia.

Through the antics of the Russian contingent in Roulettenberg, Dostoevsky sets up a serious picture showing Russians being led by their hearts, and who are thus more attuned to the irrational, more sensitive to the metaphysical than the worldly Europeans. Alexey is adamant that with adherence to a properly worked-out system, and with the will-power to quit while you're ahead, it should be perfectly possible to win scientifically at the gaming tables – and he cites examples of Europeans who he has observed doing just that. But he himself cannot submit to cold mathematics; he has to gamble with his heart, forgetting himself, losing himself in the play, heedless of the outcome. On one level we can read this as just the impassioned ravings of the addicted

---

[10] *The Gambler* p47 (Chapter 5)

gambler, but it's also Dostoevsky taking the opportunity to start floating some of his ideas about the Russian character.

The Slavophile philosophy is addressed more directly through the character of Ivan Shatov in *The Devils* who has been converted to Slavophilism from his previous membership of a radical socialist group by the dubious and highly persuasive influence of Nikolai Stavrogin (to whom we'll return in Chapter Five). Echoing the Russian historian Danilevsky, Shatov explains how each nation fashions a god for themselves in their own image.[II] The Greeks worshipped nature, and gave us art and philosophy; the Romans, then later the French, deified the State, which is why, says Dostoevsky, the Catholic church has been corrupted by temporal power. Furthermore, in order to qualify as 'great', a nation's people must believe that only they possess the truth, and must believe that they alone have the ability to rise up and save the world; indeed, if they lose that faith, they cease to be a nation. Dostoevsky thought that Danilevsky missed the point here: Danilevsky is considering the situation from an anthropological standpoint, interpreting what he has observed, whereas for Dostoevsky, the universal mission of the Russian people is a deeply held truth, requiring an unquestioning faith in their God. Dostoevsky cannot admit that other nations could even possess such a faith; only the uniquely Russian God, living in the hearts of the Russian people can accomplish mankind's redemption. Shatov's Slavophilism fails him in the end because neither he, nor, more importantly Stavrogin, actually have the living faith in God that it demands: the best that Shatov can manage is to say, rather lamely, that he will believe at some point in the future. Even his name hints at this fatal weakness, for Dostoevsky derived it from the verb *shatat'* meaning 'to waver'.

That native faith had been lost by the educated Europeanised elite, but it could still be found embedded in the heart of the

---

[II] This in itself is a development of Feuerbach's belief that we make god in our own image, an idea that will be discussed in Chapters Two, Three and Twelve.

Russian peasant. Dostoevsky believed firmly that the Russian people, more than any other nation, had a natural and unshakeable faith in Christ, and that by this faith, they would enlighten the world and bring salvation to all. There is little organised religion in Dostoevsky's novels and very few references to people going to regular Sunday church services, but we do get examples of the simple folk beliefs of ordinary Russian people: there is no elaborate theology, just heartfelt faith expressed through actions like the exchange of crosses, or praying in front of an icon at home. The importance of the people's faith is summed up in the sermons of Father Zossima in *The Karamazov Brothers:*

He who does not believe in God, will not believe in God's people. Yet he who believes in God's people will behold the holiness of God, even if he has previously not believed at all. Nothing but the people and their innate spiritual power will convert our atheists who have broken away from the land of their birth.[12]

Dostoevsky's unquenchable trust in the Russian people and its close connection to his own religious faith is vividly summarised in a touching little story, *The Peasant Marey,* that he published in *Diary of a Writer* in February 1876. It's a short, simple piece of writing, little more than an extended anecdote, yet it gets right to the heart of what Dostoevsky believes, and is his public statement of how he came to that belief. It is preceded by the article *On the Love of the People* quoted earlier, and it is intended to illuminate the ideas about the people which Dostoevsky has already been attempting to explain, (as a by-product the juxtaposition of the two pieces vividly illustrates the vast difference in quality between Dostoevsky's journalism and his literary work). Because this story deals with what has often been described as Dostoevsky's conversion experience, it assumes an importance in the critical literature far beyond what one might expect from

---

[12] *The Karamazov Brothers* p367-8 (Book 6, Chapter 2)

what is, as Dostoevsky himself describes it 'an anecdote, no not even an anecdote, just a distant memory.'

The story begins with a rare instance of Dostoevsky directly recalling his years in prison.[13] It's Easter and the prisoners have been given a few days holiday. The illicit alcohol that the prisoners have been smuggling in and hoarding has been brought out, the guards will not be visiting and the prison hut has become a scene of drunken mayhem, with fighting, gambling, coarse songs, and men comatose from drink or beatings. To Dostoevsky, the entire scene is repulsive beyond endurance. He goes outside, where he encounters one of the Polish political criminals. *Je hais ces brigands,* mutters the Pole, and these words make Dostoevsky even more disturbed, so he returns to the orgy inside and pretends to sleep. As he lies on his bunk, trying to work out why the Pole's hatred is so offensive to him, a childhood memory arises unexpectedly in his mind. He is nine years old, and is playing in a wooded ravine on his father's estate. Suddenly he thinks he hears someone cry out that a wolf is nearby: he is struck with terror and rushes into the nearby field where he knows that one of his father's peasants is ploughing. The peasant, Marey, soothes and comforts him with tender words and gestures, not concerned that this is the master's son, but simply recognising the need to be kind to a terrified child. Having calmed the boy, Marey sends him on his way, with Christ's blessing and, understanding the fantasy world of the child, a promise to keep him safe from the imaginary wolf. Refreshed by this memory, receiving Marey's comfort a second time, the adult Dostoevsky opens his eyes and looks around:

---

[13] Although *Notes from the House of the Dead* taken from Dostoevsky's experiences in prison, he takes pains to emphasise that this was a fictionalised memoir. Unfortunately, this was mostly forgotten, to the extent that Dostoevsky frequently found people believing that, like his narrator, he had been imprisoned for murdering his wife!

I suddenly felt that I could behold these unfortunate men with a wholly different outlook, and, suddenly, by some miracle, all the hatred and anger completely vanished from my heart. I went along, gazing attentively at the faces which I encountered. This intoxicated, shaven and branded peasant with marks on his face, bawling his hoarse drunken song – why, he may be the very same Marey; for I have no way of peering into his heart.[14]

Dostoevsky realises then that he pities the unhappy Pole; he thinks the Pole could not have had any memories of a Marey, and thus has had no opportunity to see the true souls hidden within the monsters who surround them. In the *Love of the People*, and in earlier pieces in *Diary of a Writer,* Dostoevsky has been commenting on the depravity of the Russian people, they are 'coarse and ignorant, addicted to darkness' and the pages of the *Diary* for January 1876 are filled with anecdotes of gratuitous violence, drunkenness, and bestial behaviour. By writing the *Peasant Marey*, Dostoevsky has returned to his own recollections of the Russian people at their absolute worst, and remembered how, at that very dark moment, he found the path that was to lead him back to the light and to his own faith.

It's very easy to read the story of Marey and apply it not just to Russians, but to humanity as a whole. Whatever Dostoevsky may have liked to think, there is nothing uniquely Russian about Marey; such incidences of spontaneous kindness occur everywhere, all the time. It's one of the things that makes us human, and it's memories of such kindnesses that frequently make being human so much easier to endure at times when life looks bleak. For Dostoevsky, the memory of Marey gave him just that, allowing him to find an escape from the black depths of despair. His own despair came from the shock of seeing his beloved Russians behaving little better than animals, and his particular need at the time was to find a way to recover his faith in the Russian people.

---

[14] *Diary of a Writer* p210 (Feb 1876, Chapter 1, section 3)

Reading Dostoevsky's journalism, I find his obsessive messianic nationalism very sad, because it seems so much at odds with what he actually achieves in his novels. One of the beauties of Dostoevsky's work, and something which contributes towards his enduring appeal is his ability to combine the specific and the universal, as we've already seen in the case of the *Peasant Marey*. Whilst Dostoevsky is exercising himself with the particular concerns of a Russian Christian living in the 19th century, he is simultaneously considering the great questions that have vexed humanity for time immemorial. How do we identify good and evil? What is the relationship between the logical and the irrational? Is there an afterlife? Why does suffering exist? And, in the end, the question on which so much happiness hinges: just how do human beings manage to muddle along together despite all their flaws? As Rowan Williams points out, Dostoevsky never needs to set out an argument himself, he simply lets the narrative, and the words and actions of his characters do it for him. His technique is to allow his characters to take a moral position to its extreme, to turn up the volume of human interactions to a devastating intensity, and then leave us to make our own judgement. It is with this in mind that we can now meet the man who is probably best known of Dostoevsky's Russians: the deranged murderer, Rodion Romanovich Raskolnikov.

On a very hot evening at the beginning of July a young man left his little room at the top of a house in Carpenter Lane, went out into the street, and, as though unable to make up his mind, walked slowly in the direction of Kokushkin Bridge.

(opening lines: Crime and Punishment)

TWO: RASKOLNIKOV

Meeting Rodion Romanovich Raskolnikov for the first time is just like being introduced to any other Russian: they don't tend to mess around too long with the polite preliminaries, they get straight down to the serious questions of life, religion, politics and money, and before you know it, you're becoming intimately acquainted, discussing these things on a level that friends in England can sometimes take years to reach. It's one of those things that makes life in Russia so exciting: a chance conversation with a stranger always carries the possibility of lifelong friendship, because you quickly discover what really makes the other person tick, instead of wasting time discussing the weather. The random cruelties of Russian life are such that every opportunity has to be seized immediately, because you may not get a second chance. As Dostoevsky puts it, when describing Raskolnikov's first encounter with Mr Marmeladov:

There are meetings with total strangers in which we take an interest from the very first moment, all of a sudden, as it were, before a word has been spoken.[1]

---

[1] *Crime and Punishment* p28 (Part One, Chapter 2)

Raskolnikov listens at length to Mr Marmeladov's drunken ramblings, hears his life story with some very personal details, then takes him home, is introduced to the rest of the family, gives them all his money and meets Sonya, the woman who will change his life. This chance encounter in a dingy bar may seem like a rather crude plot device, designed to bring the different characters together, but for Russia, it's completely plausible. It happens again at the beginning of *The Idiot* when Prince Myshkin readily engages in conversation with Rogozhin and Lebedev in the train returning to Russia; we get a useful resumé of the Prince's history, an introduction to Rogozhin, and Nastasya Filippovna indirectly makes her first appearance.

And so to our own meeting with Raskolnikov. Within a few short sentences we know that he's scared of his landlady because he owes her money for the rent; that his poverty has reduced him to a life of solitude; and that consequently he's become absorbed in himself, overwrought and anxious. By the second page, we're getting the first hints about his mad plan. We're plunging into the depths of his soul and we don't even know his name yet. It's very intense and I'm sure I'm not the only reader who has ended up with an enduring passion resulting from that chance encounter on the street with a disturbed young man. Every time I reread Crime and Punishment I become once again that seventeen year-old girl, who fell just a little bit in love with Raskolnikov. He's intelligent, good-looking and the ultimate in hopeless lost causes: absolutely unobtainable, totally unsuitable, but so dangerously attractive. It's easy to become so absorbed that you become as obsessed with his salvation as Sonya herself, rejoicing every time it seems that Raskolnikov might recover himself, and falling into the abyss with him time and again, until he finally grasps that he has the means to save himself, and lucky, patient Sonya finally reaches his soul.

To many people, Raskolnikov represents the archetypal Dostoevskian hero, and we often find him used as a shorthand for miserable disaffected youth. *Crime and Punishment* is easily the most accessible and best known of Dostoevsky's major novels, such that it becomes used as a cultural reference point – Adrian Mole reads it, Sartre uses Raskolnikov's name as a pseudonym for one of his revolutionaries in *Les Mains Sales*, and the hero of *Catch-22,* John Yossarian, is compared to him. In a 2006 poll by the Guardian[2] of 'the novels that move men', *Crime and Punishment* came in third after Camus's *L'étranger* (itself influenced by Dostoevsky) and Conrad's *Heart of Darkness* – results that clearly reflect the reading habits of teenaged boys. Raskolnikov's character is brilliantly and convincingly drawn, but there a great deal more to him than the glib idea that he just represents youthful male angst. Although Dostoevsky builds on ideas of alienation that he has already introduced in *Notes from Underground*, Raskolnikov is a more fully-formed character than the Underground Man, and the narrative technique is carefully constructed so that we are exposed to all the complexities of Raskolnikov's mind, whilst still being able to see beyond the character to the author's own thoughts.

Dostoevsky began *Crime and Punishment* writing in the first person, as he had done with many of his previous works, but this soon posed him with some serious problems. How could he portray the mind of a deranged and confused man, but still maintain a coherent narrative? How would the reader be able to trust anything that such a narrator tells them? How can Dostoevsky reveal to us those parts of the murderer's motivation that are not yet understood to Raskolnikov himself? Dostoevsky tried at one point to distance the narrator from the events by having him recounting his story after his release from prison, but it still left him with the problem of why the narrator would be telling us all this. Eventually, Dostoevsky devised a unique and intimate third-person narrator, who remains with Raskolnikov throughout the story, telling us what he sees, what he thinks and what he does, almost through Raskolnikov's own eyes, whilst remaining

---

[2] http://gu.com/p/hvbn

detached enough to resolve the problems that Dostoevsky encountered with the first-person narrative. Dostoevsky had experimented with a similar technique in *The Double* but in *Crime and Punishment* he takes it to a daring new level of sophistication, and succeeds brilliantly.

The intimate relationship between the narrator and Raskolnikov immerses us in the hero's mind and builds the tension and excitement throughout the novel. To begin with, he doesn't really know whether or not he's really going to murder the old woman, so neither do we. In fact, to begin with, we don't even know what the plan is, and we only slowly realise the truth, with horror, as he muses over the details; he says to himself:

Am I really capable of doing that? Is that serious? Not a bit of it! It isn't serious at all. Just amusing myself by indulging in fantastic dreams. Toys! Yes, I suppose that's what it is – toys![3]

On the next page, he's fretting that his distinctive battered hat will give him away, then he's visiting the old woman, and expressing his disgust that he could even think of such a foul deed, but we still have no clear idea as to what's going on. It's not until halfway through the fifth chapter that we finally have it spelt out to us, and by this time we've seen Raskolnikov's good qualities: his kindness, on his very first meeting with them, to the unfortunate Marmeladov family; his pride and independence when he learns of the sacrifice that his sister Dunya is planning to make on his behalf; and we learn how he is haunted in his dreams by a terrible childhood memory of drunken peasants flogging a horse to death. It's quite clear that this young man is not a psychopathic monster, and so, when his gruesome plan is finally revealed, it's all the more shocking.

The gut-wrenching sense of anticipation grows stronger on the evening of the crime, as Dostoevsky dwells on all the details of Raskolnikov's preparations, really bringing it home to the

---

[3] *Crime and Punishment* p20 (Part One, Chapter 1)

reader that the crime has all been carefully and obsessively planned, that Raskolnikov really did mean to do it. The suspense continues with the theft of the axe, which becomes a whole little drama in itself, and so it goes on, as we follow him through the streets, up the stairs, to the door of the flat, inveigling his way in, right up to the gruesome climax: Dostoevsky does not spare us the details here, and the unexpected second murder is particularly unpleasant. Even after all this, the tension still doesn't let up as Raskolnikov first realises that he's left the door open, is then caught, trapped inside the flat, by the other visitors, then successfully dodges them on the stairs, and when he finally gets back to his room and flings himself on the bed, the reader is almost as mentally exhausted as the murderer himself. The feeling of intense emotional involvement continues as Raskolnikov gradually accepts the consequences of his actions, and we're so close to him that we, too, feel the excruciating psychological torture exacted by the examining magistrate, Porfiry, as he plays games with Raskolnikov, slowly reeling him in.

The acceptance of punishment and the acknowledgement of guilt is a theme to which Dostoevsky returns frequently and by the time his fiction reaches its dizzying climax in *The Karamazov Brothers,* he has developed it far beyond his initial thoughts about criminal behaviour. The Karamazovs ask every single one of us as readers to consider our own behaviour and our own responses to the suffering we inflict and that we see around us; and it has become nothing less than our own humanity and salvation that is under the microscope. At this stage, however, Dostoevsky is concerned more with the straightforward question of crime and criminality, and he draws on his own experiences, gained from living among hardened criminals, for the development of Raskolnikov and later, Dmitry Karamazov. In fact, Dmitry's own story has its origins in the case of Dostoevsky's fellow prisoner D.I. Ilyinsky, who was wrongly convicted of having murdered his father to obtain an inheritance.

The nature and cause of crime was a topic of growing interest in the nineteenth century, as people began to move away from purely religious notions of sin and evil, and began to look at environmental effects, and how an individual's nature responds to its surroundings. Raskolnikov's own article *On Crime* is introduced to the story by way of Razumikhin and Porfiry reigniting a heated discussion on the question of nature versus nurture – in this case whether environment causes crime or whether the criminal is born that way. Dostoevsky also took an interest in matters of justice, another particularly topical question, as the emancipation of the serfs required a complete overhaul of the Russian judicial system to accommodate the new social arrangements. From the time of his own imprisonment, he was musing on the unique circumstances of each crime and he is unable to accept that crimes which may be legally identical, and attract the same sentence, such as a pre-meditated murder, may have been committed for different reasons and thus carry a different moral weight:

What most exercised my thoughts was the problem, which haunted me throughout my life in prison – an almost insoluble problem, one which I cannot to this day resolve – that of the inequality of the punishment for one and the same crime. It is true that crimes cannot be equated with one another, even approximately. This man and that, for instance have both killed a man; all the circumstances of both cases are weighed and almost the same punishment is meted out to one and to the other. One man, for example, has committed murder casually, for nothing at all, for an onion. ... The other killed protecting the honour of his beloved or his sister or his daughter from a lustful tyrant. One man kills because he is a vagrant, beset by a whole regiment of pursuers, trying to protect his liberty. ... What happens? Both the one and the other get the same penal servitude.[4]

---

[4] *Memoirs from the House of the Dead* p58-59 (Part One, Chapter 3).

He goes on to explain that even varying the punishment by imposing different sentences doesn't solve the problem, because individuals do not respond in the same way to their punishment. Some may pine away and truly suffer whilst in prison. Others, particularly peasants who already have a wretched existence, find that prison life is no worse than life outside, and may even be more comfortable; the prisoner has food, a roof, no responsibilities and is surrounded by his peers. Some survive prison through a refusal to acknowledge that they have done wrong, but for others the punishment of prison cannot exceed that which they have already imposed on themselves:

The pain in his own heart is alone enough to kill him with its agonies before any punishment begins. He condemns his own crime more harshly, more pitilessly, than the cruellest of laws.[5]

Raskolnikov clearly falls under the latter category because he has discovered that he has a conscience which he is unable to overcome. It's worth remembering that the title of the novel is *Crime <u>and</u> Punishment*: it's not just about Raskolnikov's crime, it's also about the subsequent punishment which is engineered by his own soul, not by any outward legal process – he would surely have got away with it if it hadn't been for that pesky human conscience. And it's through the awakening of Raskolnikov's conscience that we discover what Dostoevsky is really doing with his simple tale of a murder and its consequences.

As we gradually unravel Raskolnikov's true motivation for the crime during the course of the investigation, we realise just how well Porfiry has understood his man. He is confident that it's perfectly safe to let Raskolnikov go free until he can bring himself to confess voluntarily and submit willingly to his punishment, because he is certain that Raskolnikov won't kill again. He accepts that there's a risk that Raskolnikov may commit suicide, and rather awkwardly asks Raskolnikov to leave a note explain-

---

[5] *Memoirs from the House of the Dead* p59-60 (Part One, Chapter 3).

ing everything if he were to kill himself, but I think Porfiry knows that Raskolnikov wouldn't actually do this – he guesses correctly that no punishment can touch Raskolnikov until he conquers his egoistic pride and accepts his wrongdoing but when he does, then he will submit to punishment, not attempt to escape it by suicide. Dostoevsky continues, of course, to keep us guessing, right up until the end, and the conclusion of the novel's last proper chapter is, to my mind, one of the most dramatic moments in all of literature: even if I'm just flicking through the book looking for something else, I always get a little thrill from reading that page.

Because Dostoevsky has taken us right inside the very frightening corners of Raskolnikov's head, we feel as if we are experiencing his terror and madness ourselves. We all have dark, scary places in our minds, cupboards that we don't like to open, and when you re-read *Crime and Punishment*, knowing what's coming, it's hard not to feel frightened, however positive and cheerful one may feel in general. Dostoevsky examines madness time and again in his fiction, and looks particularly at how external demands from society such as the need to conform to certain expectations of behaviour or lifestyle, or to fit into a predetermined career path, can cause a delicate psyche to break under the pressure. In *The Devils* we see poor von Lembke, the district governor, shattered through over-promotion. He's trapped in a job that he's not capable of doing and burdened with responsibilities that he cannot handle. His slow disintegration is abetted by his nasty, scheming wife who is more concerned about raising her own social position than her husband's well-being: as so often in Dostoevsky, it all sounds very modern. In the same book, Stepan Verkhovensky is driven to madness by a finely tuned persecution complex which is exploited viciously by his own son, Pyotr (one of Dostoevsky's most evil creations), who knows precisely how to play on the weaknesses of his father and his friends.

Dostoevsky's first detailed analysis of a descent into insanity is to be found in his second published work: the absurdist short story *The Double*. The story recounts the collapse of a lowly civil servant, Yakov Petrovich Golyadkin, who, broken by his own social shortcomings and by failure to advance in his career, is haunted by his exact double, a second Yakov Petrovich Golyadkin, who gradually usurps his life. In his reaction to this apparent double, Golyadkin's behaviour becomes increasingly erratic, until he is eventually carried off to an asylum leaving his double to complete his triumphant ascent through the alternative life that Golyadkin could have chosen to live. *The Double* is one of Dostoevsky's earliest stories; he was still developing his style, and the work owes a lot to his immediate predecessor, Nikolai Gogol (if you think a man being shadowed by his own double is weird, try *The Nose* by Gogol, in which a man's nose assumes a life of its own and wanders around St Petersburg causing havoc).

Already in *The Double*, we see Dostoevsky's ability to get inside the head of his victim; the whole story is told through Golyadkin's eyes, so we see how, to him, his hallucination appears perfectly plausible, and we're never quite sure whether the double is supposed to be real or the product of a sick mind – a trick that Dostoevsky employs again, to brilliant effect, in Ivan Karamazov's nightmare visitation by the Devil. Because we're slightly detached from Golyadkin, we can clearly see just how the situation must appear to the rest of the world. To his colleagues, the matter is simple: a new employee has arrived, who turns out to be a distant relative of Yakov Petrovich. This accounts for the physical similarities and the fact that they have the same name. The new Yakov Petrovich Golyadkin happens to be rather better at playing the system, so his career flourishes and the original Yakov Petrovich responds with an acute persecution complex and loses his mind. We the readers are torn between the rational explanation and the irrational imaginings of Golyadkin's mind. The idea of doubles and split personalities comes up time and again in Dostoevsky's work; almost every major character can be matched to his or her double, albeit more subtly than in this early, experimental story.

This fascination with insanity, and his brilliant ability to depict it so terrifyingly has its origins in Dostoevsky's own unstable mental state, particularly in his younger years, before Siberia. He was notoriously sensitive, desperate to be loved, suspicious, and horribly vain. The success of his first novella, *Poor People,* went to his head and his behaviour became insufferable to his fellow-writers, who promptly launched a campaign of mockery and persecution. The writers Turgenev and Nekrasov circulated a malicious poem satirising Dostoevsky, further destabilising him, and he took any criticism of his work very personally. Time and again, we see his characters fighting the same battle between morbid sensitivity and a desire to be liked and accepted in the world. The most extreme example has to be the so-called Underground Man, narrator of *Notes from Underground.* He has cut himself off completely from society, even avoiding seeing his doctor 'out of spite', as he puts it, and there can surely be no more bitter an opening line than this:

I am a sick man. ... I am an angry man. I am an unattractive man. I think there is something wrong with my liver.[6]

The Underground Man tells us about several incidents from his past to illustrate his inability to cope with the world, and his failure to reconcile his inner feelings with his outward reactions to people. His solution has been to give up and retreat from society: he has quit his job and lives utterly alone. In the course of the events that led to his final detachment from society, he visits an old classmate, who, he discovers, is organising a farewell party for another former classmate, Zverkov, who is leaving for a distant posting. The Underground Man invites himself along to the dinner, even though he hates Zverkov, and he persists in ignoring all attempts to dissuade him, even though he can clearly see that he isn't wanted. He then behaves abominably at the dinner, and ends the evening pacing back and forth across the room,

---

[6] *Notes from Underground* p15

clattering his heels, whilst the others try to ignore him and keep up a semblance of normality. It's excruciating to read, particularly as we know that the Underground Man is fully aware of what he is doing, to himself and to his acquaintances. His attendance at the dinner is his own way of proving to himself that everyone hates him – he could have made an effort, but chose to sabotage his last chance at normal human companionship.

The Underground Man is able to take social alienation to an extreme position because there is no-one who cares enough about him to stop him. Both Raskolnikov and Dostoevsky are saved from their worst traits, like so many of us are, by the fact that they are surrounded by people who love them, despite their exasperating behaviour, and this gives them the security to find a balance between sensitive pride and a longing to fit in. Without that safety net, such people can all too easily fall through the cracks, and descend out of civilised society into a lonely, private, underground world – even Raskolnikov recognises this. The sudden growth of large industrialised cities in the nineteenth century, drawing people away from their family networks, and disrupting traditional social structures, allowed people like the Underground Man to drop out, unnoticed. It struck me recently when filling my car from a self-service petrol pump that today it would be even easier for the Underground Man: he would be able to conduct all business necessary to survival via the internet and self-service machines, without ever having to speak to another human being.

Raskolnikov could have become another such dropout; he is desperately ashamed of his poverty and has even tried to push away his devoted friend Razumikhin (despite the fact that Razumikhin is just as poor as he is), and he is beginning to live so anonymously that he could probably have got away with the murders completely unnoticed. In his terror and shame at what he has done, he starts closing himself off even more from his friends and family, but the persistent love of his mother, his sister, Razumikhin and Sonya is what eventually brings him to repentance and redemption, leading to:

The story of the gradual rebirth of a man, the story of his gradual regeneration, of his gradual passing from one world to another, of his acquaintance with a new and hitherto unknown reality.[7]

Perhaps because of the anxiety caused by his behaviour, because of his own internal conflicts and the pain inflicted on him by others, Dostoevsky suffered from nervous attacks and minor fits that later manifested themselves as full-blown epilepsy.[8] Dostoevsky vividly describes his symptoms in *Humiliated and Insulted* through the voice of his narrator, Ivan Petrovich:

At the first approach of dusk I would gradually, almost imperceptibly, enter that spiritual state (so familiar to me now at night-time in my illness), which I call mystical terror. It is a most dreadful, agonising fear of something I cannot define, something unfathomable and non-existent in the normal course of events, but which may at any given moment materialise and confront me as an unquestionable, terrible, ghastly and implacable reality, making a mockery of all evidence of reason. This fear, totally confounding all rationalisation, normally increases inexorably, so that in the end the mind – which oddly enough on such occasions can function with particular lucidity – nevertheless loses all capacity to counteract the senses. It becomes unresponsive and impotent, and the resulting dichotomy only heightens the fearful agony of suspense. It seems to me that something similar must be experienced by those who suffer from necrophobia. But on the occasion in question the vagueness of the apprehension merely served to intensify my torment.[9]

---

[7] *Crime and Punishment* p559 (Epilogue)

[8] Freud claims that Dostoevsky's epilepsy was entirely psychosomatic and without any physical cause but he presents no medical evidence for his argument.

[9] *Humiliated and Insulted* p51 (Part One, Chapter 10)

Raskolnikov suffers from similar torments which intensify as the novel builds to its climax. His fear manifests itself in predictable physical symptoms – fever, weakness and insomnia – and Raskolnikov becomes locked in a vicious downward spiral of physical and mental deterioration, wandering the streets of St Petersburg in a delirium, apathetic to everything, like a sick man approaching death. There is a double who shadows Raskolnikov through his madness, torturing him with hints and suggesting tempting escape routes and in fact in his first physical appearance in the novel he seems to manifest himself, ghostlike, out of Raskolnikov's troubled dreams. It is only when this double, Svidrigaylov, has been destroyed that Raskolnikov is able to shake himself out of his stupor and act.

Raskolnikov excites our sympathy because, unlike Golyadkin or the Underground Man, he is basically a nice person, and Dostoevsky goes out of his way to show us this. We are told about his random acts of kindness, helping strangers he meets during his wanderings, and these vignettes give Dostoevsky the social-commentator an opportunity to sketch out the squalid horrors of life on the St Petersburg streets. My favourite moment is when we suddenly get a glimpse of Raskolnikov as an ordinary bloke, having a laugh with his friend when he inflicts some good-natured teasing on Razumikhin about his feelings for Dunya. He's still trying and failing not to giggle as they go up the steps into Porfiry's office, and you can't help but join in with it. The knowledge that Raskolnikov isn't an inhuman monster means that his collapse has a particular power to shock and frighten the reader, just as his crime did. Dostoevsky's explorations of madness culminate in the terrifying sophistication of Ivan Karamazov's breakdown, which I'll be examining in more detail in Ivan's own chapter at the end of this book.

It's possible to read and enjoy *Crime and Punishment*, as I did that first time, without any knowledge at all of 19th century political thought. We can take the story at face value, and simply accept the justifications for murder that Raskolnikov himself presents to us. Initially, Raskolnikov gives us the Robin Hood argument, that the old woman is fleecing the poor and she's not even using the proceeds for herself – how much better it would be if Raskolnikov had that money himself to do good deeds, and to save his sister from a mercenary marriage to the hideous Luzhin. Just after his first visit to the old woman to borrow money, and the idea of murdering her has begun to hatch in his head, he overhears a student and a soldier in a pub, discussing, in purely theoretical terms, exactly the same idea:

Kill her, take her money, and with its help devote yourself to the service of humanity and the good of all. Well, don't you think that one little crime could be expiated and wiped out by thousands of good deeds? For one life you will save thousands of lives from corruption and decay. ... And, when you come to think of it, what does the life of a sickly, wicked old hag amount to when weighed in the scales of the general good of mankind? It amounts to no more than the life of a louse or a black beetle, if that, for the old hag is really harmful.[10]

Later, in his feeble and hysterical attempts to justify his crime to Sonya and to Dunya, Raskolnikov returns to this image of a louse crushed underfoot and Dostoevsky uses it again in *The Karamazov Brothers* when Dmitry talks about his father in the same terms. The idea that killing the old woman, or Fyodor Karamazov, amounts to no more than killing a louse vividly sums up the futility of both murders. No-one ever has gained anything from killing a louse except for a minor relief from discomfort, and for every louse that is killed, there are always plenty more to replace it. It's like trying to eliminate cockroaches from a Moscow flat. There will always be lice and cockroaches, there will always be nasty little human beings, and attaching any importance to eliminating them is a crazy delusion.

---

[10] *Crime and Punishment* p84 (Part One, Chapter 6)

We discover later on that there is, in fact, much more to Raskolnikov's motives than a desire to improve his situation and help his family. Porfiry unearths an article that Raskolnikov had written six months previously, and which has since, apparently unbeknown to Raskolnikov, been published. In this article, *On Crime*, Raskolnikov suggests that there exists on earth a special class of people, who are so extraordinary that they have the right, or even the duty, to eliminate anyone who gets in their way: he cites Napoleon and Mohammed, among others, as particular examples. For this extraordinary class of people, the normal moral rules do not apply; they are permitted to commit terrible crimes, but only provided that they are acting for the better good of mankind. For example, he says, if Kepler or Newton would only have been able to make their discoveries known by eliminating dozens of people, then that bloodshed would be perfectly acceptable because of the greater benefit to all of their scientific advances. The last thing that Dostoevsky is doing here is actually justifying murder himself – in fact nothing could be further from Dostoevsky's own views on suffering and from the colossal value that he places on human life. This article of Raskolnikov's is actually Dostoevsky's answer to the extreme ideas being propounded by the Russian radicals of the far left in the 1860s.

The emancipation of the serfs in 1861 unleashed a fresh period of optimism and feverish political activity in Russia, as this one concession by the Tsar led to the hope of further reform, and we see the atmosphere and events of this time, compressed into the hothouse of a small provincial town, vividly recounted in his later novel *The Devils*. The critics Chernyshevsky and Dobrolyubov and the contributors to their journal *The Contemporary* represented the radical end of the political spectrum and were pitted against the liberal elite and the older generation, whilst Dostoevsky and his brother Mikhail with their theory of *pochvennichestvo,* attempted to plot a middle way. The Dostoevskys were broadly sympathetic to the desire of the Radicals to construct a better society, free of injustice and inequality; Dostoevsky spent four years in a Siberian prison camp because of his involvement in a left-wing revolutionary group, which he had joined with the aim of working towards the liberation of the serfs, and he was particularly sensitive to any displays of mindless cruelty.

Where Dostoevsky's views diverged from those of the Radicals was broadly in the means by which each side thought that mankind could achieve this happier, more just society, and how that society would eventually look. The views of the Russian Radicals were derived from those of European writers such as Ludwig Feuerbach, Jeremy Bentham and Max Stirner, and consisted of a strictly atheist utilitarianism. Feuerbach, for example, took the dialectical principles of his mentor, Hegel, and applied them to Hegel's own thinking about God. The conclusion he, and others, reached was that humanity had alienated itself from its own essence by projecting its best qualities onto an imagined god, and that the only way to retrieve these virtues is to concentrate solely on immediate, corporeal existence and obedience to the laws of nature – theology had to become anthropology. Bentham and other English Utilitarians based their philosophy on the principle that the greatest good is the maximisation of human happiness, with, importantly happiness and security taking precedence over individual liberty. Legislators should be capable of making laws that bring about the greatest happiness of the greatest number. All these ideas fed into early socialism, and the process of reclaiming the human spirit back from God was undertaken collectively so that the metaphysical heaven of Christianity could be replaced with an earthly paradise based on the greater good. For example, when the young Friedrich Engels was cataloguing the horrors of industrial Manchester, he was seeing the suffering of the working class not just as physical misery, but also as something that alienated them from their very humanity. This alienation then explained, for Engels, the degraded and immoral behaviour that he witnessed in the slums.

Dostoevsky saw the socialism of the Radicals and the idea that everything was determined by scientific rules, as being a principally Western European solution to mankind's sufferings, and with its Feuerbachian denial of God, utilitarian Socialism was indisputably atheist. For Dostoevsky this simply reflected all the evils of Western industrialised society and he considered it to be entirely unsuitable for the deeply Christian Russians. Dostoevsky's own solutions sprang from the traditions of the Orthodox church and the Russian people, particularly the organisation of village life in Russia, with its culture of shared responsibility.

Chernyshevsky and his radical colleagues believed that the salvation of mankind lay in a crude form of utilitarian socialism, and their ideas were set out most famously in Chernyshevsky's novel *What is to be Done?* – a work that was hugely successful when published and enjoyed continued popularity during the years of the Soviet Union. It is a naïvely optimistic story which claimed to show how the solution to all social problems lay in what was known as rational egoism. The rational man believes that all human conduct derives purely from the laws of nature, and that human self-interest in fact automatically aligns with whatever action will bring the greatest good to the greatest number. This philosophy, and the ideological conflicts of the time are more vividly illustrated in the characters of Turgenev's 1861 novel *Fathers and Sons*, in which his hero, the young radical Bazarov, faces the old-school liberal gentry of the Kirsanov family. Bazarov is the son of a humble army doctor, and his origins and beliefs are typical of the left-wing intelligentsia of the 1860s. Bazarov is, his friend Arkady Kirsanov explains, a nihilist,

A person who does not take any principle for granted, however much that principle may be revered.[11]

Nihilists, we are told, look at everything critically, and then judge everything according to whether or not it serves the greater good of humanity, including their own emotions and will, and every

---

[11] *Fathers and Sons* p36 (translated by Rosemary Edmonds, Penguin Books, 1975)

irrational feeling must be conquered. The word nihilist was already being used, but it was Turgenev's novel that brought it into general circulation, and although his application of the word was intended to be derogatory, as so often happens, a word used in criticism gets turned around and neutralised as it becomes adopted by those against whom it was initially aimed. One leftwing critic, Dmitry Pisarev, failed completely to see that Turgenev was making fun of the Radicals and he wrote an article praising the novel, recognising Bazarov as being a member of an elite class that struggles on behalf of the general mass of population, whilst simultaneously despising it. In fact Turgenev himself dramatically changed his political views later in his life, and was conveniently able to use Bazarov as evidence to substantiate his claim that deep-down he had always been a socialist.

In *Crime and Punishment* Dostoevsky examines the full extent of the nihilist creed, taking it to its logical conclusion to see whether it stands up. This is his most complete consideration of radical politics, and having satisfied himself that radicalism was a moral dead end, Dostoevsky confined himself in subsequent novels to satire. In *The Idiot* and *The Devils,* the young radicals are portrayed as over-enthusiastic and fervent young men who are caught up in the excitement of clandestine activity without having really thought through the full implications of what they are doing. In a wry bit of irony, even in *Crime and Punishment* Razumikhin puts his friend's increasingly erratic and evasive behaviour down to the fact that he must have become involved in some political conspiracy. The irony rebounded on Dostoevsky a decade later as the political situation in Russia in the 1870s deteriorated towards violence and anarchy, when, as we will see in Chapter Ten, a new generation of young terrorists seemed to be taking the ideas of Raskolnikov and the nihilists more and more literally.

What Dostoevsky in fact does with Raskolnikov is to take one small step onwards from Pisarev's article and from the characters in Chernyshevsky's novel, to bring the nihilist creed to its awful, logical conclusion. He sets this out in Raskolnikov's article *On Crime* and it becomes Raskolnikov's true motivation for the murder. If the nihilists believe that every action is justified if it is undertaken for the greater good of humanity, then why should conventional morality stand in the way? Alyona Ivanovna, the old woman, is deemed to be a menace to society, getting rich at the expense of others, then hording her cash: her death would release that money to give happiness to others.

Although the ideas of the nihilists are inspired by altruism and a desire to alleviate suffering in the long term, they cannot in fact ever work, because, we discover, when they are taken to the extremes that Raskolnikov demonstrates, they require an insurmountable conquest of free will. For Dostoevsky any denial of human freedom and the repression of individuality was impossible. He had seen first-hand in the prison camp that people strive for freedom and self-expression above all else, even when the exercise of their free will results in actions that are in fact harmful to them. In *Notes from the House of the Dead,* he talks about how the prisoners will, when they get the opportunity, break the rules, get drunk and bully their fellow-convicts, despite the terrible penalties for such misdemeanours:

The prisoner dearly likes to swagger – that is, to pretend to his fellows (and even to convince himself, for however short a time) that he has more will-power and authority than he appears to have. In a word, he may play the rake and the bully, crush whomever he chooses into the dust with a single word, and prove that he can do all this. ...Yet perhaps the whole cause of this violent break in a man from whom it wasn't in the least to be expected, was a mournful desire for an abrupt display of personality, a longing to be his own self, a wish to declare himself and his own lowly personality, appearing suddenly and developing into fury, insanity, the eclipse of reason, paroxysm, and convulsion.[12]

---

[12] *Memoirs from The House of the Dead* p 95-96 (Part One, Chapter 5)

Dostoevsky first sets out his thoughts about the need of the human ego to assert its free will in *Notes from Underground*, using the Underground Man to demonstrate that however much a man may try to live rationally, the overwhelming power of man's free will rises up in contradiction, and the result is absolute moral paralysis. The Underground Man is a vicious parody of rational egoism; he is attempting to bottle up and suppress all irrational human emotions, but this just cuts him off from the world. The supreme desire of the human soul is to exercise free-will, even if this results in apparently irrational, damaging behaviour, and this holds the clue to explaining the behaviour of many of Dostoevsky's flawed heroes and heroines – we'll be looking at the greatest example of this in Chapter Four.

The desire to exercise free-will and to assert the personality is what makes human beings resistant to being simply cogs in a machine. Dostoevsky was familiar with the works of Utopian Socialists such as Charles Fourier, who came up with elaborate schemes for the perfect ordering of a just society. Fourier imagined people living in perfectly ordered colonies, in buildings of his own design, which he called phalansteries. Dostoevsky demolishes the idea of the phalanstery in *Notes from Underground*, in his famous crystal palace image, which was inspired by his visit to the World Exhibition in London in 1862. Seeing the crowds thronging the real Crystal Palace gawping at visions of the future, he had been fascinated and horrified:

The Exhibition is indeed amazing. You look at those hundreds of thousands, at those millions of people obediently trooping into this place from all parts of the earth – people who have come with only one thought, quietly, stubbornly and silently milling round in this colossal palace; and you feel that something final has been accomplished here. ... You feel that a rich and ancient tradition of denial and protest is needed in order not to yield, not to succumb to impression, not to bow down in worship of fact.[13]

---

[13] *Winter Notes on Summer Impressions* p50-51 (Chapter 5)

Everything in the crystal palace has been plotted out with mathematical accuracy; all problems are eliminated; but, as the Underground Man points out, it will be unbelievably boring, and the human desire to assert its freedom will always end up fighting against the predetermined, prescribed happiness. This is why Golyadkin and von Lembke both collapse: neither of them are able to follow along the groove of a pre-determined career. Golyadkin feels that he should be advancing, but can't bring himself to do the necessary schmoozing with colleagues and superiors that is required for promotion. Von Lembke would have been more than happy in a quiet little job somewhere in the provinces, enough to earn his keep and allow him to indulge his delightful hobby of making intricate cardboard models. It's the same process that makes prosperous middle-class British people to drop out of the rat-race, and seek self-fulfilment through running a bed-and-breakfast in rural France, or an organic bakery, or writing books about Dostoevsky: a desire to say no, this is what I am, and this is what makes me happy and therefore this is what makes me me. And of course, it's the same human desire to smash the crystal palace that causes such problems for the heroes of the great twentieth century dystopian novels: *We, Brave New World* and *Nineteen Eighty-Four*.

The Underground Man is mostly theorising, sitting in his little hole, too scared to do anything: he's come into some money and therefore has the financial means to drop out of society altogether, but Raskolnikov takes the extreme logical conclusion of the nihilist position out into the world and gives it wings. Dostoevsky is saying that if any action is acceptable when it's done with the utilitarian belief that mankind will benefit from it, then what's to stop a poor student from murdering an unpleasant old woman for her money? The result would be anarchy, as Raskolnikov himself discovers in his dream at the end of the novel, in which a plague has spread across the world, and its symptoms are that every person believes himself to be completely possessed of perfect rationality to the exclusion of everyone else – in other words, every infected person believes that they alone are one of the extraordinary people who can do as they like. It ends, of course, with social breakdown and wholesale destruction.

Fortunately, Raskolnikov's reaction to his crime demonstrates that this horrific outcome could never actually come to pass, because it is, Dostoevsky hopes, beyond the capabilities of human nature to allow such a thing to happen. In his biography of Dostoevsky, Joseph Frank describes *Crime and Punishment* in terms of a classic detective novel, but one in which the mystery is not the identity of the killer, but rather the killer's true motivation, as even Raskolnikov himself doesn't fully understand why he has committed the crime. Frank explains how we are given clues and false leads, until eventually we discover that Raskolnikov is testing himself to see whether or not he is one of the great men. According to Raskolnikov's own article though, this actually does make him a criminal because, despite what he claims, he's not really using the murder to achieve anything for society, he's only doing it to test himself – Raskolnikov has entangled himself in a circular argument from which he cannot escape.

Before the murder, we see him thinking about why criminals are almost always caught. He concludes that it's not due to the physical difficulties of concealing a crime, but that the criminal will invariably suffer from a breakdown of his critical faculties, and become amazingly careless and irrational; this loss of control attacks the criminal like a disease, reaching its climax at the moment the crime is committed, and then gradually subsiding. But of course, Raskolnikov is confident that this won't happen to him, because according to the precepts of his article, what he's doing isn't a crime.

Of course what actually happens during the course of Raskolnikov's crime is a whole catalogue of disasters and near-misses. He fails to steal anything significant after murdering the old woman, he inadvertently kills the innocent Lizaveta, and even forgets to lock the door of the old woman's flat, only bolting it later when other visitors arrive – thus betraying his presence in the flat. Immediately after the murders, he is overcome with revulsion at what he's done, revulsion to the point that he makes himself ill and finds himself unable to face the company of his friends and family because he is so disgusted with himself. Napoleon, he later realises when explaining his ideas to Sonya, would never have worried about these sorts of trifles, and so he finally accepts that he has failed his own test, and that he is not one of the extraordinary men. Porfiry sums it up, in his kindly way:

He's invented a theory, and now he's ashamed that it has proved a failure and turned out so very unoriginal. It's turned out rotten, that's true, but you're not such a hopeless rotter, after all. Not at all such a rotter! At least you haven't been deceiving yourself long; you've reached the end of the road all at once.[14]

Dostoevsky does not, at this stage, propose his own alternative to the rational egoism of the radicals; it is simply enough at this point to demonstrate the internal weakness of their thinking and to destroy it by exposing the logical consequences. Dostoevsky thinks that the solution is to be found in the figure of Jesus Christ, but first he has to expose this theory to the same test that he applied to nihilism. He has to take it his idea to its extremes, throw it into the world and see what happens. The surprising result is Prince Myshkin: *The Idiot*.

---

[14] *Crime and Punishment* p471 (Part Six, Chapter 2)

You have no tenderness: only truth, and that's why you're unfair.

(Aglaya to Prince Myshkin)

THREE: PRINCE MYSHKIN

Prince Myshkin is one of Dostoevsky's strangest and most haunting characters, and perhaps also his most puzzling. He's clearly supposed to represent Christ in some way, in his meekness and in his generous, loving nature, but why is his brief sojourn in the world such a disaster? Why is it that whatever he does, however pure his motives, he seems to create nothing but heartache and chaos? And what is such an innocent doing with Nastasya Filippovna, the epitome of corrupted worldly beauty? To understand how Dostoevsky created Prince Myshkin, and his literary successor, Alyosha Karamazov, we should first step back and look briefly at some points of Orthodox theology, before moving on to explore Dostoevsky's own ideas about Christ.

Dostoevsky himself had a fairly conventional middle-class upbringing, and unlike his aristocratic literary contemporaries Turgenev and Tolstoy, he spent his childhood among ordinary Russian people. The landed gentry paid lip-service to religious observations, but for Turgenev and Tolstoy religious education was not part of their upbringing and they both regarded the faith of the people as something a bit strange or exotic. Dostoevsky, on the other hand, was immersed in Orthodox Christianity from an early age. His parents were devoutly Christian; he was taught to read from a book of Bible stories; and one of his earliest memories was of reciting prayers before the household icons. He spent his childhood in Moscow, amid the splendour of the city's ancient cathedrals and churches, and although we usually associate Dostoevsky with European St Petersburg, the great 'Window on the West', it is important to remember that he grew up in the city that considered itself the world centre of Orthodox Christianity and the spiritual soul of Russia: Moscow, the Third Rome.

After centuries of bickering, allegations of heresy, and power struggles over arcane theological points, the Eastern and Western churches finally divided irreconcilably in 1054 in what became known as the Great Schism. In the West, the Catholic church continued to take leadership from the Popes in Rome, while the Eastern Orthodox church looked to the Patriarchs and to the divinely anointed emperors in Constantinople who now styled their city the Second Rome. Constantinople and much of Eastern Europe fell to the Ottomans in 1453, just as the princes of Muscovy were emerging as a newly powerful and unified nation after throwing off Tartar oppression. Russia was thus in a natural position to take up leadership of the Orthodox church, and the church was woven into the national mythology, becoming an inseparable part of Russia's identity.

In response to the unremitting physical hardships of life in Russia, and to the endless horrors inflicted on her people, Russian Christianity places considerable emphasis on self-sacrifice and suffering, following the example of Christ, who is seen as having emptied himself of all his divinity to become fully human.[1] The first martyrs of the Russian church, Boris and Gleb, were not particularly holy, but they are venerated because they willingly gave themselves up to political assassination in an attempt to preserve peace and stability. This sanctification of innocent suffering and the veneration of those whose lives were pointlessly cut short by violence, has continued down the centu-

---

1 This doctrine is known by the Greek word *kenosis*, meaning emptying.

ries, up to the canonisation by one branch of the Russian church of the last Romanovs.

The theological historian Diarmid MacCulloch sees a three-way connection between this doctrine of self-emptying, the Orthodox attitude to the ancient problem of original sin, and God's grace.[2] Following the teachings of St Augustine, the Western church has tended to believe that the sin of Adam tainted the whole of humanity, that because of Adam's sin, we are all born sinful, and only through the gift of God's grace can we hope to overcome that sin. For some, this has led to belief in predestination – the idea that only those actively chosen by God will be saved, and that all the rest are irredeemably damned. By contrast, theologians such as Pelagius (writing in Rome, in the early 5th century), and later the Byzantine monk Maximus the Confessor, saw the story of Adam's fall as merely an isolated incident, a warning to humanity of the perils of sin rather than an irrevocable corruption of human nature. The sin of Adam, says Pelagius, is not inherited, and therefore humans still have within their nature the ability to achieve perfection. According to Maximus, the aim of the human spirit is a constant search for the path back to God, to become a living image of Christ[3]. The result is a much healthier attitude in Orthodox Christianity to the problems of sin and guilt – we all have within ourselves the power to overcome our own evil and draw closer to God, rather than having to rely on an externally bestowed grace, which may not even be available to all.

A popular Orthodox technique in striving towards a closeness to God is the mystical doctrine known as Hesychasm – the name comes from a Greek word meaning 'to keep stillness'. It's a practice that has a particularly Eastern feel to it, consisting as it does of contemplation, correct physical posture and repetition of formulaic prayers, but what is interesting in the context of *The*

---

[2] Diarmid MacCulloch, *A History of Christianity* Penguin 2009 p509
[3] Quoted MacCulloch p440

Idiot is the importance of light as a route towards knowing God. That great passage from the opening of St John's Gospel introduces the metaphor of Christ as the light 'that shineth in the darkness' and Hesychast theologians placed particular importance on this; the light illuminates our knowledge of God, and because we are born with the ability to overcome sin, we all have within ourselves the power to find the transforming light of God. Prince Myshkin experiences something of this during his epileptic fits:

In an epileptic episode there was a stage, almost immediately preceding the attack ... when suddenly amidst overbearing sadness, spiritual despondency and depression, there were moments when his brain seemed blaze up and all his vital forces would be exerted in one extraordinary effort of will. His mind and heart were illumined with an uncommon glow; all his anxieties, all his misgivings, all his uncertainties appeared to be resolved in an instant and transformed into some kind of a higher serenity, suffused with bright, harmonious joy and hope, replete with wisdom and the consciousness of an ultimate purpose.[4]

One final point to note here is the difference between Western and Eastern churches in their use of images. As is immediately obvious the moment you set foot inside an Orthodox church, images reign supreme. The walls and ceilings will usually be covered with paintings or sumptuously beautiful mosaics that depict scenes from scripture or from the lives of the saints; and across the body of the church, cutting off the holiest sanctuary, stands the iconostasis – a great wall bedecked with painted icons. What is notably absent is sculpture, and even the wall paintings and icon pictures are distinctly two-dimensional and stylised. Now consider the great cathedrals of Europe and the Western religious art that fills galleries around the world: the churches, Catholic ones in particular, are resplendent with sculpture, from

---

[4] *The Idiot* p233-4 (Part Two, Chapter 5)

pretty cherubs, to serene virgins, to gruesomely realistic crucifixion scenes, and the paintings run parallel to developments in the secular world, as artists developed the technical abilities to create more and more life-like representations.

The difference in the treatment of images in the two churches arises from how the Old Testament commandment against 'graven images' is interpreted. At times, this commandment has been taken literally to mean no images, full stop: the Jews and Muslims take this line, as did Puritan Protestants. In the 10th century, the Orthodox church went through a brief period of iconoclasm (literally, 'icon smashing'), during which much magnificent Byzantine ecclesiastical art was destroyed. Following the iconoclastic ransacks, the Orthodox compromise was take the commandment literally: 'thou shalt make no *graven* image' – i.e. no carved image. So paintings and mosaics are fine, sculpture is out, and the two-dimensional, highly stylised iconography of the Orthodox church maintains a significant distance between the image and reality. It's also important to note the significant role that images play in Orthodox worship; despite the prohibition on bowing down to idols, worshippers in Orthodox churches will pray directly to icons and even kiss them, and before the revolution, every household maintained a 'beautiful corner' where the family's icons were kept, permanently lit by a candle.

Living in 1840s St Petersburg, before Siberia, Dostoevsky was exposed to all the latest European debate and thinking about Christianity, particularly through Belinsky, the most influential critic of the day, and the man whose lavish praise of his first novel, *Poor People,* launched Dostoevsky's literary career. When they first met, Belinsky was advocating the ideas of French Utopian Socialism and the New Christianity, as set out by Saint-Simon, who held that human society should be governed primarily by Christ's teachings about justice and love and that the organised church had perverted these ideals beyond all recognition into a religion of fear, repression and damnation. This variant of socialism focussed on the morality of the Gospels and Jesus's message of love and equality, and advocated a return to the values actually preached by Jesus, rather than following the distortions that had grown up over 1500 years or more of organised religion. The Christian and Utopian Socialists also held the common masses in high regard, believing that ordinary folk were morally superior to the oppressor upper-classes, and some, such as Robert Owen in Scotland, endeavoured to put their ideas into practice by building workers' communities that prioritised the welfare and morality of their inhabitants.

Shortly after this, the writings of a more radical generation of German philosophers, such as Feuerbach and David Strauss, began to appear in Russia, and Belinsky, never known for his consistency, quickly changed tack. This German group, known collectively as Left Hegelians or Young Hegelians, built upon the work of the philosopher Hegel, and as we have already seen, they applied his dialectical ideas to their own work. We considered the political consequences in the previous chapter, and now Dostoevsky turns his attentions to the theological implications. Feuerbach thought that God was simply an artificial vessel created to contain mankind's best qualities, whilst Strauss destroyed the myth of the gospels with his explosive *Life of Jesus,* in which he examined the historical realities of Jesus, and explained how the real-life prophet and teacher had become a figure onto which certain members of the Jewish community had been able to project their own spiritual desires. Strauss's book had a devastating impact, giving substance to the growing degree of religious scepticism in Europe, and causing great distress to fervent believers. The English translator was Marian Evans (better known as George Eliot), who wept over it, but consequently lost her own faith and adopted left-Hegelian humanist principles in her own novels.

Feuerbach and Strauss still held that Christian moral values should govern behaviour, but one of the more extreme proponents of Left-Hegelianism, Max Stirner, maintained that the acceptance of *any* externally imposed moral value system hinders freedom and that people can only ever act to satisfy the desires of the individual ego: for example, crime only happens because society is organised so unfairly that the criminal has no choice but to commit a crime in order to satisfy his needs. From these ideas evolved the rational egoism of the radicals – egoistical desires should, in theory, align with what is good for the whole of mankind. Although Belinsky and others wavered for a while over the question of God, Russian socialism eventually adopted a strictly atheist and rationalist character.

What exactly Dostoevsky believed during this period is not entirely clear. Many years later, in *Diary of a Writer,* he wrote two articles about Belinsky, and the story as he told it then was that Belinsky converted him to socialism and atheism, setting him on the path that would eventually lead to imprisonment in Siberia; and it was only in the prison camp that he underwent a conversion back to the faith of his childhood, as recounted much later in his story *The Peasant Marey.* The truth is almost certainly more complicated than that, and although the new ideas to which he was exposed caused him to question his beliefs, Dostoevsky probably never completely abandoned some sort of faith in Christ.

Shortly after the death in 1864 of his first wife, Maria Dimitreyevna, deep in grief, (and also plagued by guilt, for whilst his wife was ill, he had been indulging in an affair), Dostoevsky set out in his notebook his own thoughts about God, immortality, Christ, and the purpose of life on earth. The man who had just finished writing *Notes from Underground* with its powerful portrayal of the ego's desire to assert its independence no matter what the consequences now considers Christ's command to 'love your neighbour as yourself', which seems so contrary to the demands of the ego.

As we have seen, the rationalists believed in responding exclusively to the desires of the human ego, because enlightened self-interest means that the best possible course of action will automatically be for the benefit of mankind. The ego rules because it apparently knows what is best for the community. Dostoevsky took a different approach, saying that the ego must be overcome and completely annihilated, meaning that the soul must be emptied of all desires, emptied of self, and filled instead with absolute, unselfish love for everyone else in the world. Only Christ has truly achieved this, making him the perfect example to which everyone must aspire. We may be beset along the way by the sinful demands of the ego, but by following Christ's example and his teachings, we can take steps on the road towards his ideal. Dostoevsky sees glimmerings of this in the communal organisational structures of Russian peasant life, underpinning his belief that the ordinary people of Russia hold the key to mankind's salvation. The importance placed on self-sacrificing love, and the Orthodox attitude to original sin jointly support Dostoevsky's argument here, as both imply mutual co-operation. This is a social faith, not the solitary path of the hermit, and all must strive together to achieve Dostoevsky's vision of paradise. Orthodoxy allows that we all have within us the means to be good, whereas belief in predestination can lead to those who believe that they are chosen setting themselves apart from the irredeemably damned, and the recognition and reception of God's grace becomes a distinctly individual effort. The importance of collective responsibility for sin and for love is elaborated by Father Zossima, in *The Karamazov Brothers*, but its origins can be traced back to these notes of 1864.

As ever, Dostoevsky takes his ideas through to their logical end, and he concludes that if mankind were to achieve a perfect state of unselfish love, there would be nothing left to strive for. This cannot happen on earth, because it is in our nature that we must always have something to aim at, a sense of purpose and development. Dostoevsky saw clearly during his prison years what happens to human beings when they can see no point in their own existence: he talks sensibly of the need to give prisoners meaningful tasks, and describes how most of the prisoners undertook their own black market trading activities primarily so that they had work of their own that meant something to them. Some of these thoughts in *Notes from the House of the Dead* are not far removed from modern management theory, and anyone who has been subjected to 'smart' goal-setting will immediately recognise the passage in which the men are asked to dismantle an old barge and are hopelessly overwhelmed by it until one of the leaders breaks the task down into smaller pieces, telling them what they actually need to do, and in how much time. Dostoevsky uses his practical experience of human nature and transforms it into a higher vision; he astutely observes what actually moves people to act, and then uses this knowledge of human behaviour to consider how mankind can make the best of itself.

According to Dostoevsky, the continual need of human beings to strive for something means that the perfect conquest over the personality can never be achieved during earthly life; it is not for nothing that Christ says in St John's gospel 'My kingdom is not of this world'. In his essay, Dostoevsky thus concludes that there must be a paradise, a future world, where this state of perfection can finally be attained, a paradise that is founded on perfect Christ-like love, where all individual egos are joined together in a great communion. He refers also to another gospel passage in which Christ talks about there being no marriage in heaven, which is somewhat at odds with the intensely loving family life that Dostoevsky found for himself in later life, and with the importance he places on stable families in his novels, but we have to remember that under the circumstances in which he was writing this essay, happy family life must have seemed like a distant dream. Human sexual love, or even the love of a human family is basically selfish, he says, because it represents the satisfaction of individual desires, whereas the pure love of Christ that will reign in paradise has to be born from a sacrificial renunciation of those desires.

These notebook ideas find a voice again seven years later in *The Devils,* as Stepan Verkhovensky lies dying. He's been a pathetic, ridiculous figure throughout his life (his friend Varvara

Stavrogina is surprised that he seems to be capable as doing something so definite as dying); he's a caricature of the 1840s liberals, and he has duly renounced God until the moment when he receives the sacrament on his death bed. Though the narrator treats this with a fair amount of cynicism, saying that the beauty of the rite must have appealed to his artistic sensibilities, Stepan Trofimovich himself now acknowledges God as being the only being that it is possible to love eternally, and that therefore there must be an immortal life where that love for God can continue:

If I have come to love Him and rejoice in my love – is it possible that He should extinguish both me and my joy and turn us into nothingness? If God exists then I, too, am immortal![5]

I'm not sure that Dostoevsky's vision of heaven is any more satisfying than any other solution that has been offered to explain the mystery of what eternal life would really entail. One only has to read Dante to realise that an exploration of hell can be much more interesting than trying to fathom out the mysteries of heaven, but whatever we think of it, Dostoevsky's ideas about love and immortality serve as a useful guide for understanding how his mind is working, and why some of his characters act as they do.

It's with all this in mind that we can now return to Prince Myshkin. *Notes from Underground* and *Crime and Punishment* both demonstrated that fulfilling the needs of the ego ultimately leads to misery and destruction, and in both novels Dostoevsky demolishes the political theories of those who aimed to create perfect egalitarianism – the would-be architects of phalansteries and crystal palaces, and the believers in the benign authority of the ego. Now he turns his attention to his alternative solution: the complete elimination of the ego, through perfect self-sacrificing love for all of humanity. His aim when he set out to write *The Idiot* was to create someone who comes as close as

---

[5] *The Devils* p656 (Part Three, Chapter 7)

humanly possible to the perfectly beautiful man that is Christ, then to throw him out into the world and see what happens. In a letter to his niece, Sofya Ivanova, Dostoevsky explains that, in his view, the only perfectly beautiful figures in Christian literature are Don Quixote, Mr Pickwick, and Jean Valjean (from *Les Misérables*). The first two, he says, are only good and beautiful because they are also ridiculous, and Valjean achieves goodness through the immense sympathy for his misfortunes that he generates in the reader. Like these predecessors, Prince Myshkin is perceived by the world around him as a rather ridiculous figure, and is frequently laughed at. Dostoevsky makes the point directly when Aglaya stashes the letter she receives from Prince Myshkin inside a book, and then bursts out laughing when she realises that the book is *Don Quixote*. The comedy that surrounds Don Quixote or Mr Pickwick is absent, although like them, Prince Myshkin maintains his dignity in the face of ridicule, and is compassionate to those who mock him.

Prince Myshkin's open and simple nature is quickly sketched out in the first chapter of the novel and is immediately placed in contrast with that of his double, the worldly playboy, Parfyon Rogozhin. It's another of Dostoevsky's great opening chapters: two strangers meet on a train returning to Russia and strike up a conversation (and I cannot help but wonder how much Dostoevsky, writing the novel whilst stranded in Europe, longs to be on that train). Rogozhin's questions to Prince Myshkin are, we are told, scornful, irrelevant and frivolous but the Prince answers them willingly and simply, either oblivious to Rogozhin's sneering, or rising above it. Myshkin then plunges straight into St Petersburg life, with all its marriage intrigues and scandals, where everyone is driven by the search for wealth and status, and where no-one can take the Prince's goodness at face value. Everything he does is assumed to have an ulterior motive, because that's how everyone else acts, which explains, for example, Ganya's fury and confusion over the business of Aglaya's note in Part One. To set Prince Myshkin firmly in context, the narrator wanders off into descriptions of the daily life of the Yepanchin, Ivolgin and Lebedev families, and reflects at length on 'men of action' and 'ordinary people'. These digressions make the novel a bit disjointed, structurally, but they play an important part in creating a picture of the messiness and ugliness of the world through which Prince Myshkin is wandering.

The Idiot is made up of several overlapping triangles of love, or at least marriage prospects, and Prince Myshkin's simultaneous love for Nastasya Filippovna and Aglaya Yepanchin forms the heart of the book. In David Magarshack's translation, Prince Myshkin says of Nastasya Filippovna that he was not 'in love' with her, but that he loved her because he pitied her[6]. Pity can seem rather a soft word because it has become debased and overused, but what Prince Myshkin feels for Nastasya is not just the momentary, passing pity such as we might feel when we see another news story about suffering people in a far-off country, and which we forget the moment that the television is turned off. If we want to remember what 'pity' really means, we need only think of the equivalent Italian word *pietà* and its specific use in art as the name for any image of Mary weeping over her son's crucified body: that crushing, heart-breaking anguish that only the best artists can portray. This is what Prince Myshkin feels for Nastasya Filippovna, and for everyone else in the world too, but Nastasya is the focal point, because at this particular moment she is the one who needs him.

In his book on Dostoevsky, Rowan Williams talks about how Prince Myshkin seems to exist independently of time: he lives in the moment, with no memory and no sense of the consequences of his actions, which is why he can respond with love to each situation as it presents itself to him. When Myshkin does attempt to consider the longer term consequences, he tries to suppress his love for Nastasya Filippovna by expressing it instead as hatred –

---

[6] Avsey opts for 'compassion', but I like the simplicity of 'pity', The Russian word here is *zhalost'* – like 'pity', it's a short simple word, with a great deal of punch.

one of his most convincingly human moments – but when faced again with her suffering, he has no choice but to respond to it.

The Prince's relationship with Aglaya Yepanchina is outwardly more conventional than the one he has with Nastasya and he ends up being formally engaged to her, despite the misgivings of her family, who have a peculiarly elevated view of Aglaya, and imagine a glorious future for her. She is invested with an almost angelic status and her sisters are prepared to sacrifice their own marriage prospects for Aglaya's glory:

Aglaya's fate, from the vantage point of the elder two, was with the utmost sincerity imagined as nothing short of paradise on earth. Aglaya's future husband had to be the acme of all accomplishments and perfection itself, not to mention his wealth of course.[7]

It is Aglaya who makes all the moves in her relationship with the Prince, but having seen Dostoevsky's vision of Christ-like perfection, she becomes confused about whether this is really what she wants. She taunts and teases the Prince, who all along offers her the same generous brotherly love that he gives to Nastasya Filippovna, and indeed to everyone else. Aglaya's tragedy is that, just like the crowds in Jerusalem on Palm Sunday who think that Jesus has come to fight and overthrow the Romans, she misunderstands the Prince, and cannot understand his passive, gently loving responses to everything that happens to him. At the beginning of Part Three, she sets him up as a chivalrous, medieval knight, linking him mockingly to Don Quixote, and she teases him with Pushkin's poem *The Poor Knight* which she recites one evening, omitting several verses and twisting its meaning to suit her own vision of the Prince.

Pushkin's poem depicts a crusading knight who prays exclusively to the Virgin Mary, and carries her colours into battle. When he dies, the Devil attempts to claim his soul because he has

---

[7] *The Idiot* p40 (Part One, Chapter 4)

never actually prayed to God or Christ, but Mary intercedes for him. In her recital, Aglaya omits these verses, and substitutes Nastasya Filippovna's initials for the words *Ave Mater Dei* on the knight's shield, thus painting a more traditional picture of the chivalrous knight fighting for his lady. We can assume that Dostoevsky's Russian readers knew their Pushkin well enough to see exactly what Aglaya has done to the poem, and how she has twisted its meaning. She thinks that the Prince is fighting for Nastasya Filippovna's virtue, and declares:

At first I failed to understand him and I sneered at him, but now I love the [Poor] *Knight and, most of all, I respect him for his chivalry and valour.*[8]

Later she expects the Prince to defend his own dignity too, becoming infuriated on his behalf when he apparently won't protect his fortune against Burdovsky's scheming.

Prince Myshkin's failure is manifested in the way that he bungles his relationships with Nastasya Filippovna and Aglaya, and as far as public opinion is concerned, his behaviour towards the two girls is positively scandalous. The problem is that Prince Myshkin simply tries to love everyone, in a pure and Christ-like way, but he is forced to shoehorn this utterly selfless love into the models that society expects. For the Prince, there should be no need to choose between Aglaya and Nastasya, and he simply responds to the needs of each woman as they are presented to him. The Yepanchins at least were given some indication of what to expect, for in his first meeting with them, he artlessly tells them about the poor abused girl Marie whom he befriended in Switzerland. He is blithely unaware of how his attempts at kindness towards Marie would be misconstrued, and at first the consequences for her are dire, until the Prince convinces the villagers, via the children, that Marie is innocent and deserves their kindness in her dying days. He thus sees nothing wrong in

---

[8] *The Idiot* p258 (Part Two, Chapter 6)

loving Nastasya Filippovna in the way he does, but, just as it was in the case of Marie, his pitying love is incomprehensible to the world which can only understand possessive sexual love.

For Myshkin, there is absolutely no question of sexual attraction, and just to make sure that cynical readers are in no doubt about his motives, he suggests that his illness has rendered him impotent. Crucially, Nastasya and Aglaya cannot understand or accept the Prince's generous love, and in another of Dostoevsky's jaw-dropping set pieces, in the presence of both Myshkin and Rogozhin, the rivals confront each other and explode into the sort of vicious cat-fight of which only young girls are capable. In their hysteria they force Myshkin to choose between them, failing to understand that this is not a choice that he is capable of making. It is his attempt to glide innocently through the world that has brought them all to this, and by forcing him to decide, the girls set in place the train of events that leads unstoppably to the novel's great tragedy, and to Prince Myshkin's retreat from the world.

Haunting Dostoevsky's attempt at portraying a perfect man is a painting of the real Christ: not an icon, but a real and all too human Christ. The painting is *The Body of the Dead Christ in the Tomb*, by the great Renaissance humanist painter Hans Holbein the Younger. Rogozhin has a copy of this painting in his apartment, and its appearances in the novel coincide with the most destructive events of the narrative: Rogozhin stabbing Myshkin; Ippolit's suicide attempt; and the novel's shocking ending. It is, without doubt, one of the most disturbing paintings that I have ever seen. It depicts Christ, God made man, the most perfect human being, but very obviously dead, and already decaying. The face is green, the wounds on his hands are horribly bruised, and the open eyes stare vacantly upwards. This is no idealised, pretty crucifixion scene for decorating a church; it's not a gorgeous icon covered in gold; this is human death in all its ugliness – but it's Christ. If I found this painting shocking, despite the casual irreverence of the modern age, in which nothing is sacred, I cannot imagine the effect it would have had on a sensitive Russian, accustomed to revering two-dimensional stylistic portraits of Christ that are heavy on symbolism, adorned with beauty and wholly lacking in realism. Dostoevsky was profoundly moved by Holbein's painting when he saw it in Basel, and spent so long transfixed in front of it, that his ever-sensible wife, Anna, had to drag him away from it for fear that it would provoke an epileptic fit. It must surely be Dostoevsky's own words when Prince Myshkin exclaims:

Why, some people may lose their faith by looking at that picture.[9]

This painting serves as a pointed reminder to Dostoevsky's readers of Christ's humanity, and makes a connection between the hideous violence done to Christ on the cross to the violent acts that follow each of its appearances in the story. We see in it all the awfulness of humanity, the depths to which the flesh can sink, physically and morally, and of just how much we have to do ourselves to overcome our sin. By looking at the painting, we are forced to confront what we have done to Christ and those like Rogozhin and Ippolit, who simply cannot bear it, are driven to despairing acts of destruction. However, Prince Myshkin responds to the painting with his anecdotes about faith and explains that the essence of faith is something innate, no matter what the surface is like:

Surely God must know what goes on in the hearts of these drunken weaklings.[10]

Myshkin goes on to assert that this innate faith is stronger in the hearts of Russians than in those of other nationalities – the same conclusion to which Dostoevsky arrived in his prison camp.

The relationship between Prince Myshkin and his creator is, amongst Dostoevsky's work, uniquely intimate. The Prince is in

---

[9] *The Idiot,* Magarshack p236 (Part Two, Chapter 4)

[10] *The Idiot* p228 (Part Two, Chapter 4)

no way autobiographical – and there are little bits of Dostoevsky's personality scattered all over his work – but he allows Prince Myshkin a peculiar access to his own soul. Dostoevsky created Prince Myshkin in order to test his own deeply held conviction about Christ and to find out whether it is possible to live a perfectly beautiful life on earth, but it seems that because he has invested so much emotion in his strange creation, and because his own life at the time he wrote *The Idiot* was so desperately unhappy, he has chosen Prince Myshkin as a conduit for some of his own most personal memories. So, just as Dostoevsky takes us deep into the psyches of his heroes, so Prince Myshkin takes us right back into Dostoevsky's own mind. We see the horror of an epileptic fit as it happens, with the dizzying moments of glory that precede it, in a long passage that can only be Dostoevsky's voice, telling us exactly what happens to him. And it is in *The Idiot* and speaking again through the voice of Prince Myshkin, that Dostoevsky quietly tells us what was going through his mind during those awful moments on 22 December 1849 when he and his fellow prisoners were brought out onto a scaffold in Semenovsky Square and heard their sentence of execution. The Prince tells it to the Yepanchins as a conversation he had with 'a man he once met'. The man had been sentenced to death, and told the Prince in intimate detail how he felt during and after those agonising twenty minutes, the time between hearing the sentence and the reprieve:

He recollected everything with extraordinary clarity, and said that he would never forget anything that happened. ... He had no more than five minutes left to live. He recounted that those five minutes were like an eternity for him, a priceless treasure. He felt that in those five minutes he would be able to live so many lives that it was quite unnecessary to think about the final moment, such that he was even able to apportion them appropriately. He allotted enough time to say goodbye to his friends – this would take about two minutes, then two minutes to think back on his own life for the last time, and then the rest to cast one last look around. ... The uncertainty and revulsion of what was imminently in store were agonizing. But in his own words nothing was more insupportable than the persistent notion, "What if I were not to die! What if I were to have my life back again – a whole infinity! And all would be mine! I'd make every moment last for ages, nothing would be wasted, every moment would be accounted for, everything would be taken care of". He confessed that eventually this thought incensed him so much that he wished they would hurry up and shoot him.[11]

Alexandra asks Prince Myshkin whether his friend, having been granted an eternity of life, succeeded in counting every minute separately, and the Prince replies that he also asked the same question. The answer, of course, is that the reprieved man lived like any other man, and wasted many, many minutes, just as we all do. Prince Myshkin says he can't believe that it's impossible, but even he can't entirely admit to achieving it: it's too much for us to count every single minute. Think of those moments when you are so extraordinarily happy, and life is wonderful beyond all belief, especially when it happens for no particular reason; try as you might, they are all too fleeting, and just like the dazzling glory before Dostoevsky's epileptic fit, we do not have the strength to sustain them. Prince Myshkin walks in that glory, removed from ordinary time, far more than the rest of us.

It is clear at the end of the novel that Prince Myshkin has failed, and that it's simply not possible to live Dostoevsky's dream of a supremely perfect life amidst the materialism and selfishness of life on earth. The Prince's behaviour clashes with all the desires of the human ego for status, power and sexual gratification, and it is just as incompatible with that love for one's own family that comes from deep within us, from our selfish genes. The misunderstandings that arise from the clash of the divine with the mortal give rise to disaster. We know from Dostoevsky's notebooks that he had no idea how *The Idiot* was going to fin-

---

[11] *The Idiot* p63 (Part One, Chapter 5)

ish; he was writing in instalments, and constantly changing his mind about the plot, so it's clear that he was letting his characters take the lead, he's throwing them into a petri dish to see what happens. We also have to remember again that most of it was written during an intensely difficult period of Dostoevsky's life; he was living in exile in Europe, perpetually in debt, crippled with an addiction to gambling, and then enduring the death of his cherished first-born daughter at just three months old. Does Prince Myshkin fail because Dostoevsky himself couldn't, at the time, come to any other conclusion?

I think this must be the case, because ten years later, Dostoevsky is giving us a far more positive image of the perfect man in the figure of Alyosha Karamazov. Alyosha appears to be almost impossibly good: not only is he devout, chaste, physically handsome and abundantly healthy, but he is also an extremely likeable young man, wholly lacking in sanctimony, and these attributes are even more surprising when we remember the rest of his family, and his chaotic upbringing. He's outgoing, friendly, and deals with people in an honest and straightforward manner. He gets things wrong sometimes, particularly when he gets carried away with his good-natured, youthful enthusiasm: the scene in which he tries to fix Katerina up with Ivan is almost as embarrassing for the reader as it is for the three protagonists, but when he's made a mistake, he doesn't dwell on it, but simply acknowledges his error and gets on with life.

Alyosha's bleakest moment comes after the death of Father Zossima. Everyone in the monastery and town was expecting a miracle, but in fact the body has begun to rot, horribly, obviously and sooner than expected, recalling the shock that we experience when we see Holbein's putrefying Christ. Alyosha is already heartbroken that his hero and only true father-figure has died, and is also facing the prospect of leaving the monastery, so the scandalous scenes at the open coffin and the imputed disgrace to Zossima's memory are just too much for him to bear. The cynical and scheming Rakitin takes advantage of his despair and tempts him, not as Jesus is tempted with miracle, mystery and authority, but with sausage, vodka and sex at Grushenka's house. Alyosha lets Rakitin lead him to Grushenka, where he expects to find only wickedness, but instead he finds a sister, for it is in the home of the fallen woman, the she-devil, that Alyosha starts to learn how he can in fact do good in the world, and how simple Christian love can make a difference to people.

Immediately after his visit to Grushenka, he is comforted further by his dream of the wedding at Cana, the scene of Christ's first miracle, when he turned water into wine. It's a miracle that demonstrates Christ's humanity, his love for everyone, and his delight at seeing people taking pleasure from life. Alyosha's spiritual crisis has come about because all his love has been concentrated on one person, Father Zossima, but the visit to Grushenka and the dream show him how he must love and welcome all people unconditionally, just as Christ did. He embraces the earth and weeps, but arises with renewed strength and a firm resolution. During the remainder of the story, the newly fortified Alyosha gains a quiet confidence and assertiveness as he helps to bring reconciliation within the complicated quartet of Dmitry, Ivan, Katerina and Grushenka, and gives his much-needed blessing to the escape plan that has been hatched. It is significant too that the others now seek his authority, that they feel the need to have his blessing.

Christians have long debated over the exact nature of Christ, whether he is God or Man, whether he has two simultaneous natures, one human and one divine, and so on, down to hairsplitting complexity. The early medieval Church was continually riven by debates on the subject, and the Byzantines took their theology so seriously that arguments over the nature of Christ could lead to riots in the streets. It's not a problem that exercises us much these days, and the question of exactly what substance the divine nature of Christ took has been usurped by more elemental doubts over whether there was ever any divine aspect to Jesus at all. In Dostoevsky's day, the historical, human and humanist Jesus was beginning to emerge from behind the myth and mystery, and so the figures of Myshkin and Alyosha can be read as reflections, at this turning point in our understanding of Jesus, on the human and divine aspects of his nature.

Christ as represented by Prince Myshkin, is an idealised, perfect figure, a distant saviour, gazing benignly down from an icon or from the dome of a cathedral, but not a figure that can engage successfully with the world. Rowan Williams, in his discussion on the timeless aspects of Prince Myshkin, also remarks on his physical resemblance to Christ as depicted in Orthodox iconography[12] and he suggests that it is this resemblance that makes Nastasya think that she has seen him somewhere before. Myshkin is a purely divine Christ, an intense, illuminated beauty as depicted by the greatest icon painters, but there's also something unwholesome about him, in his sickness and strangeness. He is detached from the world and unable to engage with the problems of the world, and this is why, in the end, he fails.

Alyosha, on the other hand, is a fully-formed and very human Jesus, not a sickly mystical figure, but a healthy historical person. Practical goodness and morality take precedence over mysticism: this is the Jesus of Saint-Simon's New Christianity. In his novel *The Good Man Jesus and the Scoundrel Christ*, Philip Pullman imagines a Jesus who is rather like Alyosha, a historical Jesus who is simply an itinerant preacher, and a good man but who, in the end, is executed because the message that he preaches is simply too radical. Pullman's figure is a Jesus who has had his simple message of love and freedom distorted by his alter-ego 'the scoundrel Christ' into a religion of miracle, mystery and authority that becomes the realm of the Grand Inquisitor.[13]

---

[12] *Language Faith and Fiction* p48

[13] This short novel makes an excellent complement to Ivan Karamazov's Grand Inquisitor, essentially dramatizing the same story, the perversion of the original Gospel message. Pullman himself said in an interview published in the Guardian that he deliberately avoided reading the Grand Inquisitor passage whilst writing his own book.

The bridge between the distant divine beauty of Myshkin-Christ and the robust, loving humanity of Alyosha-Jesus comes in Ivan Karamazov's Grand Inquisitor poem where they both meet, as they have to, in Dostoevsky's brief, and very brave, imagining of the real Jesus Christ. On the steps of Seville Cathedral, before his arrest, he is the Jesus of the Gospels, healing the sick, inspiring people with his love, and scaring the authorities. But the Grand Inquisitor doesn't see this, he sees only the impossibly perfect Son of God, who places a great burden on the weak sinners of the human race. The Grand Inquisitor sees only the Christ who gives his people the freedom to choose between good and evil, a freedom that they cannot handle because they only have the unattainable perfection of Christ to guide them. He knows too that Christ understands all this, as he looks on with his gentle eyes, not saying a word. The final, perfect action of Dostoevsky's Jesus Christ is the silent kiss he gives to the Inquisitor as he leaves. He won't give the old man the satisfaction of hearing himself condemned by God's own son. Instead, Christ demonstrates his love and his pity, for the Inquisitor and for all mankind, by silently kissing him, and such is the power of the kiss that the Inquisitor has no choice but to let Christ go free. In this moment, the human and divine Christ come together; it's a kiss of love but also of defiance, of not giving into hatred, and Alyosha takes up the challenge by kissing Ivan after he has finished telling his story.

Holbein's painting of the dead human Christ hangs symbolically over the pages of *The Idiot* and Prince Myshkin is a failure, but Alyosha is robust and cheerfully alive, and emerges at the end of the novel quietly triumphant. And whilst Prince Myshkin is a lonely figure, isolated by his inability to engage with the world around him, Alyosha's story ends for us with him surrounded by a devoted band of young followers (of course Dostoevsky can't resist making the point – just like Christ's disciples, there are twelve of them). The final words of Dostoevsky's final novel are perhaps his own feeling of rejoicing in the positive beautiful man that he has at last been able to depict, and really, he doesn't need to say anything more:

"And always all our lives, we'll walk hand in hand! Hurrah for Karamazov!" Kolya shouted again ecstatically, and, once more, all the boys echoed his cry.[14]

---

[14] *The Karamazov Brothers* p974 (Epilogue, Chapter 3)

Such beauty can turn the world upside down.

(Adelaida Yepanchina)

Four: Nastasya Filippovna

From the perfect, divine beauty, as represented by Christ, that Dostoevsky tries to capture through Prince Myshkin and Alyosha Karamazov, we turn now to his treatment of earthly beauty; how it affects those who possess it and those who desire it; and what happens when our desire for human beauty distracts us from the perfection of Christ. Dostoevsky recognises and appreciates the power of beauty and he shows vividly how it can be a demonic force that drives us to perdition, or something magnificent that lifts our lives above mere animal survival, or perhaps even both at the same time.

The Idiot is a novel that deals extensively with human desires; for money, for status, for alcohol, but above all, for sex. The story revolves around a group of young people caught in a tangled web of relationships: they are all dithering between potential partners; trying to make sense of their own confused desires; and balancing their own needs against social expectations. Parents hover anxiously on the side-lines, and for respectable society girls like Aglaya Yepanchina, there will be no second chances at conjugal happiness. Described like this, it sounds like the scenario for a Jane Austen novel, but of course this is Dostoevsky, so it's no delicate comedy of social manners, it's all far darker. *The Idiot* is a story of lust, violence, sexual jealousy and the destructive power of human beauty. It ends in death and insanity.

At the centre of the web of desire is the spectacular and tragic figure of Nastasya Filippovna. Everything revolves around Nastasya and her devastating beauty – beauty that has the power to turn the world upside down. When the novel opens, she is a fallen woman with a notorious reputation; she is kept by Totsky, a rich older man who has abused the power of care entrusted to him when the young Nastasya was left an orphan. She is seen by the men who surround her as an object that can be bought, sold and bargained over (in contrast to her high-minded rival Aglaya, who pointedly says that she does not bargain). Her monstrous ego feeds off the attention she receives, and off her notoriety, and pushes her to extremes of behaviour, regardless of what is actually rationally good for her. She knows that she can do whatever she wants and will get away with it because she is so beautiful, and so there is nothing to hold her back, no guiding hand to restrain her.

The story begins with complicated marriage negotiations. Totsky wants to shed Nastasya and make a respectable marriage, and has in mind one of the Yepanchin girls. He and General Yepanchin cook up a scheme whereby Nastasya is offered a dowry of seventy-five thousand roubles if she marries Gavrila Ivolgin (Ganya). For his part, Yepanchin gets one of his daughters married to a rich man, and gets Ganya away from his youngest daughter, Aglaya. Ganya gets the money that he thinks he needs to kick-start a successful career, and Nastasya escapes Totsky whilst remaining secure. That the marriage is a mercenary transaction matters little; it's not really any less cynical than many other marriages were at the time and seems to be a win-win situation for everyone. However, Nastasya Filippovna clearly doesn't want to slot herself conveniently into everyone else's plans, even though it is the most sensible and rational option for her – another instance of someone wanting to smash their way out of the Underground Man's crystal palace.

The arrival of Prince Myshkin and Parfyon Rogozhin, Christ and the Devil, gives her the opportunity to make her escape from the crystal palace. Rogozhin is rich, spoilt, stupid and determined to have Nastasya, whatever the price, so he ups the offer to one-hundred thousand roubles. In one of the grandly grotesque and dramatic set-pieces at which Dostoevsky excels, a bidding war for Nastasya's body unfolds at her birthday party. First there's Ganya, armed with Totsky's seventy-five thousand. Then Rogozhin turns up with his hundred thousand roubles, in cash, wrapped in a dirty newspaper, tied up with string – it's a vivid image. Nastasya, who, despite her affectation of injured pride, is obviously enjoying herself immensely, declares that she might just as well walk the streets, and that no man would take her if she had nothing, to which Prince Myshkin dramatically declares that he will. Like Christ forgiving prostitutes and adulterers, he is convinced that Nastasya has emerged pure and honest out of her suffering. He will protect and love her, and if they are poor, he will work to support them. But before he even gives Nastasya a chance to answer this extraordinary declaration, he announces that actually, he's likely to come into a large inheritance, so suddenly the price has leapt up to possible millions, plus a title and the game begins again.

The evening reaches its sordid climax when Nastasya, mocking Ganya for his mercenary ways, throws Rogozhin's hundred thousand roubles into the fire and tells Ganya that he can have it if he pulls it out. It's a jaw-dropping moment, the sort of thing we'd all love to do, if only we dared. Time and again this happens in Dostoevsky's novels, the suggestion that everything is permitted. It's so tempting isn't it, to throw off good manners and social constraint, and just do what the hell we like. The suspense as the bundle of money smoulders on the fire and we wait for Ganya's reaction is fantastic: this is Dostoevsky at his melodramatic best, one of those passages where I read on, spellbound, almost ashamed at myself for enjoying it so much; but because these moments of excess are carefully chosen, and rationed, Dostoevsky gets away with it. We know that he could fill a whole novel with this sort of thrilling drama (as he does in *Humiliated and Insulted,* for example), but like a parent deciding when a child can have sweets, Dostoevsky carefully times and rations these big moments. By doing this, he gives us, his readers, a huge amount of momentum, so that we still keep eagerly turning the pages through the more thoughtful or difficult passages. His obvious relish in telling a good story is a practical application of his own beliefs in the role of art, to which we will return later, but at this point it is worth mentioning that Dostoevsky firmly believed that in order to impart any sort of message, a work of art must first delight its audience – and in passages like this, he shows just how to do it.

In looking at how Dostoevsky develops the group of characters that I've called the beautiful whores, the women whose place in the world is defined by their bodies, we begin with the humble suffering of the actual prostitutes, Liza and Sonya, before moving on to Polina, the heroine of *The Gambler* and Nastasya Filippovna, who both think that themselves to be strong and independent, but who, in truth, are captives of their own beauty. As always, the culmination comes in *The Karamazov Brothers,* where we see the indomitable Grushenka Svetlova, who is able to rise above all the attempts to buy her and who finally learns how to love.

I think it would be a distraction to analyse the beautiful whores in a particularly feminist way; sadly the reality of life was then, and still is now, that it is women who suffer more from the exploitation of beauty, and Dostoevsky is, after all, addressing the great moral and social truths of human life. There is also little to be gained from studying Dostoevsky's own life to understand the roles these women play in his novels. For a nineteenth century artist, full of emotion and inner drama, Dostoevsky seems to have had a remarkably straightforward personal life, and his attitude to women strikes me as refreshingly simple. He suffered neither from Tolstoy's misogyny nor Turgenev's unrequited love, and his human weaknesses were displayed at the gambling table, not in the bedroom – although he had one rather unhappy and tumultuous affair during his first marriage, he seems to have recovered from it, and his second marriage to the wonderful Anna Snitkina was long and happy. He was attracted to intelligent, emancipated women, and fills his novels with strong and positive female characters such as Dunya Raskolnikova, Dasha Shatova, and Varya Ptitsyna. And all of Dostoevsky's female characters of course benefit from his remarkable gift for psychological insight and his ability to flesh out all his characters into rich, fully rounded human beings. As a woman, I respond naturally to the women in his novels, as I recognise elements of myself, past and present, or elements of the woman I wish I could be, (oh, to have Dunya's poise, dignity and self-control!) and I sometimes feel that someone has probed just a little too deeply into my own soul. Men no doubt feel the same way about his male characters, and if dogs could read they would probably relish his description of Perezvon/Zhuchka in *The Karamazov Brothers*.

In his early novels, where he is still occupied with cases of social injustice, Dostoevsky writes about young girls who are literally selling their bodies, and his portrayals of prostitutes allow him to make a spiritual point whilst also reminding his readers of the real horrors of life on the streets, the brutal and short life to which so many women were condemned, and still are, and which the Underground Man describes so vividly and cruelly to the prostitute Liza:

At any rate, your value will be less in a year's time. ... You'll leave here for somewhere more degraded, another house. A year more and you'll go into yet another, and so on, always getting lower and lower, and in about seven years you'll come to a cellar in the Haymarket. ... And you will have given up everything, everything, whole-heartedly – health, youth, beauty, hope – and at twenty-two you'll look like thirty-five, and you'll be lucky if you are not a sick woman. ... When you die, you'll be carted off in a hurry, by strangers, grumbling and impatient – nobody will say a prayer for you, nobody will sigh over you – they'll simply want to get you out of sight as quickly as they can.[1]

The spiritual point that Dostoevsky is making, first with his prostitutes, and later with his other sexually liberated female characters is that enslavement to earthly desires is what prevents mankind from fulfilling its true destiny of love. There are plenty of other earthly passions that can ensnare the weak and the unwary, and Dostoevsky makes full use of them too – we'll see in Chapter Eight how he treats alcohol and gambling. Anything is bad if it absorbs human passions to such an extent that the imperative to love Christ is forgotten, but the absolute rock bottom, the worst level to which we can sink, is to buy a tawdry simulation of real human love.

The Underground Man's description of his night with Liza shows just how deeply he has plunged into the abyss. He has boasted previously about his degrading and vicious habits, but this particular encounter is, apparently, his final grotesque attempt at having any sort of relationship with another human being. He has sex with Liza, without even speaking to her, it's simply an animal union of two bodies, without desire, but it is still human contact. It is at this moment that we first meet the spider that appears time and again to haunt those who have lost all their humanity:

I remembered, too, that for two whole hours I had not spoken a single word to this being, or considered there was any need to do so; until a few moments before I had even felt pleased about it. But now, absurd and disgusting, like a spider, there rose before me suddenly and vividly the image of lust, which lovelessly, crudely, shamelessly, begins where true love finds its crown. We lay there for a long time looking at one another, but she did not lower

---

[1] *Notes from Underground* pp97-99 (Part Two, Chapter 6)

her eyes or change her expression, and at last I was filled with an ... eerie feeling. "What's your name?" I asked abruptly.[2]

The Underground Man attempts to defend himself against his own vileness and tortures Liza's mind, breaking down her attempts to defend her way of life, forcing her to confront the humiliation of her situation and her inevitable grim fate, and to consider the joys of family life that will never be hers (or his, for that matter). Having broken her spirit in this way, he becomes carried away with the sense that he, for once, has power over another human being and it's not the purchased sex that's done this, it's his psychological cruelty. Drunk on his power game, he invites Liza to visit him, and imagines setting himself up as her saviour and putting into practice (albeit on a smaller scale) his grandiose fantasies of being a heroic benefactor. The irony is that if he had actually had the moral strength to carry though his plan, his own life would have been redeemed as well as Liza's and two lost souls would have been saved; but in the cold light of day he loses his nerve, and by the time Liza arrives on his doorstep, he is horrified at the idea of her seeing the hideousness of his squalid life. He breaks down in hysterics and in a bitter outpouring tells her that he was only using her:

It was power, power, I wanted then, the fascination of the game; I wanted to get your tears, your humiliation, your hysterics – that's what I wanted then! It's true that I couldn't go through with it, because I'm trash, and I got scared and, God knows why, was fool enough to give you my address. Afterwards, even before I got home, I was already cursing you for all I was worth because of that address. I really hated you then, because I had lied to you. Because I only want to amuse myself a bit with words, to have a few dreams in my head, but in real life do you know what I want? For you to vanish that's what![3]

---

[2] *Notes from Underground* p86 (Part Two, Chapter 6)

[3] *Notes from Underground* p116 (Part Two, Chapter 9)

As so often in Dostoevsky, utterly vile behaviour is met by sincere compassion; there are times when we long for a good fight, and behave badly with the hope of sparking that fight, only to be disarmed utterly by receiving a calm and measured response. The Underground Man expects and hopes that Liza will react with anger or sorrow, but instead she responds with love, silently holds out her arms, and embraces him with tears, just as Christ will later kiss the Grand Inquisitor in *The Karamazov Brothers*. The Grand Inquisitor, despite everything, recognises the gesture and the deep purity of the love that it expresses, and lets Christ go free, but although the Underground Man realises that Liza has understood his misery, he is unable to accept any sort of love, and responds in the only way he knows, unleashing bitterness and anger, and ruining everything yet again. They fall into bed but Liza understands that this is angry, vengeful sex, an outpouring of his hatred and a rejection of the love she has offered. To make his point, in a final, awful gesture, he thrusts money into her hand as she is leaving.

In *Crime and Punishment* it is the degradation and self-sacrifice of another prostitute, Sonya Marmeladova that finally shows Raskolnikov the failure of his own utilitarian justification for his crime. In the first of his two long late-night conversations with Sonya in her room, Raskolnikov begins with the same tactics that the Underground Man used against Liza, and paints a grim picture of the future he sees for the young children of her father's second wife, Katerina Ivanovna, predicting that little Polya too will end up following Sonya into prostitution. Sonya, he says, has ruined herself for nothing, because she cannot earn enough money to save the family, and this makes her a great sinner in his eyes because it's all such a waste. She's not related to Katerina Ivanovna or her children, because she is Marmeladov's daughter by his first wife, so her behaviour cannot even be explained by the blind altruism of genetics. In the utilitarian view to which Raskolnikov is still clinging, Sonya's sacrifice is utterly pointless, and therefore it is wrong, as wrong in his eyes as the greatest sin. He wonders why Sonya hasn't realised this and why it hasn't driven to her to despair, why she hasn't finished the job of destroying her life by throwing herself into the nearest canal, and how she has managed to retain her pure soul despite the pointlessness of her situation and all the vice that surrounds her.

Raskolnikov, we recall, had convinced himself that he had to step over a barrier, to prove that he was one of the special chosen ones that he had identified in his article *On Crime*. In his failure to cross the barrier, he has taken human life for nothing: he has broken his own utilitarian law and committed an absolutely pointless act. Raskolnikov desperately wants to believe that Sonya's crime, the destruction of her own life, is as futile as the murder that he committed, for this would put the two of them on an equal moral footing, and bring Sonya down to his level. What Raskolnikov doesn't understand is that Sonya's sacrifice of her own life is acceptable not because it is her own life and her own will – in Dostoevsky's eyes, the pointless destruction of any human life is a terrible crime – but because she has sacrificed herself in a genuine loving attempt to do good to others: we have seen already the importance that the Russian church has always assigned to innocent suffering. This is why Sonya is able to retain her sanity, but Raskolnikov is undergoing a mental collapse. Eventually after a long spiritual tussle, Raskolnikov understands that by accepting Sonya's love, and allowing her to hold his hand and guide him in the path of Christ, he can put an end to the torture that he has inflicted on himself through his own pointless act of murder.

A frequent complaint made about Crime and Punishment is that Sonya's character is too shallow, that she's just a symbol, and not really convincing. It's true that her character does not have the same psychological depth as some of the others, but according to Dostoevsky's doctrine of love and the conquest of the ego, it is because she has travelled further down the road of Christ-like love and self-sacrifice. But putting aside for a moment her symbolic role as an example of love, and thinking only about whether she is successful as a character in a story, I actually find her thoroughly convincing. Dostoevsky brings out perfectly what it's like to be a teenaged girl, full of burning truth and idealistic love, her own personality still only half-formed, and unsullied by the cynicism of age. Whenever I read the scene when Raskolnikov confesses to Sonya, and she pledges to follow him to Siberia, she's just like so many other young girls, swayed by mad passions, unrestrained by any common sense. On the first reading, I was right there with the adoring girl, but from an older and wiser standpoint, this passage provokes a wry smile of pity for Sonya and what appears to be a hopeless devotion to an utterly self-centred lost cause. Teenaged girls can be incredibly one-dimensional, which is why, in the end, Sonya is the perfect vehicle for Dostoevsky's message about the redeeming powers of self-sacrificing love. It's interesting to note that in the notebooks for *Crime and Punishment* she begins as a far more complex and contradictory personality, until Dostoevsky gradually pares her down to the pure, burning spirit of love and humility. At the end, in Siberia, she matures and grows into a practical and self-assured young woman, now that her abstract love and passion has a real human focus, and she able to offer material help and comfort to Raskolnikov's fellow-prisoners. It's as if she's taken a step back, away from the pointless sacrifice and a search for heaven, and back into the temporal world of proper human love and support. In this sense, she prefigures the failure of Prince Myshkin: in this life, it seems that there is a limit to how far we can travel along the road to Christ.

In Dostoevsky's eyes, as we have seen, Christ is the most beautiful human being, and therefore our own appreciation and love of earthly beauty must be undertaken only as part of our journey on the search for Christ. Anything else is idolatry, and can lead only to destruction, as we see in the case of those who choose to worship human beauty to the exclusion of Christ. Whilst the ability of Liza and Sonya to rise above the exploitation of their bodies shows how human beings can come closer to Christ by retaining their love and purity of soul despite the most degrading circumstances, Dostoevsky's later whore characters show how a misguided devotion to human beauty can lead to departure from the path of Christ.

Nastasya Filippovna and Grushenka are not literally prostitutes, but both are kept by richer, older men, and both have a certain reputation to deal with. This is an important part of the set-up; unlike the pure, high-minded girls they find themselves opposing, both of them are tainted by human lust, and show the power of beauty as something that can corrupt and destroy both beholder and possessor if it is not treated with respect. It's a literary cliché of course that heroines are impossibly beautiful, although in Russian literature it's always a bit more believable, because Russian girls are so overwhelmingly gorgeous. In Moscow, I frequently felt dowdy and dumpy, surrounded as I was by tall willowy girls with shiny hair and immaculate clothes, who shimmied effortlessly along icy pavements in high heels whilst I trudged around in big boots with a streaming nose and my curls permanently flattened under hats. Shopping for clothes in Moscow was impossible, because the nice shops never stocked anything as large as (horrors) my English size 10, and I could never carry off the tailored chic that all my Russian colleagues managed so gracefully. I could perhaps have taken comfort from Dostoevsky's own description of Grushenka:

Connoisseurs of Russian female beauty, looking at Grushenka, could unfailingly have predicted that by the age of thirty, this still fresh, youthful beauty would lose its harmony, become obese, her face would sag ... in a word, it was an ephemeral, fleeting beauty, which one meets so often among Russian women.[4]

And it's true that the rigours of the climate, a heavy, stodgy diet, polluted air and the hardships of life inevitably take their toll on many of those gorgeous faces and perfect bodies.

---

[4] *The Karamazov Brothers* p187-188 (Book Three, Chapter 10)

There was one exception to my claim that we cannot look to Dostoevsky's biography for the origins of his demonic women, and she is the woman with whom he had that disastrous affair: Apollinaria (Polina) Suslova. Frank describes her as a feminist, and sums up the relationship in the title of his chapter covering their affair: *An Emancipated Woman: A Tortured Lover*. Polina was living independently, attempting to make her own living as a writer and, wanting to flaunt her unconventionality, she was angered by Dostoevsky's insistence on keeping their relations discreet. The affair was not a happy one; Dostoevsky had to deal with the guilt of betraying a wife who was dying of tuberculosis, as well as many huge demands on his time, and as she was not able to see him as often as she wanted, Polina feared that Dostoevsky was merely using her. It seems that he did actually feel passionately about her, but she eventually gave up on the difficulties of being with him in favour of a sexy young Spaniard. She is quite clearly the source of inspiration for Polina in *The Gambler* and the way Polina torments Alexey in the story seems to be based on the behaviour of her real-life model. Her destructive egoism finds its way into Nastasya Filippovna, who could easily have lived her life the same way that the real Polina did, lurching from one tempestuous and unsuitable relationship to another, always demanding, but never finding happiness.[5]

The Gambler's Polina is expected to inherit a fortune, which makes her the object of Count de Grieux's attentions – with some success, for it appears that he has already seduced her. When her grandmother publicly gambles away the entire family fortune, de Grieux leaves, and insults Polina by informing her

---

[5] Polina Suslova eventually ended up married to the Symbolist writer and critic V.V. Rozanov, who spearheaded a new wave of interest in Dostoevsky at the end of the 19th century. Avril Pyman suggests that his relationship with Suslova was founded solely on his own obsession with Dostoevsky. He soon discovered that he should have heeded the warnings in Dostoevsky's fiction, for Suslova turned out to be just as unmanageable as Nastasya Filippovna. (Pyman *A History of Russian Symbolism* p134).

that he's cancelling a large debt that her stepfather owes him. Polina longs to be able to fling the money back in de Grieux's face, so Alexey (who is madly in love with her) goes straight to the roulette table and, in a streak of luck, the like of which Dostoevsky must frequently have dreamed, he wins the entire sum. Alexey is so carried away by his triumph over the odds that he doesn't think how his actions might be perceived: he runs straight to Polina in her hotel room, and thrusts the money into her hands. She accuses him of behaving just like de Grieux, but still spends the night with him, just so that the next morning she can throw the money back at Alexey, and revenge herself on both men. We see here the beginnings of a Nastasya Filippovna: Polina is disgusted by her actions, but she has now been seduced twice, and in both cases money has come into the equation and she fears what she is becoming. Nastasya Filippovna is imprisoned by her ego and consumed by hatred, but Polina saves herself from this fate by seeking the help of kind Mr Astley and it is in fact Alexey who is left ruined by her beauty. Polina has tempted him into gambling and other silly actions (such as insulting an elderly German, which loses him his job), and he does these things because he worships her beauty. Having lost Polina, Alexey blows all his winnings on Madame Blanche, in a brief liaison that they both cynically know will last only as long as Alexey's money, and then gives himself up to the passion for gambling that has replaced his passion for Polina. She ends the novel quietly recovering from the drama under the gentle care of Mr Astley's mother and sister, whilst Alexey fritters his life away at the roulette tables.

Parfyon Rogozhin and the Karamazovs become similar victims to female beauty, completely destroyed by the attractions of Nastasya and Grushenka. Rogozhin, on seeing Nastasya Filippovna but twice, at a distance, is so smitten that he steals ten thousand roubles from his father and buys her a pair of diamond earrings, whilst Dmitry Karamazov pinches three thousand from his fiancée, Katya, and blows it on a wild party with Grushenka. Dmitry and his father, Fyodor, then become locked in mortal combat over their desire for Grushenka, with the elder Karamazov also hoping that he can buy her. This struggle opens the fault lines within the family, bringing old conflicts to the surface. The outcome is the murder of Fyodor Karamazov and the arrest of Dmitry, who is seized whilst he is finally in bed with Grushenka.

Like the operatic heroine Carmen, with whom she has so much in common, Nastasya Filippovna takes a certain pride in her bad behaviour and wears her reputation like a badge of honour. The beauty that attracted Totsky caused her downfall, but she brazenly exploits it in order to continue her bad behaviour, like a child who has been told off once and who defiantly resists punishment with even more attention-seeking naughtiness. When I first read *The Idiot* I was at that age when I was trying to figure out the whole business of sex for myself, making mistakes along the way and being just a little envious of Nastasya Filippovna and her apparent power over men. What I didn't realise in my naïvety, and which is now all too clear with age and a little more wisdom, is that for all the outward appearances, she's a sad, pathetic figure, scared of love, getting love and lust thoroughly mixed up, and trying to convince herself that she's in control, when in fact she is driven by the insatiable, diabolical demands of her ego.

We see in Nastasya the ego as a wayward, destructive force, alien to reason and alien to the sacrifice required by perfect love, the antithesis of conscience. Nastasya takes the demands of the ego to a level that no-one else in Dostoevsky's novels achieves, and although she doesn't actually articulate the mantra that 'everything is permitted', she certainly lives by it, on a grand scale. She is guided only by her passions, and does things no-one else would dare to do, however much they may want to, and this is what makes her one of the great tragic heroines of literature. She's also splendid entertainment, a drama-queen *par excellence*, and it's hard not to read about her antics without a sneaky feeling of admiration and envy. Throw one hundred thousand roubles on the fire and stand calmly by whilst your victim struggles with his dignity and his avarice. Write crazy letters to the girl you perceive as your rival in love. Strike a man with a whip in a public park. Stir up trouble and scandal by shamelessly embarrassing a respectable society man in front of his potential fiancée and her family. The incidents involving Radomsky are particularly indicative of Nastasya's blind egoism; if she were acting rationally, she would see that causing trouble between Aglaya and Radomsky is not going to help her own situation in regards to the three-way relationship between herself, Aglaya and Prince Myshkin.

Prince Myshkin responds differently to Nastasya's beauty. From the first moment that he sees her portrait, he recognises that she is suffering greatly and he pities her, but he also views her with horror as he comes to understand that she is the very opposite of his own goodness, and that he cannot possibly rescue her, however much he tries. She is too much in thrall to her own beauty and its power, refuses to recognise any other reading of herself, and cannot or will not turn from her path of destructive egoism.

For the Prince there was always something painful in the very features of the woman; talking to Rogozhin, he attributed this sensation of pain to one of infinite pity, and this was true. The sight of her face even on the portrait evoked a torrent of pity in his heart. This feeling of pity, indeed of compassion for this creature, never waned in his heart. ... Only now [did he realise] *what it was that was missing from his words to Rogozhin. It was words to convey the full horror of her condition. Yes, horror!*[6]

Nastasya Filippovna can also be read as playing Magdalene to Myshkin's Christ. Mary Magdalene is traditionally viewed as either a reformed prostitute, or an adulterous woman, and she is often used in art and literature as a shorthand for the weaknesses of the flesh. One Easter Sunday, a couple of years ago, as I listened to the Gospel reading, which tells of Mary meeting the ris-

---

[6] *The Idiot* p365 (Part Three, Chapter 2).

en Christ in the garden, and Christ's gentle word of rebuke to her as she fails to recognise him, it struck me that whatever Mary's past, her greatest problem was that she was simply in in love with the man Jesus, in an ordinary human way, and Christ's response to her is a great compassion for her inability to overcome the human desires that leave her blind to his risen glory – this is why she doesn't recognise him in the garden. Prince Myshkin behaves in a similar way to Nastasya Filippovna. We have already seen that Myshkin pities her, for what she has been, and for the suffering she still undergoes, but Nastasya cannot accept this selfless, sacrificing love, and certainly cannot understand that this love is a universal love, to be bestowed equally on everyone. The only sort of love that Nastasya understands is carnal love, and it is this pure naked lust that keeps driving her back to Rogozhin, even though she knows that their unstoppable sexual passion is going to lead to disaster. They don't even like each other much, and there can certainly be no question of happy married love between them, but in the meantime, Prince Myshkin is waiting, desperate to rescue Nastasya, forgiving her when she returns to him. In the end though, he fails to hold onto her and she abandons the Christ-like Myshkin and succumbs to the demonic attraction of Rogozhin. We've seen, in Chapter Three, how, in his notebook essay on immortality, Dostoevsky discussed Christ's statement that there is no marriage in heaven, and how he understands this as meaning that human love for a partner is essentially selfish. He then takes this to the extreme in the relationship between Nastasya and Rogozhin, making sex into a symbol for all the destructive, worldly desires that keep people away from the true path of Christ.

Grushenka too has something of the Magdalene about her, and it's easy to pair her with Nastasya Filippovna through the effects of their beauty, but as in everything else, the later novel is much more optimistic and Grushenka is, in the end, a far more positive figure. Despite the fact that she too has begun her adult life by being seduced, cast out by her family and rescued by the dubious attentions of a much older man, she does not allow herself to be distracted by the blind passions of either lust or hatred. She takes the money given to her by Samsonov, her 'old man', and learns from him how to manage it, becoming a successful businesswoman (albeit of rather dubious ethics). She's rich, self-assured, independent, doesn't care about the reputation she has in the town, and is fully in control as she lets the Karamazov men do battle over her. When her Polish seducer returns, she runs to him, but when she learns that he has accepted an offer of three-thousand roubles from a desperate Dmitry, she finally sees sense and flings him out, cursing herself for wasting so much time pining for him, but with no further complications. The evening ends when she finally makes her choice, of her own free will, for Dmitry, and unlike Nastasya Filippovna she then remains firm and faithful in her decision right through to the end.

Grushenka is not above using her physical attractions to make mischief, but her behaviour stems from a malicious gleefulness and a perverse desire for fun at the expense of others, rather than the dark destructiveness of Nastasya Filippovna. It was her desire to provoke and tease that led to the rivalry between the Karamazovs, and she decides to stir the pot further by bribing Rakitin to bring Alyosha to her, claiming that she wants to try seducing him too. Alyosha, in the depths of his despair and anger at the events surrounding Father Zossima's death, goes with Rakitin, expecting, even hoping, to find nothing but wickedness, but to the surprise of both Grushenka and Alyosha, something extraordinary happens to both of them. On learning of Father Zossima's death, Grushenka offers Alyosha love and pity, which he immediately recognises and gratefully accepts. Grushenka is amazed that she has been able to help someone, and goes on to tell Alyosha a folk story about an old woman and an onion. A wicked old woman is burning in hell and her guardian angel pleads to God for her salvation. The angel is told that if the woman can be found to have done just one good deed, she can be saved. The angel struggles, but finally remembers that the woman once gave an onion to a beggar. God says that if the onion is strong enough to pull her out of the lake of fire, she can go to heaven, but as she grasps the onion, the other sinners in hell grab hold of her hoping to be rescued too. She selfishly tries to kick them off, and in the course of the struggle the onion breaks and they all fall back to eternal damnation. Grushenka, through her compassion, has given Alyosha new strength to resume his mission in the world and she modestly likens this to the gift of an onion; the one good deed that might save her.

The worldly, cynical Rakitin cannot comprehend what has happened: he laughs at them, insisting that they've fallen in love (doubtlessly he really means lust) but Alyosha and Grushenka know that what they have found is a mutual love and support that will give them both strength through the trials ahead. Grushenka, who is assumed to be little better than a whore, has redeemed Alyosha, saved him from temptation and given him a new vision for his life after the monastery, and he offers her a kindness and pity that has been absent from her life for many years. At this crucial stage in the drama, she recognises that she has given Alyosha an onion, but it is not yet clear to Grushenka whether the onion will be sufficient to redeem her from her wickedness. As the story progresses, we find that by being shown love by Alyosha, Grushenka is then able to love Dmitry, and theirs is at last a genuine, mutual love that has finally transcended the superficial attractions of beauty and desire.

Dostoevsky is often credited with the famous phrase 'beauty will save the earth', and Alexander Solzhenitsyn took it as the title for his Nobel Prize acceptance speech. Dostoevsky does use this line twice in *The Idiot,* but, as he often does, he buries his passionate beliefs deep within several layers of narrative. Ippolit asks Prince Myshkin whether it's true that he once claimed that beauty will save the earth, and the Prince does not answer the question. Later, Aglaya warns him before the disastrous dinner party at her parents' that he is not to start raving about beauty saving the earth. And that's it – Dostoevsky's great statement is never actually spoken by the character who is supposed to believe it. Dostoevsky puts what he doesn't believe into eloquent speeches by his greatest characters. To find his deepest, most heartfelt beliefs, we often have to listen to the fools, or look at what isn't said.

Dostoevsky believed deeply in the power of beauty, particularly the beauty of art, and he passionately defended artistic freedom against Radicals such as Chernyshevsky and Dobrolyubov, who thought that art would be redundant once the injustices of life had been swept away, for according to them, its only purpose was to convey a social message. Although he flirted in his youth with romantic ideals about the mystical purity of art, the mature Dostoevsky does not dispute the importance and usefulness of art, but he elevates it to a higher plane than the narrow utilitarian view expressed by Chernyshevsky and Dobrolyubov. The Radicals saw art as a vehicle for escaping from the discomforts of life: Chernyshevsky said that a man may dream of magic gardens and trees laden with jewels but once he has a comfortable orchard of his own, he will no longer dwell on his dream of paradise. But Dostoevsky, in his reply, says that people need beauty as much as food or drink. Genuine beauty embodies the eternal ideals of mankind, and a truly beautiful piece of art can become useful or important to society in ways not foreseen at the time of its creation. Therefore, any attempt to dictate what sort of art should be produced is narrow-minded and short-term, and it doesn't lead to good art that survives the test of time. Does anyone beyond specialists in Russian literature remember the names of any officially sanctioned writers from the Soviet Union, who wrote what was prescribed? No, but the works of Pasternak, Akhmatova, Solzhenitsyn and Bulgakov, among others, survive and continue to delight and amaze us.

More importantly, Dostoevsky says that people respond most deeply to the beauty of art when they are seeking something themselves; when there is a gap in their own lives between the real and the ideal. The results can be either a representation of the beauty and perfection that the artist yearns for, or a response to what he or she is trying to escape. It's a commonplace observation that art is often easier to create when the spirit is yearning for something: it is the great human tragedies of loss, death, exile and pain that produce the most powerful works of art, such as the utterly sublime anguish of all the music that has ever been written for Good Friday.

The beauty in Dostoevsky's own works is not always immediately obvious, and he himself thought that his artistic powers were inferior to those of Turgenev or Tolstoy, with their lyrical descriptions: Molchulsky says that for Dostoevsky, artistry meant the ability to paint, whether with brush or words.[7] The beauty of Dostoevsky's own art comes not from a sublime use of language, or beautiful descriptive passages, but from the craft of his storytelling and characterisation, and the intensity of the human emotions that he sets out so skilfully. It manifests itself in the sheer delight that comes when you lose yourself in one of his novels. On this foundation he builds his discussions of the political, social, psychological and theological themes that interested him, and so we can either read his novels for the sheer pleasure of their stories, or we can delve deeper, as I am doing in this book, to discover what Dostoevsky wanted to achieve through his art.

Dostoevsky is right too when he says that we respond better to beauty when we aren't wholly absorbed in ourselves and our own satisfaction: it's possible to become so dangerously soaked in happiness that we have no room to absorb any extra stimulation. We'll see in the next chapter what can happen to us when we think we have everything we could possibly desire and stop seeking for anything better. Even more dangerously, when we stop responding to good, wholesome beauty, we stop seeking Christ, who is of course the pinnacle of beauty, and we become confused, bewildered, like Dmitry Karamazov:

---

[7] Mochulsky p434

Beauty's an awesome, terrible thing! It's awesome because it's indefinable; as indefinable and mysterious as everything in God's creation. It's where opposites converge, where contradictions rule! ... Man is beset by too many mysteries on this earth. Fathom them as best you can, and survive unscathed. Beauty! Sometimes it's just too much to bear, to see a man of noble heart and high intellect begin with the ideal of the Madonna and finish with that of Sodom. ... What the intellect finds shameful strikes the heart as sheer beauty! Is there beauty in Sodom? Take it from me, that's just where it lurks for the vast majority of people – you didn't know that, did you? The awesome mystery of beauty! God and the devil are locked in battle over this, and the battlefield is the heart of man.[8]

Nastasya Filippovna's beauty is so dangerous because she represents everything that draws people away from the perfection of Christ and anyone who mistakenly worships human beauty to the exclusion of Christ is necessarily doomed. To spell it out explicitly, both Nastasya and Grushenka are described in diabolical terms – for Dmitry, Grushenka is, to begin with, depending on your translation, a hell-cat or a she-devil,

The queen of all the she-devils that you can imagine in the world! She's delightful in her way...[9]

And he uses the word 'infernal' to describe her famously distracting curves.

We're accustomed from religion, legend and literature to the idea of men being driven to madness by their enslavement to female beauty, and Dostoevsky can hardly be criticised for adding to the canon; it's a convenient device to get his message across. It may seem that, like so many men, he has fallen for the old cliché, from Genesis onwards, that it's always the woman's fault, that sexually assertive, seductive women are creatures to be feared.

---

[8] *The Karamazov Brothers* p136-137 (Book Three, Chapter 3)

[9] *The Brothers Karamazov,* Magarshack p181 (Book Three, Chapter 11)

But to find a study of a truly evil, demonic beauty that corrupts everything it touches, we have to turn to one of Dostoevsky's most troublesome male characters: Nicholas Stavrogin.

I was also struck by his face: his hair was just a little too black, his light-coloured eyes a little too calm and clear, his complexion a little too tender and white, his colour a little too dazzling and pure, his teeth like pearls, his lips like coral – he would seem to be a paragon of beauty, yet at the same time there was something hideous about him. People said that his face reminded them of a mask... [10]

---

[10] *The Devils* p57 (Part One, Chapter 2)

> *In my opinion, this document is a morbid work, the work of the devil who took possession of that man. It reminds me of a man who is suffering from an acute pain and is tossing about in bed to find a position to relieve his pain even for a moment.*
>
> *(Father Tikhon)*

FIVE: NIKOLAI STAVROGIN

The Devils, (or *The Demons*, or *The Possessed*, depending on your translation) is more firmly rooted in its own time than Dostoevsky's other major novels. The setting is quite definitely Russia of the 1860s, and it couldn't possibly be anywhere else. It contains references to contemporary events and debates, and savage caricatures: Dostoevsky cannot resist poking fun at some of the major political movements of his time – the Slavophiles, the nihilists, socialists of various hues and, in the elderly Stepan Verkhovensky, the European romanticism and liberalism of his own youth. Several of the characters can be traced to real people, and there is a vicious and undisguised attack on his old enemy and former friend, Turgenev, in the character of Karmazinov; an attack which is so prolonged that it makes the reader quite uncomfortable. And if you aren't familiar with all the fine details of 19th century politics and culture, the effect is a bit like that of the Literary Quadrille that takes place during the novel's disastrous fete[1] – you know that something's being mocked but you're not really sure of all the details.

It's probably this specific sense of time and place that makes *The Devils* the toughest of Dostoevsky's four major novels, and I

---

[1] The fete itself was inspired by a real event which took place in Moscow in 1862

confess that it was with some degree of trepidation that I picked it up to re-read it when writing this book. It had been a long time since I last read it, and I had but a vague memory of pages and pages of incomprehensible philosophising, followed by a melodramatic bloodbath in which most of the major characters are killed off in a few pages. It's true that *The Devils* requires a bit more effort than the other novels, but it's worth persevering, because beyond the satirical surface (parts of which are actually really funny), we return to the same ideas that thread their way through all of Dostoevsky's writing: good and evil, personal salvation, and how to live a life that is not devoid of meaning. It's also the home of Nikolai Stavrogin – hypnotic, seductive and absolutely, irredeemably evil.

Frank says that although scholars have long debated whether or not Stavrogin was inspired by the Russian anarchist Mikhail Bakunin, he suspects that a more likely candidate is Nikolai Speshnev, the leader of the inner circle of plotters within the Petrashesvky Society, whose malign influence led Dostoevsky to imprisonment in Siberia – it is probably no coincidence that the two men share the same first name and initials. Although some of Stavrogin's moral views do echo those expressed by Speshnev, he is less directly committed to political action than either of his supposed prototypes, and as we shall see, he is, as W.J. Leatherbarrow so brilliantly describes him:

A highly 'artificial' character, ectoplasm summoned up from the European literary tradition and trailing clouds of literary illusion.[2]

Stavrogin plays revolutionary politics as an amusing game, like so many other rich youngsters through the ages, who go in for radical political activities, safe in the knowledge that they can bail out and go home whenever things get too uncomfortable. Stav-

---

[2] *Dostoevsky's The Devils: A Critical Companion* p44, ed. W.J. Leatherbarrow. (Northwestern University Press, 1999)

rogin is happy to infect other people with his warped political ideas, but he leaves them to face the consequences alone. He willingly goes along with Pyotr Verkhovensky's schemes as long as they don't inconvenience him, but he remains coolly detached, and apparently lacking in any firm convictions of his own.

Unlike the Machiavellian Pyotr Verkhovensky, who is unremittingly nasty, with no positive features whatsoever, Stavrogin is a complex and enigmatic character. His role in the novel has been distorted and confused by the omission of one significant chapter – *At Tikhon's*, which is now generally published as an appendix and usually referred to as 'Stavrogin's Confession'. In this chapter, Stavrogin visits Tikhon, an elderly monk and gives him a document to read in which he recounts how he once seduced a twelve-year old girl, drove her to suicide and calmly stood by while she hanged herself. It's a repulsive story, even to modern readers who are more accustomed to such shocking tales: Stavrogin's description of how he sat looking out of the window, swatting a fly, and watching a tiny red spider on a plant, guessing what little Matryosha is doing, doing nothing to stop her, and even wondering whether she's had enough time to die, is truly chilling. It's not surprising that Katkov, Dostoevsky's editor, refused point blank to print it, and his friends agreed that it went beyond what the public would tolerate, persuading Dostoevsky to suppress it. Dostoevsky toyed with other possibilities for Stavrogin's crime, and eventually submitted a new version which suggested that Stavrogin's document was not entirely truthful, but even this was too much. In the end the chapter was omitted altogether, and was not published until a copy was found among Dostoevsky's papers in 1921. Although he adjusted other elements of the novel so that it could be read without the confession, everything up to that point had already been published in serial form, so couldn't be retrospectively changed. So although *At Tikhon's* is usually printed as an appendix, there is a case to be made for skipping straight to it, after the chapter *Ivan the Crown Prince*, which is where it was intended to go, for there are still allusions and hints to it throughout the remaining pages that make far more sense when you know about Stavrogin's sordid history.

Dostoevsky's original plan for *The Devils* was that Stavrogin should be clearly seen as the source of all the evils that have infected the small town where the story is set, and by extension, Russian society as a whole. In literary terms, Stavrogin is the descendent of the so-called 'superfluous men' of the 1820s and 1830s who populate the novels of Pushkin and Lermontov, a literary generation before Dostoevsky. The most famous of the superfluous men are Pushkin's eponymous hero Eugene Onegin, and Pechorin, Lermontov's *Hero of our Time*. They are defined by a hopeless lack of purpose, by their ennui, and a perpetual but futile search for stimulation. They are rich and educated, but having lost their enjoyment for the easy pleasures of life, they find they simply don't know what to do with themselves. They search for intellectual stimulation but once again become disillusioned and sink into an egoistic self-hatred. Their lives are empty and all they can do is to continue behaving badly by fighting duels, breaking hearts, and going nowhere. The first part of *Eugene Onegin* describes him, 'oppressed by emptiness of soul', bored first with the glitter of the ballroom, and then with the books to which he turned: 'he'd given up girls – now gave up letters'. And here's Pechorin, who is even more embittered and cynical than Onegin:

My imagination knows no peace, my heart no satisfaction. I'm never satisfied. I grow used to sorrow as easily as I do to pleasure, and my life gets emptier every day.[3]

Dostoevsky saw Onegin in particular as symptomatic of the division in Russia between the Westerners and Slavophiles, and diagnosed that the problems of the superfluous men were rooted in their European education and their growing disconnection

---

[3] *Hero of Our Time* p54 (translated by Paul Foote, Penguin Books 1966).

from the Russian soil and Russian values. Even in literary terms, the superfluous men derive from a European prototype: the Byronic hero. Dostoevsky expands on this theme in the first part of his Pushkin speech, describing Onegin, and Aleko, the hero of Pushkin's poem *The Gypsies,* as spiritual wanderers, blades of grass blown in the wind, who are unable to anchor themselves in their native land. The ideas of the European Enlightenment have alienated the wanderers from their Russian Christianity, leaving them vulnerable to the cold blasts of atheism and egoism, and unable to find peace or happiness. Pushkin's Aleko thought that he would find the truth by running off with a band of gypsies: now, says Dostoevsky, it's socialism that draws the young and disenchanted. Dostoevsky had already touched on this in *The Adolescent* when he reverses our idea of what it means to be a wanderer. Makar Dolgoruky, the legal father of the narrator, Arkady, lives a simple life as a spiritual wanderer, roaming Russia and living among the people. He returns to St Petersburg, dying, and when his doctor snootily describes him as a vagrant, a tramp, Arkady hotly points out:

The vagrants are sooner you and I, and everybody else here, and not this old man, from whom you and I have something to learn, because there are firm things in his life, and we, all of us here, have nothing firm in our lives.[4]

Makar's simplicity and spiritual wholesomeness are contrasted with the soul-sapping entanglement of lust, fraud and blackmail in which Arkady finds himself caught up, and from which he is unable to escape, but his meeting with Makar gives him new hope, and an understanding that there is an alternative to the corruption that surrounds him.

Nikolai Stavrogin is the direct successor of Onegin and Pechorin; just to make the point abundantly clear, Dostoevsky even throws in a duel for him, a sordid little affair that takes place on a

---

[4] *The Adolescent* p371 (Part Three, Chapter 2, Section 3)

patch of waste ground between the town and the factory. Interestingly, there is just one other duel in Dostoevsky's major novels: in his pre-monastic life as a young army officer, embroiled in a thoroughly hedonistic lifestyle, the man who is to become Father Zossima gets into a duel over a woman, and as he faces his opponent, it dawns on him that there is a better way of life, and he immediately resigns from the army to become a monk. Stavrogin, as we shall see, never gives himself the chance to make the same discovery. He commits random and inexplicable acts of violence; he has a reputation for womanising; and he has been mysteriously living amongst the low-life of St Petersburg, despite his wealth. And like Onegin and Pechorin, his good looks and impeccable manners, combined with an air of tragic gloominess, make him irresistibly attractive to women, thus giving him ample opportunity to perpetuate his bad behaviour. To Dasha Shatova and Liza Tushina he comes across as a sad, tortured soul; a rescue project. Dasha is a sensible, intelligent girl, one of Dostoevsky's frankly likeable characters, but she is enthralled by Stavrogin, despite knowing most of his secrets and she is prepared to stand by him right to the end, firm in her own egotistic delusion that she alone can save him from his demons.

Stavrogin's terrible crime, his written confession, and his stark denial that he understands any difference between good and evil, goes further than anything that had gone before in the literature of the superfluous man. By raping a child, he has done something far worse than anything Pechorin or Onegin even dreamed of, and yet by writing down his hideous confession and claiming that he will have hundreds of copies published and distributed, he also goes further than them in his ostentatious self-loathing. If the problems of contemporary Russian society can be traced back to the pernicious effects of European influences on the intelligentsia, as exhibited in the superfluous men, then Stavrogin is the highly contagious carrier of that infection.

Stavrogin's influence can be seen on two of the most ideologically important characters in *The Devils* – Kirilov and Shatov and his incredible charisma enables him to shape the views of weaker men, without requiring him to hold onto any firm convictions himself. He inspires devotion without effort, without even really appearing to seek it, and yet can express ideas in such a compelling way that he is able simultaneously to inspire Kirilov and Shatov with diametrically opposing views. Rowan Williams describes Stavrogin's role as being that of a 'diabolical author'. The Devil, he says, cannot act directly, he can only cause human beings to do his will for him (we will return to this idea in Chapter Eleven). Stavrogin is characterised with the same impotence, and to underline the point, there are suggestions that he is sexually impotent too: he can only act indirectly by creating his characters and letting them loose in the world, and once they've been released, he refuses to engage any further with them.

Rowan Williams explains further that the significance of the confession lies in the fact that it's a written document, and as such presents no opportunity for any further dialogue. The sacrament of confession requires confessor and penitent to engage in a conversation. Recounting one's sins can be cathartic, but once those sins are let out, they must be dealt with, tamed and then carefully packed away, and there is no progress unless the penitent is open to receiving something back and willing to work in dialogue with the confessor to reach repentance and absolution. By presenting his confession in writing, Stavrogin closes off that possibility, just as he refuses to engage in any discussion with Shatov and Kirilov about the beliefs that he has bestowed on them.

Pyotr Verkhovensky, another devil in his own right, recognises Stavrogin's potential as a political figurehead, and is desperate for him to lead his revolution so that the two of them together can unleash a tale of destruction: indeed the only time Pyotr ever shows any sign of emotion is in his hysterical outpouring of adoration to Stavrogin:

I love beauty. I am a nihilist but I love beauty ... To sacrifice life – yours and another man's – is nothing to you. You're just the sort of man we need. I – I, especially, need a man like you. I don't know of anyone but you. You're my leader, you're my sun, and I am your worm.[5]

Demonstrating that his own personal philosophy consists of nothing but a lust for power at any cost, Pyotr Verkhovensky proposes setting Stavrogin up as a mythical pretender to the Tsarist throne, Ivan the Crown Prince, (possibly a reference to Ivan the Terrible's son and heir, murdered by his father). Earlier, Stavrogin has complained to Shatov that Pyotr wants to make him into a new Stenka Razin, referring to the notoriously bloodthirsty leader of a Cossack rebellion in the 17th century. Interestingly Stenka Razin is also referred to by the Underground Man during his discussion of gratuitous violence and the smashing of crystal palaces, and this slender thread ties Stavrogin firmly to ideas about the desire to destroy paradise. Pyotr's plan is to create a web of stories and legends, and there is little doubt that he is capable of it, but Stavrogin calmly, laughingly, refuses. He's not interested in power, or in subjecting himself to Pyotr Verkhovensky's will, and Pyotr is devastated by his refusal.

Pyotr has attempted to set Stavrogin up as a god, but we've already seen what happens to the worshippers of false idols, and so Stavrogin shatters Pyotr's dreams – and everyone else's too. He has infected Kirilov with the disease of atheist rationalism, leading him to believe in the cult of the man-god and the ultimate power of the rational human ego over all spiritual and irrational tendencies, a belief that leads Kirilov to sacrifice his life unnecessarily. On Shatov, Stavrogin has bestowed a crude Slavophilism, a nationalist version of the man-god doctrine, raising the people, the nation, to the level of a god. If there is only one god, there can only be one true god-bearing nation at any one time, and that nation is, of course, Russia. Shatov himself admits to Stavrogin that he doesn't actually believe in God – he squirms around the question, professing belief in Russia, in the Ortho-

---

[5] *The Devils* p420 (Part Two, Chapter 8)

dox Church and even in the second coming, but he can't actually believe in God. Like Pyotr Verkhovensky, he is relying on Stavrogin to help him make the final step:

I'm a man without talent, and I can only give my blood, and nothing more, like every man without talent ... I've been waiting here two years for you. I've been dancing naked before you for the past half-hour. You, you alone could have raised the banner.[6]

However, his conversion from socialism to Stavrogin's brand of Slavophilism has driven him to break with the secret revolutionary society, and therein lie the seeds of Shatov's destruction as the group of five plot to murder him. Shatov and Kirilov both perish as a result of the ideas that Stavrogin has planted in their minds, just as Dostoevsky himself nearly perished because of Speshnev's ideas.

Like the other superfluous men, Stavrogin attempts to fill the emptiness of his life with pure physical pleasure, but while the heroes of Pushkin and Lermontov succumb to apathy and depression when pleasure loses its lustre, Dostoevsky's depraved sensualists resort instead to ever more extreme vices in order to achieve the same degree of sensation and excitement. Our first example of this character type is, more or less, a real person – the convict known as 'A' in *Notes from the House of the Dead*.[7] 'A' was based on a man called Pavel Aristov who had been a police informer in order to fund a lifestyle of depravity. He was convicted of embezzlement and making false denunciations, but continued his vicious behaviour as best he could whilst in prison. Dostoevsky's description of him is positively stomach-churning:

Simply a lump of flesh with teeth and a stomach, and with an insatiable thirst for the grossest and most bestial physical pleasures. ... He was an example of the lengths to which the purely physical

---

[6] *The Devils* p259 (Part Two, Chapter 1)

[7] In the Russian text, Aristov is referred to only by his initial. Some translators blur the boundary between fact and fiction by supplying Aristov's full name.

side of a man could go, unrestrained by any internal standard or discipline. ... Add to all this that he was sly and clever, handsome, had even a certain amount of education and possessed some talents. No, better fire, better plague and famine, than such a being in society![8]

Pavel Aristov undoubtedly provided Dostoevsky with a useful model when he was creating the likes of Valkovsky, Svidrigaylov, Stavrogin and Fyodor Karamazov, and Dostoevsky echoes this with a smile in *Humiliated and Insulted* when Valkovsky says to the loosely autobiographical narrator, Vanya:

You ought to be grateful ... you could model one of your characters on me you know, hahaha.[9]

Aristov and the fictitious debauched monsters who follow him show the ego when it has gained complete mastery at the expense of all other concerns. The fate of Nastasya Filippovna showed us how the demands of the ego can make us act irrationally, but Nastasya at least knows that she is miserable, and probably understands in her deepest heart that she is behaving stupidly, even though she is powerless to stop herself. The decadents of this chapter, on the other hand, are following their instinctive animal urges for physical pleasure; they are enjoying themselves immensely and are utterly oblivious to the damage that they are doing to their souls.

Dostoevsky first discusses what Frank calls his 'psychology of decadence' in an essay on Pushkin's *Egyptian Nights,* written in 1861 and published in Dostoevsky's journal *Time*. Pushkin's poem, embedded within a frustratingly incomplete story of the same name,[10] tells how Cleopatra promises a night of unlimited

---

[8] *Memoirs from the House of Dead* p90-91 (Part One, Chapter 5)
[9] *Humiliated and Insulted* p248 (Part Three, Chapter 10)
[10] Dostoevsky himself considered the story to be perfectly complete in its own right, and in the same essay criticised Katkov, the editor of the *Russian Messenger* for calling it an incomplete fragment.

passion to any man who is then willing to forfeit his life the next morning. Pushkin doesn't explicitly spell out Cleopatra's motivations, but Dostoevsky in his essay puts her firmly in the camp of the depraved decadents, as she seeks ever more extreme thrills. She can no more stop herself than the black widow spider, to whom she is inevitably compared. There's another comparison though: as Nastasya Filippovna leaves her house in her bridal finery, an onlooker calls out 'My life for a single night', quoting Pushkin's poem, and although Nastasya doesn't actually indulge in Cleopatra's lust for pleasure, the implication is clear.

Dostoevsky diagnoses the cause of Cleopatra's state to be the absence of any guiding faith that might give purpose to life:

Life exists with no goal. Hope is a useless fraud. Thought is no longer illuminated by the divine flame: it flickers and goes out. The world has gone astray, and in cold disappointment senses itself on the edge of the abyss, ready to plunge into it.[11]

By Cleopatra's time, the moral and spiritual discipline offered by the old classical gods was losing its force. Corrupt emperors identified themselves with the deities, raising themselves up as equals to the gods, yet by doing so, their own terrible behaviour weakened the power of religion to hold society in check. With the moral weakness came political and military weakness, and all the problems of the dying classical world can be seen in the antics of Cleopatra and her imperial lovers. It was among such people that Jesus Christ lived, preaching his message of redemption to a world that was becoming hopelessly lost in pleasure seeking and hungry for spiritual renewal:

You understand much more clearly now what sort of people it was to which our divine redeemer descended. And you understand much more clearly the meaning of the word: redeemer.[12]

---

[11] *Collected Works,* Vol 19 p 135 , my translation.
[12] *Collected Works*, Vol 19 p 137, translation Frank p312

The great liberal Russian writer, Alexander Herzen had already made the connection between the late Roman-Graeco world and what he saw as a similar moral decline in Western Europe in the 1840s and 50s, and he foresaw that a socialist revolution in Russia could shake the world in the same way that Christ's coming had revolutionised the ancient world. It's no great surprise that Dostoevsky then takes Herzen's analogy literally, and suggests that it would in fact be Russian Christianity that would revitalise a corrupt and sickly Europe, raising her from the morass into which she had sunk. In this context, it therefore makes perfect sense to me that I find Dostoevsky's sensualists to be decidedly un-Russian. Life for most people in Russia has always been too chaotic, too unpredictable to sustain such dedicated and single-minded hedonism. Pleasure in Russia has to be seized enthusiastically when the occasion arises, like the prison debauches that Dostoevsky describes in *Notes from the House of the Dead* or the mad nights of partying indulged in by Parfyon Rogozhin and Dmitry Karamazov. A warm summer night begins with a quiet beer in a park after work and ends in drunken chaos. An evening at the opera somehow turns into an all-night clubbing extravaganza with American soldiers, followed by frantic attempts to sober up in McDonalds on the way to church. These things aren't planned, they just happen by accident, and that's why they get so out of hand.

Stavrogin and Valkovsky are both clearly linked to Europe, by their education and by their personal histories, and Dostoevsky wants to imply that, just like Cleopatra's, their behaviour is the product of a sick and decadent society; a society that has lost its sense of purpose, and its spiritual direction, and which is now spreading its deadly germs into Russia, infecting the likes of Arkady Svidrigaylov and Fyodor Karamazov. In the latter case, Dostoevsky allows himself a bit of fun, and so the disgusting sensualist parodies European Enlightenment ideas, peppers his conversations randomly with Diderot and Schiller, and tries to articulate a mocking religious scepticism. Just to make the point, he even, in Magarshack's words, has the features of:

An ancient Roman patrician of the decadent period.
or, more wittily, from Avsey:
This face has got decline and fall written all over it[13].

A few years after his essay on *Egyptian Nights,* Dostoevsky returns to Cleopatra in *Notes from Underground* when the narrator discusses the way in which people gain pleasure from pain and violence. He astutely observes that, although the shedding of blood has become abhorrent to modern man, society still secretly glories in it, just as Cleopatra was said to be fond of sticking golden pins into the breasts of her slaves so that she could watch them writhe in agony. The enthusiastically lurid crime reports in the media, both in Dostoevsky's time, and even more so now, when 'misery-lit' has its own section in bookshops, testify to our horrible desire to salivate over the sufferings of others. In theory, when the golden age of pure rationality arrives, no-one will stick pins into anyone, but the Underground Man, in telling the story about Cleopatra, reminds us that this will never be the case, that the desire to ruin paradise, to smash the crystal palace, will always prevail.

Dostoevsky's first truly fictional decadent, Count Valkovsky, understands this completely. He shocks Vanya, who is rather an innocent, by insisting that really everyone is as perverse and depraved as he is, but that he alone is not ashamed. He wears his depravity with pride, and insists that any right minded person would do the same:

My friend, if you're a real philanthropist, you'd recommend to any sensible person exactly the same kind of delectation I enjoy, even down to the filthy bits, otherwise anyone who's got his head screwed on would soon find there's nothing for him in this para-

---

[13] *The Karamazov Brothers,* Book One, Chapter 4 *(*Avsey p29, Magarshack p23). Magarshack is more accurate, if more prosaic.

dise for fools. ... I know I live in an empty society. But it offers me creature comforts and I'm only too happy to support it.[14]

Valkovsky claims that by being open about his thoughts and actions, he is more honest, perhaps more true to his human nature than those like his mistress, the Countess, who are openly pious and sanctimonious but who secretly indulge in the very vices they condemn. We all know about this – we so frequently see politicians and others in the public eye falling short of the virtues they claim to represent that it's a cliché, but yet we all know that, in truth, they're no different to the rest of us. How often are we surprised to learn just exactly what our friends, acquaintances or colleagues get up to when they think no-one is looking? What secret vices do we all harbour? Dmitry Karamazov blames his behaviour on his Karamazov nature, inherited from his father, but what is surprising is the admission by the apparently saintly monk Alyosha that he sees in himself the same nature; he has just not progressed as far up the ladder as Dmitry, but he is still a Karamazov. Dostoevsky forces us to recognise that there is a bit of Svidrigaylov, of Valkovsky, of Fyodor Karamazov in everyone, and in his short story *The Dream of a Ridiculous Man*, he spells it out explicitly, describing:

Those impulses of <u>cruel</u> voluptuousness which affect virtually everybody on our earth – everybody, and which are the sole source of almost all sin in our human race.[15]

He simply magnifies these tendencies to grotesque proportions in the monsters that he creates.

The decadents are all plagued with a desire to share too much information, getting an extra kick from causing outrage, provoking disgust and trying to pervert the innocent. Valkovsky horrifies Vanya as he regales him with tales of his behaviour; Svidrigaylov pours it all out to Raskolnikov; Dmitry Karamazov

---

[14] *Humiliated and Insulted* p255 (Part Three, Chapter 10)
[15] *Diary of a Writer, p684* (April 1877, Chapter Two)

does it to Alyosha and finally there is Stavrogin going further than everyone, of course, with his awful confession, which he intends to inflict on the general public. Tikhon, the monk who reads the document, surprises Stavrogin (and perhaps any reader who hasn't yet encountered Father Zossima) with his astute and worldly assessment of Stavrogin's motives, and cleverly deflates Stavrogin's colossal ego. He begins not by judging, or with outrage, but simply suggests that Stavrogin's atrocious writing style could be improved. Under questioning, Stavrogin eventually admits that he will delight in the hatred that his confession will arouse, to which Tikhon points out that the most unbearable thing for Stavrogin will be if the manuscript is greeted not with derision, but with laughter; disgusting crime and self-loathing made merely the subject of ridicule. Finally Tikhon, foreseeing Stavrogin's suicide, predicts that Stavrogin will go on to commit a greater crime, purely to avoid publishing his confession, and Stavrogin storms out of the monk's cell in fear and rage. Liza makes a similar threat; suspecting that Stavrogin has done something really awful, but she counsels him not to tell her, because if he does, she'll make him a laughing-stock.

Although Valkovsky seems to breeze through life utterly untroubled by what he has done, Svidrigaylov and Stavrogin both find themselves troubled by their consciences, and haunted by intimations of the afterlife. Svidrigaylov is visited by ghosts, and recognises that healthy people don't see ghosts, only the sick. In Stavrogin's case it becomes clear as the novel progresses that he is desperately looking for a way out from his moral dead-end. He is haunted by what he did to Matryosha because, like Raskolnikov, he has discovered that he cannot step over the moral barrier after all, that in fact it is not true that everything is permitted. For all his boasting that he doesn't recognise any difference between good and evil, it's clear that he is deeply troubled. His crazy marriage to Maria Lebyatkina is nothing but an extravagant attempt to abase himself, and Shatov attributes it to Stavrogin's passion for cruelty in a succinct character assessment:

I don't know why evil is bad and good is beautiful either ... but I do know why the feeling for the distinction between them becomes blurred and is lost in such gentlemen as the Stavrogins. Do you know why you got married to that woman in so infamous and despicable a fashion? Just because the infamy and absurdity of such a marriage reached the pitch of genius! Oh, you never walk at the edge of the abyss, but precipitate yourself over it boldly, head downwards. You got married because of your passion for cruelty, because of your passion for remorse, because of your moral turpitude. It was a case of morbid hysteria. The challenge to common sense was too tempting to be resisted ... you idle, loafing son a of a nobleman.[16]

Stavrogin is, however, genuinely kind to Maria, visiting her and supporting her financially, and trying to protect her a little from the cruelties of her brother. In marrying Maria, and in writing his confession, Stavrogin is looking for an act of martyrdom, something that would adequately atone for his crime against little Matryosha. He realises however that both these actions would only make him look silly, and expose him to laughter, when what he wants is to be torn to pieces by lions. A man with the pride of Stavrogin can face physical pain or death, (as he does when he duels with Gaganov), but he would rather be thrown to the lions than face ridicule. This is why he backs away from publicising his marriage, and why, in the end, he will not publish his confession. He must silently suffer the same torment of shame that drove Matryosha to kill herself.

Stavrogin is paralysed because he realises that whatever does, or wherever he goes, Matryosha will continue to torment his dreams, and her memory taints his subsequent relationships with women. Dostoevsky inflicts on Stavrogin the spider image that he first uses when the Underground Man is in bed with Liza, and which symbolises a hopeless loss of faith, and the terrible behaviour that is unleashed in the absence of a guiding spiritual light.

---

[16] *The Devils* p 260-261 (Part Two, Chapter 1)

Svidrigaylov imagines hell to be a dirty bathhouse full of spiders, Ippolit's hideous dream that he is being visited by a giant spider spurs him on in his decision to take his life, and Liza Tushina, the morning after her night with Stavrogin, tells him of her own vision of a giant spider that would taint any relationship that they might have. For Stavrogin, plagued by the memory of the little red spider he watched whilst Matryosha hanged herself, and whose dream of paradise is interrupted by that same spider, her words must have struck terror into his heart.

After Dostoevsky's failure to publish *At Tikhon's*, he recycled Stavrogin's paradise dream, in slightly different guises, in *The Dream of a Ridiculous Man* and in *The Adolescent*. All three passages were inspired by Claude Lorrain's painting *Acis and Galatea,* which Dostoevsky saw in Dresden, and which he referred to as 'the Golden Age'. Stavrogin and the story's nameless narrator both dream of a prelapsarian paradise, whose inhabitants live simple lives filled with beauty and love. Stavrogin awakens from his dream filled with a happiness that he has never previously experienced, his eyes wet with tears, but as he wakes, and tries to retain the happiness of the dream, he sees instead the red spider, and then Matryosha herself and at this point he knows that he is doomed, and that he will never be capable of freeing himself from what he has done. The Ridiculous Man fell asleep whilst contemplating suicide, with a loaded gun ready beside him, and although in his dream he infects the happy society with all the evils of human life – lies, jealousy, possessiveness, sensuality, and the rest, he wakes with a new vigour and zest for life and for goodness. His dream and the initial hesitancy to shoot himself have also come about as a result of his dealings with a young girl – in his case a beggar girl who he met on the way home but refused to help. He realises that he pities the girl, and is puzzled because such pity seems to him pointless in one who is about to die. This is on his mind as he falls asleep and dreams, and the story ends with him saying that he sought out that little girl, who has brought him redemption – unlike Stavrogin's little girl who comes unbidden and brings damnation.

The Ridiculous Man begins his story in the same vein as the Underground Man: proud and touchy, suffering from a loss of faith in humankind, caring nothing for the existence of the world, losing all feelings. His dream pierces his heart; he alone has been responsible for infecting an entire world with pain and suffering but it brings him sharply back to life and gives us an idea of what Stavrogin could have become if he had had the spiritual strength to overcome his devils. The Ridiculous Man takes up a life of preaching, humbling himself, learning happily from his mistakes, so that he can bring more people to share his own new-found faith. He doesn't fear humiliation but happily makes himself ridiculous, in a way that Stavrogin was unable to do.

I think Dostoevsky genuinely pities Stavrogin and recognises how hard it is for him to find salvation, and for me, the clue to deciphering the author's attitude to his suffering demon lies buried in words Stavrogin apparently spoke to Shatov, and which are quoted back to him by Shatov at the beginning of their midnight conversation:

Didn't you tell me that if it were mathematically proved to you that truth was outside Christ, you would rather remain with Christ than with truth? Did you say that? Did you? [17]

Compare this with a famous passage in a letter that Dostoevsky wrote to his friend Mme Fonvizina on his release from prison, in which he firmly sets out his belief that Christ is the pinnacle of perfection, and that nothing can be more beautiful than Christ:

More than that – if someone succeeded in proving to me that Christ was outside the truth, and if, <u>indeed,</u> the truth was outside Christ, then I would sooner remain with Christ than with the truth. [18]

---

[17] *The Devils* p 255 (Part Two, Chapter 1, Section 7)
[18] *Selected Letters* p68 (15 February- 2 March, 1854, to N.D. Fonvizina)

Why would Dostoevsky put his deeply felt words, his most cherished belief, into the mouth of this monster? It's true that he does distance himself from what Stavrogin says through several layers of narration, but recall that he did exactly the same thing with Prince Myshkin on the subject of beauty. Like Myshkin, Stavrogin refuses to confirm or deny what he said, but it's a hint that even Stavrogin once knew the answer to his problems, that the seed is there in his own soul. All he has to do to escape from the tyranny of his ego is to turn to the truth of Christ, but he cannot do it. To borrow from the symbolism of *The Karamazov Brothers* and its epigraph, the seed will not bring forth fruit, because it is has been planted not in the fertile spiritual ground of Russia, but has been left high and dry on what Dostoevsky sees as the barren wastes of European rationalism.

As far as Stavrogin himself can see, there is now only one way out of his mess, and that is to commit the 'even greater crime' that Tikhon predicted and take his own life, just like Matryosha did. For Dostoevsky with his boundless love for life, suicide is the worst punishment that he can inflict on his characters, and it is reserved exclusively for the irredeemable, for those who have fallen so far from Christ that there is no possibility of return. Even Ippolit is allowed a last minute reprieve for he still retains a few shreds of faith. Kirilov attempts quite calmly and even cheerfully to reverse Dostoevsky's logic: he will kill himself because he has no faith and because he believes that by doing it without fear, he will raise mankind to the status of god. In the end though, his death is not really a suicide, it's a murderous farce, manipulated by Pyotr Verkhovensky, and, as Joseph Frank so eloquently puts it, Kirilov becomes a 'terrified sub-human creature,' negating his own desire to conquer the fear of death.

Like Stavrogin, Svidrigaylov also takes his own life, but his suicide is calmer, his exit carefully orchestrated. This is an act not of despair, but of sheer boredom. He's done everything that he wants to do, there are no close ties to bind him to the earth, and he has no responsibilities. He's simply finished, so he quietly departs. While he still thought that he could seduce Dunya, he had some purpose in life, but once that's over, he realises that he has no other goal left. We've already seen that, for Dostoevsky, an essential part of the human spirit is the need to have something to strive for, but Svidrigaylov's life is so empty that he has died spiritually long before he pulls the trigger. He tells everyone that he's going to America, (while Stavrogin talks about going to Switzerland), and invites Raskolnikov to go with him, for he thinks that the only way out for Raskolnikov is for him to kill himself as well. But Raskolnikov has Sonya to guide him away from the path of spiritual death and so he is able to avoid Svidrigaylov's fate. The notebooks show that Dostoevsky considered suicide as a possibility for Raskolnikov, but that would, I think, have been entirely inconsistent with Raskolnikov's character and the nature of the novel.

The third suicide to consider is that of Smerdyakov in *The Karamazov Brothers*. It's hard to write about this in too much detail, for fear of giving away too much of a story that keeps us in as much suspense as any great thriller, but like Stavrogin and Svidrigaylov, Smerdyakov is a man whose spiritual life has led him into such a dead end that there is nothing more for him. Like the other two, Smerdyakov has lost any sort of morality; he's absorbed some of Ivan's atheism, but only the parts he finds convenient: that everything is permitted (of course), or that if there is no God, then there's no such thing as virtue or even any need for it. And just as Svidrigaylov's suicide enables Raskolnikov to take his first steps to spiritual freedom, so Smerdyakov's suicide forces Ivan and Dmitry to confront their own roles in the murder of their father, and prepares them for the future.

If the suicides of Svidrigaylov and Smerdyakov have a profound effect on the events that follow, Stavrogin's suicide leaves no such legacy. He has lost all the characters that he has created, and his own death is the closing of the book, quite literally: after his death, there is nothing. Rowan Williams writes that the Devil is out to stop history, and in *The Devils* that is exactly what happens. The ends of the other novels all have some sort of sense of the future, (even the bleakness at the end of *The Idiot* is mitigated by Lizaveta Prokofyevna) – after finishing these novels I always find myself sitting quietly for a few moments before I put down the book, in acknowledgement of the fact that the story goes on. *The Devils* isn't like that: it finishes very firmly, story done, Stavrogin dies, the book snaps shut.

Stavrogin's frank and honest final letter to Dasha is one of the saddest parts of the novel, comparable to the tenderness of Stepan Verkhovensky's last days. It is so sad because Stavrogin is still struggling to come to terms with the fact that his life has been devoid of all meaning, but now he's run out of steam. He feels nothing, he believes in nothing, and realises that he has nothing left to him but a hopelessly proud emptiness.

From me nothing has come but negation, with no magnanimity and no force. Even negation has not come from me. Everything has always been petty and lifeless. ... I know that I ought to kill myself, to brush myself off the earth, like some loathsome insect; but I am afraid of suicide, because I am afraid of showing magnanimity. I know that it will be another delusion again, a delusion in an infinite sequence of delusions. What is the use of deluding oneself merely in order to play at magnanimity? Indignation and shame I can never feel, therefore not despair either.[19]

These terrible monsters conjured up by Dostoevsky are exaggerations of ourselves; we all lose the way from time to time, we've all done things that we know we shouldn't, but by and large we all have a moral compass that keeps us in line, that brings us back to where we should be. Some are lucky enough to have a firm religious faith to guide them, which for Dostoevsky is to be found exclusively in Christ, but it doesn't have to be. The moral compass doesn't even have to come from a god: I know atheists who have a much stronger personal morality than many

---

[19] *The Devils,* p 667 (Part Three, Chapter 8)

religious people. The rest of us muddle along, trying to do our best, but often making mistakes along the way, and causing unnecessary suffering to our fellow humans, and to ourselves. Dostoevsky dwells on the extremes; he draws out the chaos and instability of society that he saw around him, and points us to the worst things that can happen.

Commentators often draw our attention to the fact that Dostoevsky was writing at a time of great social upheaval, when the old ways of life and the old certainties were being questioned, and this is no less the case today, when it is easier than ever to get lost in material comforts, to give ourselves up to the desire for more and more pleasure, and when morality is increasingly left to the individual. It's easy to see how such a decadent world can produce the legions of Stavrogins, Raskolnikovs and Karamazovs. Alternatively we could try to attain the impossible heights of spiritual perfection exhibited by Sonya, Alyosha or Father Zossima, by retreating into a protective cocoon of religious faith.

What is harder to understand is how the average person manages to live amid chaos and disintegration, either in Dostoevsky's time or our own, or in the far more terrible years that separate them, and retain basic human decency. But the Dostoevskian world is not always about extremes, and its reputation for being a place of hopeless misery is unjust, because amidst all the vice, the misery, the confusion and the instability, Dostoevsky gives us some really decent men and women, nice people who you'd be happy to go to the pub with or live next-door to, the miracles of ordinary life whose combined force is what actually keeps everything together.

It was hardly possible to be on anything but friendly terms with Razumikhin, who was an extraordinarily cheerful and communicative young fellow ... everybody was fond of him.

SIX: RAZUMIKHIN AND DUNYA

Raskolnikov's close friend Razumikhin is one of those people who it's very hard to dislike. He bounds through the pages of *Crime and Punishment* like a big shaggy dog, sometimes overenthusiastic, sometimes getting the wrong end of the stick, but nevertheless devotedly loyal, and sadly confused by Raskolnikov's erratic behaviour. His impulsiveness often leads him to speak his mind before he's thought about what he's saying, especially after a few drinks, so he frequently puts his foot in it. His behaviour around the Raskolnikov women is exacerbated by the fact that he is embarrassed and flustered by their uncommon dignity and beauty, but happily he also possesses a great deal of natural charm and is thus able to wriggle out of the sticky situations in which he lands himself – such as being grossly (but understandably) rude about Dunya's fiancé. He also has a wicked sense of humour, as in this case where he's clearly decided that his discussion with Porfiry about the origins of crime is getting far too serious:

"Very well, if you like", he roared, "I'll prove to you at once that your eyelashes are white because the church of Ivan the Great is two hundred and fifty feet high, and I shall prove it clearly, ex-

actly, progressively, and even with a liberal twist! I promise you I will. Want a bet?"[1]

As the story unfolds, Razumikhin becomes a rock of support for the whole Raskolnikov family. Even though he's as poor as Raskolnikov, he works to support himself and generously offers to share his translation work with his friend: he is so considerate that he pretends that his German isn't up to scratch, so that Raskolnikov has the opportunity to accept help without wounding his own pride. He helps Raskolnikov's mother and sister with the practical arrangements for their life in St Petersburg once they have freed themselves from the odious Luzhin, and he comes up with a well-thought out, if optimistic plan for them all to set up a publishing business. Mrs Raskolnikov, despite her alarm at his madcap ways, quickly recognises his efficiency, and above all his kindness. Rock seems the most apt word to describe Razumikhin, for he reminds me time and again of Christ's apostle Simon Peter, the Rock on which the church was to be built. Like Razumikhin, Peter is always charging ahead, blundering about, saying really silly things and making promises that he might not always be able to keep; but despite his impetuosity, he is well-meaning and sincere in his devotion to Jesus, and his response to the suffering of his friend is to find in himself a new degree of maturity and responsibility. The story of St Peter is, above all, the tale of a perfectly ordinary man who suddenly finds himself in the middle of extraordinary events, and the message that we are left with is that if Peter can conquer his human foolishness, then so can we all. If we were to re-tell *Crime and Punishment* from Razumikhin's point of view, the result might be similar.

It's easy to overlook Dostoevsky's good people, his ordinary human beings, people like Razumikhin and Dunya, or like Varya Ptitsyn, Radomsky or Dasha Shatova, in favour of the semi-fantastical, larger than life characters, the Stavrogins, the Kara-

---

[1] *Crime and Punishment* p274 (Part Three, Chapter 5)

mazovs, the Verkhovenskys or Nastasya Filippovna, but like St Peter, the normal folk have important roles in the drama. It is their destinies that give us a hint as to where Dostoevsky's own sentiments lie, and they become quiet morals behind the fireworks of tragedy. They stand as striking contrasts to the larger figures: they magnify the grotesque, they emphasise the gulf between ordinary and extraordinary and they show us what effect the fantastical characters can have on the world around them. Some survive their encounter with Dostoevskian excess seemingly unscathed, but others, like Aglaya Yepanchina and Katerina Verkhovtseva, crash against it, and find their lives changed. One step further from the action, there are the anonymous crowds of other ordinary people who are, by turns, puzzled or angry or disgusted, and their responses dictate how the action develops. Out of these crowds step the frail human narrators who deliver Dostoevsky's stories to us, again, ordinary people who are sometimes bemused by what's going on and coloured by their own ignorance and prejudices, but who nevertheless try to tell us about the strange things they have seen.

Dostoevsky himself acknowledges the importance of the ordinary people in his narrative in his digressive introduction to Part Four of *The Idiot*:

Nevertheless we are faced with dilemma – what is a novelist to do with ordinary people, people who are completely featureless, and how to make them the least bit interesting to readers? One cannot possibly avoid them altogether in a story, because ordinary people form an essential and vital link in the chain of life's events; were we to miss them out, this would be at the expense of verisimilitude. To pack novels with types alone or even simply for interest's sake with strange and unusual people, would be to violate reality, and, come to that, would be uninteresting.[2]

---

[2] *The Idiot* p484 (Part Four, Chapter 1)

Dostoevsky makes a sound point here, but there is more to his portrayal of ordinary people than simply a desire for realism: quite frankly, I think that if Dostoevsky had wanted to create a thoroughly fantastical narrative, he would have been quite capable of doing so. *The Devils* comes close at times, with only Dasha Shatova and Mrs Virginsky providing any hint of normality – and they're fairly minor characters. Ordinary may seem too harsh a word, especially for such personable characters as Razumikhin and Dunya, but in the context of Dostoevsky's odd and fantastic creations, yes, these are indeed ordinary, realistic human beings. They are blessed with balanced minds, are firmly grounded in the real world, and psychologically equipped to live there.

Dostoevsky claims, in that passage in *The Idiot*, that all ordinary people want to believe themselves better than they are. Psychologists call this phenomenon 'illusory superiority' and it famously manifests itself in surveys of how people perceive their own skills, such as driving ability, and in which a mathematically impossible number rate themselves as being above average. Dostoevsky talks first about those who he considers to possess limited intelligence but who themselves firmly believe that they are in fact quite extraordinary and original, because they are able to delude themselves that they have come up with their own clever ideas, when in fact they have simply absorbed them from others. Dostoevsky often pokes fun at this type, and Pyotr Luzhin and Andrei Lebezyatnikov (*Crime and Punishment*) make for particularly good comic examples. Luzhin is thoroughly unpleasant, and is certainly not very bright: he fails to see how grossly he has treated Dunya and her mother, and after the break-up puzzles over whether he would have done better to give them more gifts so that they would feel indebted towards him. On his arrival in St Petersburg, he has felt the need to ingratiate himself with the progressives and the younger generation, not out of any firm political beliefs, but simply because he has a terror of what he refers to as 'exposure' – he doesn't really understand anything, but has picked up a few fashionable phrases, so that he can sound convincing. Lebezyatnikov, his younger room-mate and his guide to radical society, is, we are told, 'a bit stupid', and Dostoevsky goes on, using rather cruel language to describe such hangers-on, who grasp on to the latest ideas, but who end up vulgarising the causes that they think they sincerely believe in. Lebezyatnikov guiding Luzhin is plainly a case of the blind leading the blind, and the consequences are made clear in the first chapter of Part Five in which the pair attempt to discuss the question of women's emancipation. The misunderstandings and cross-talking that litter this conversation are incredibly funny – I tried to find a passage to quote, but really the whole scene needs to be read to get the full comic effect.

The conversation between Luzhin and Lebezyatnikov and Luzhin's subsequent attempt to frame Sonya for theft is one of those few episodes when the narrator steps away from his close shadowing of Raskolnikov, so there must be a reason for this digression into the lives of other people, other than to provide the reader with some light relief. What Dostoevsky is doing here is not simply exposing radical nihilist ideas to ridicule and making us laugh at them – he's being a bit more subtle than that. Whilst Raskolnikov's theories, his crime and later his nightmare about the future, all illustrate how dangerous utilitarian ideas could be in the hands of an extremely intelligent, single-minded man, Luzhin and Lebezyatnikov are there to demonstrate the dangers of putting complex ideas about the organisation of society into the hands of people who clearly don't understand them at all. If the likes of Lebezyatnikov, with their confused grasp of socialist theory, were in charge, the results would be a muddle-headed awfulness, just as it would be if the amateur conspirators of *The Devils* had ever got anywhere. We know this, because we've seen it time and again, across the world, in all the failures of communism and its mutations, when the shrewd political operators have triumphed over the thinkers – Dostoevsky saw it coming.

The other type of ordinary person who appears in this essay in *The Idiot* belongs to the class of those who are smart enough to know that they are ordinary, but who cling desperately to the belief that if things had been different they could and should have done better. If they'd been to a better school... if they'd had better connections... if they'd had enough capital... if they hadn't had children... It's an insidious train of reasoning, and it tempts the thinker into a dangerous abnegation of responsibility. These people are driven by a desperate desire to rise above their mediocrity. They are not content with the happiness that they could find in their lives if they only looked for it, and they fail to recognise the value of their own small good deeds, their particular talents and the jobs they've done well. The narrator says that Ganya Ivolgin has begun along this path, and it's the crippling mixture of ambition and fear of failure common to this type of person that leads him into his entanglements with Nastasya Filippovna and his failure to win Aglaya. He ends up having a nervous breakdown and living off his sister, when he could have had a perfectly respectable career in the service of General Yepanchin, for he is clearly has the makings of being a competent administrator. Von Lembke, the governor in *The Devils,* is forced onto a similar road of destruction by his ambitious wife, whereas he himself would have been quite content to settle for a post suited to his abilities and that allowed him the time and energy to devote to his model-making hobby.

Dostoevsky puts Ganya's sister, Varya and her husband, Ivan Ptitsyn, into his category of clever ordinary people, but really they're a third type, because he makes it clear that they actually do recognise and accept their ordinariness. They understand that they can be happy as they are, they don't worry about their mediocrity and they take practical steps to make their lives comfortable. Ptitsyn occupies himself with the grubby but necessary business of moneylending, but he tries to treat his clients honourably, and is rewarded with a steadily growing business. Ganya is angry that Ptitsyn refuses to squeeze his customers mercilessly in the hope of becoming a 'Rothschild' – Dostoevsky's standard shorthand for what he sees as fantastic and dubiously earned wealth – whereas in fact Ptitsyn limits his dreams to a perfectly achievable ambition of owning a couple of houses in a nice part of town. Dostoevsky is particularly sympathetic and kind to the Ptitsyns, and makes it clear that even though they have married for boringly sensible, practical reasons, they will find happiness together – and four houses. Adelaida and Prince Sh. are a similar case, albeit from slightly higher up the social scale – Prince Sh. is:

One of those men ... who are honest, decent, who conscientiously strive to do good and are distinguished by the fortunate quality of always being able to find employment for themselves.[3]

In other words, definitely not a superfluous man. In the words of Radomsky, although Prince Sh. and Adelaida are 'not yet intimate friends', they too will learn to be happy together.

Radomsky himself is another extremely attractive character – good looking, successful, charming and pragmatic. He remains unflustered by Nastasya Filippovna's hysterical attempts to embarrass him, and after the events of the novel reach their tragic conclusion, it is Radomsky who takes practical steps to pick up the pieces. Like the Ptitsyns, one of the reasons that he is so likeable is because of his perceptive understanding and acceptance of himself. On the terrace of the Yepanchins' house, he talks about the Russian landowning class, of which he is a member, and its detachment from the rest of the Russian nation. All the Russian liberals and socialists hail from the landowning class, maintains Radomsky, and they all hate everything that is truly Russian despite thinking that they care deeply. Radomsky obviously includes himself in this honest description, because by the end of the novel he has gone abroad. In his own words, he is 'a superfluous man in Russia' – and unlike Stavrogin, he recognises this, and understands that he is better off in Europe, rather than becoming a stranger in his own country.

---

[3] *The Idiot* p192 (Part Two, Chapter 1)

These ordinary people can be held up as a mirror to the Dostoevskian big guns, reflecting their circumstances but offering a human alternative to the choices and mistakes made by the heroes. Razumikhin, as we have noted, is in an almost identical position to Raskolnikov, in fact he is even poorer than his friend, but he knows that his only chance to escape from poverty lies in relentless hard work and patience. His name is derived from the word *razum,* meaning reason, but there is a further subtlety that is not always included in translations: in Part Two, Chapter 3, Razumikhin says that his real name is actually Vrazumikhin. The verb *vrazumit'* means to make someone listen to reason, or to convince, thus implying that Razumikhin should really have an active role to play – but as it is, Raskolnikov's stubbornness and refusal to accept help or advice mean that Razumikhin cannot influence him, and he simply stands instead as an example of the reasonable behaviour that Raskolnikov should have adopted. Raskolnikov thinks he can overcome all the obstacles in his way by being a superman: he is looking for a quick fix, and fails terribly, but Razumikhin's example shows him that he would have had more chance of success by being a decent, ordinary, man.

The ordinary folk, on the whole, manage to handle their problems and are able to deal competently with whatever life throws at them. Characters like Razumikhin and Dunya avoid the difficulties experienced by Dostoevsky's heroes and heroines who cannot cope when their ideals clash with the reality of the world; they understand the world and they are prepared to make compromises to their own ideals in order to fit in and be happy. When faced with the suffering of humankind, they are not overwhelmed by it, like Ivan Karamazov, and they strive to help those around them in small, practical ways instead of trying to grapple with the enormity of the whole earth's misery. They do not fool themselves that they are great people to whom everything is permitted, but rather they try to overcome their own material shortcomings with the resources available to them. And when relationships become difficult, as they inevitably do for even the most outgoing, cheerful people, they struggle on, instead of taking the route of the Underground Man and retreating from the world.

Dunya exhibits this sensible, pragmatic approach to life when dealing with her proposed marriage to Luzhin. There are, of course, obvious parallels to be drawn between Dunya and Sonya, particularly in Raskolnikov's reactions to their behaviour. He fully understands that Dunya is marrying Luzhin not for personal gain, and certainly not for love, but purely in order to support her family – specifically him. Dunya is essentially doing exactly the same as Sonya, with the only difference being that she is selling her body in a way that is sanctioned by society. The important point to make about Dunya here is that although she is prepared to suffer when she thinks that by doing so she can help her family, she will not sacrifice herself pointlessly, and she will not embrace suffering for the sake of it, so when it becomes clear that Luzhin will not allow her to use his money to support Raskolnikov, she promptly breaks off the engagement. As we will see in the next chapter, Dostoevsky utterly detests unnecessary suffering, and he eventually rewards Dunya for her sense in avoiding it. Varya Ptitsyn, like Dunya, finds herself in a position where she needs to marry in order to support her rather hopeless family when the breadwinner, her brother Ganya, suffers a nervous collapse after his disastrous entanglement with Nastasya Filippovna. In contrast to Nastasya, who takes a perverse pride in the fact that her body is up for auction, Varya doesn't marry Ptitsyn with a stubborn self-righteousness, and she doesn't make a fuss of the fact that she is selling herself for her family's sake. Like Dunya, she too is rewarded by Dostoevsky with a happy marriage and a modestly comfortable life.

Dostoevsky has an obvious admiration for Dunya and for the other spirited, practical and intelligent women who grace his pages, and the bitter complaints of Katerina Nikolaevna in *The Adolescent* would not, I imagine, have been applied to Dostoevsky himself:

In society they never talk with us women like that [she has been recalling how she and Arkady would examine and discuss statistics published in the newspapers]. *Last week I tried to talk with Prince ___ v about Bismarck, because it interested me very much, but I couldn't make up my own mind, and, imagine, he sat down beside me and began telling me, even in great detail, but all of it with some sort of irony, and precisely with that condescension I find so unbearable, with which "great men" usually speak to us women when we meddle in what is "not our business".*[4]

Unlike some men, Dostoevsky was not at all afraid or intimidated by clever and emancipated women, and this is borne out in the women wrote about, and by his choice of friends in real life – women such as Anna Korvin-Krukovskaya. She was the daughter of a retired army officer who had very strict ideas about how young ladies should behave, but both Anna and her sister Sofya broke away quite impressively from the bourgeois strictures of their upbringing. Anna eventually ended up married to Charles Victor Jaclard, a well known French communist. She fought alongside her husband on the barricades of the Paris Commune and translated Marx into French; whilst Sofya became one of the first female professors of mathematics in Europe. Anna met Dostoevsky after he had published some stories that she had secretly written. They struck up a close friendship, and very nearly became engaged, despite the disapproval of her father (Frank suggests that aspects of Aglaya Yepanchina and her relationship with Prince Myshkin are modelled on Korvin-Krukovskaya). The relationship broke up because of their political differences and because Anna sensibly realised that their strong personalities would be better suited to friendship than marriage, and they remained close friends.

Dostoevsky's sensible women also bear a striking resemblance to his second wife, Anna Snitkina: she lacked the intellectual fire of women like the Korvin-Krukovskaya sisters, but she was

---

[4] *The Adolescent* p254 (Part Two, Chapter 4, Section 1)

blessed with great practical abilities and strict morals. (She was part-Swedish, and it shows!) Unlike his first marriage, which was founded on passion, and on the sort of desire that comes only with unavailability,[5] this second marriage was long and happy and was one of the few bright lights in Dostoevsky's biography. Anna arrived on his doorstep at a moment of crisis: he had to produce a novel for Stellovsky, a notoriously rapacious publisher, in payment of a debt, and the penalty for not delivering it on time was to be forfeiture of his copyrights. He was suffering physically under the strain, and time was rapidly running out, so his friend Milyukov urged him to hire a stenographer to help with the workload. Milyukov made all the arrangements, and Anna Snitkina duly reported for work on 4 October 1866.

The first meeting was not a success. Dostoevsky was irritable and distracted, and was still not convinced that using a stenographer would work, but when Anna returned for a second visit, he was more relaxed and they soon settled down to an orderly pattern of working, managing together the minor miracle of completing *The Gambler* before Stellovsky's deadline. The publisher then attempted to prevent Dostoevsky from submitting the novel in time by leaving town and instructing his subordinates that the manuscript must be delivered to him alone – but his deviousness was thwarted by Anna who, anticipating trouble, took legal advice and arranged for a notary to receive the manuscript.

Anna's side of the story too has a certain fairy-tale ring to it. She had been studying at the Women's Pedagogical Institute in St Petersburg, but had to drop out of her studies to nurse her sick father. At his encouragement, she enrolled in a stenography course only because the classes were held in the evening and so she was able to attend after her father had gone to bed. In her *Reminiscences*, she writes that she had long dreamt about work-

---

[5] Maria Isaeva was still married when she and Dostoevsky first met, and after her husband's death she vacillated for some time between Dostoevsky and another suitor.

ing and was delighted when her stenography teacher recommended her for a job with the famous writer.

> *I was quick to agree. The name of Dostoevsky had been known to me since I was a child. He was my father's favourite author. I myself had been enraptured with his works and had wept over 'Notes from the House of the Dead'. The very idea, not only of meeting this gifted writer, but also of helping him in his work, filled me with excitement and elation.*[6]

In lengthy conversations in between the dictation sessions, Anna and Dostoevsky quickly became friends, and before long, she had been transported from being an avid reader of each new instalment of *Crime and Punishment* to being engaged to its author and working with him on the final chapters. At this stage in the story, one is tempted to say lucky, lucky Anna. However, the luck was just as much on Dostoevsky's side. Anna brought him calm, stability and immense practical common sense, and settled his chaotic working habits into a regular daily routine. After her triumph over Stellovsky, she then took care of his business arrangements and drove hard bargains with publishers and creditors who had previously taken advantage of Dostoevsky's own hopelessness in this area. Eventually she set up two successful businesses: first a publishing company to publish Dostoevsky's novels, then a mail-order bookselling enterprise offering readers in the provinces the opportunity to buy books that were only obtainable in St Petersburg. On top of all the practical comforts that she brought, she also loved him faithfully and devotedly, despite the disaster of his selfish gambling addiction and the poverty and personal tragedies that were to befall them. Throughout his biography, the spirited but sensible personality of Anna rings out, and it is surely to her that we owe the creation of all his later novels, for she gave him the support that he so badly needed, creating the atmosphere in which he could write as well as con-

---

[6] Anna Dostoevskaya, *Reminiscences* p14-15

tinuing her invaluable stenographic work to prepare his manuscripts for publication.

In his speech at the unveiling of the Pushkin statue in 1880, Dostoevsky makes his admiration for such steadfast and strong women abundantly clear, although, given the tenor of the rest of the speech, and of Dostoevsky's general line of thought, it all becomes inextricably bound up with his blinkered nationalist ideas about Russia. He talks about Tatyana, the heroine of Pushkin's great poem *Eugene Onegin*, calling her:

A strong character, firmly standing on her own soil ... an apotheosis of Russian womanhood.

And, in a hugely generous gesture to Turgenev, he went on to say that:

So beautiful and genuine a type of Russian woman has virtually never reappeared in our literature – save, perhaps, for the image of Liza in Turgenev's A Gentlefolk's Nest.[7]

Tatyana is presented by Dostoevsky as a contrast to Onegin, who is the lost wanderer and archetypal superfluous man. She has grown up in the depths of the Russian countryside, under the care of a Russian nanny; she is steeped in Russian traditions and is modest and virtuous (although Dostoevsky conveniently overlooks the fact that Tatyana's Russian is so weak that she has to write her famous letter to Onegin in French). She falls in love with Onegin, but he makes it clear that he thinks she's plain and boring and rejects her. When they meet again, she has been married off by her family to a rich general, and now, decorated with a few jewels, she is miraculously transformed in Onegin's eyes.

---

[7] The speech was later published as a special edition of *Diary of a Writer* in August 1880. Some witnesses claimed that Dostoevsky had also mentioned Tolstoy's Natasha Rostov (*War and Peace*) alongside Turgenev's Liza, but this was lost in the tumultuous applause produced by his praise of Turgenev, and the reference was omitted from the printed version of the speech (see *Collected Works,* v. 26 p496).

He suddenly discovers that he loves her after all, but she, while admitting that she still loves him, refuses him, stating firmly that she is bound to her husband, and cannot break the sacred bond of marriage. In Dostoevsky's eyes, this steadfast commitment to the vows she has made, coupled with her professed hatred of the glittering life that her marriage has brought her, is what makes her the perfect Russian woman. I am sure that Dunya is Dostoevsky's own attempt at recreating Tatyana's virtue for his generation. She refuses to be corrupted by either Luzhin or Svidrigaylov, remains steadfast in her love for her family, and is quietly courageous throughout the story.

Dunya and Razumikhin have the moral strength to survive their intimate contact with two of Dostoevsky's monstrosities – Raskolnikov and Svidrigaylov – but not everyone is so lucky. Aglaya Yepanchina and Katerina Verkhovtseva are both described as high-minded, intelligent, virtuous girls, and both would have been destined to make good marriages and live uneventful lives until they wake up one day to find themselves in the middle of a Dostoevsky novel. When they are confronted with Prince Myshkin, with Nastasya Filippovna, and with the Karamazovs, the two girls find themselves behaving in ways which they would ordinarily consider to be despicable, and they emerge from the experience profoundly changed.

Aglaya is still very young – only twenty, and has lived a life of comfort, being petted and adored by everyone. Her encounter with Prince Myshkin and Nastasya Filippovna magnifies all her own worst characteristics, and the more she tries to play at being a grown-up rival to the worldly Nastasya, the more her own immaturity shows through. We've already seen how her adolescent imagination attempts to turn Prince Myshkin into a virtuous knight, a real fairy-tale prince: she mocks him with Pushkin's poem *The Poor Knight* and becomes angry when she thinks he's not standing up for himself against Burdovsky's attempts at slander and extortion. The strange episode where she quizzes him about duels and urges him to learn how to use a pistol are linked to her girlish romantic notions about the Prince: I suspect that she cherishes a secret fantasy that he (or someone else) will one day fight a duel for her.

Aglaya is continuously cruel to the Prince, laughing at him, squabbling with him, and as Myshkin is a child himself, albeit a wiser child than Aglaya, he lacks the emotional depth and experience of life to recognise her attention-seeking for what it is. His kindness and patience with her only encourage her behaviour, which comes to its climax in the great confrontation with Nastasya Filippovna. Aglaya is trying painfully hard here to be adult and dignified, but faced with Myshkin and Nastasya she loses all self-control and indulges in petty name-calling and unjustified unpleasantness. Her words remind the Prince how everyone perceives Nastasya, forcing him again to pity her for her unhappiness, and it is thus Aglaya who engineers Myshkin's final fateful decision.

Aglaya is left frozen in her childlike ways because Prince Myshkin's timelessness has atrophied her character so that she can now no longer grow and develop into a mature woman. She ends the novel in a disastrous marriage to a Polish émigré, separated from her family, involved in Polish relief work and probably converted to Catholicism – such a wholehearted conversion to European ways is Dostoevsky's way of implying that she has cast off her native land and all her innate Russian virtues. For her though, it must have seemed to answer her childish fantasies about running away and trying to do good deeds, and the dubious Polish Count probably also appeared to meet her requirements for a knight in shining armour. Sometimes merely admitting a dream to another person makes it more achievable, especially if that person is as trusting as Prince Myshkin, to whom Aglaya confessed all her secret desires. If she hadn't met Myshkin, she would have grown up, married Radomsky, or perhaps Ganya, and settled down as a tyrannical but ordinary mistress of a comfortable household, just like her mother.

Like Aglaya, Katerina (Katya) Verkhovtseva, Dmitry Karamazov's fiancée, is rich, clever and beautiful, and seems to want for nothing. Her family background is not as stable as Aglaya's though: her father has been caught pilfering regimental funds, attempts to shoot himself, and is saved only by the timely intervention of Katya's sister. Her entanglement with Dmitry Karamazov begins at this terrible point in her life. Dmitry has let it be known that if Katya comes to his room, alone, he will give her the money that her father needs to repay his debt. The implications are quite clear, but Katya bravely submits to his demands and arrives at Dmitry's lodgings, fully prepared to pay the necessary price for the sake of her father. Dmitry is so amazed that she is actually willing to sacrifice herself in this way that the various Karamazov thoughts (as he puts it himself) that initially go through his head are quickly banished, and he instead finds himself touched by her bravery. He simply hands the money over to her without condition, she bows down to him and now a fateful bond of obligation has been formed between them that will taint all their subsequent relations.

Katerina's dilemma, when faced with the Karamazovs and Grushenka is that she finds herself in a situation that she can no longer control. When we first meet her, she has the self-assurance that comes to someone who is accustomed not just to having her own way, but to being able to anticipate people's behaviour and respond accordingly. From the very beginning, she is wrong-footed by Dmitry, and she has to confront the unpredictable, chaotic, Karamazov side of human nature. In our first meeting with her in the novel, she is trying to master her rivalry with Grushenka. She knows that Grushenka's first love, the Polish officer, has returned for her, and she convinces herself that Grushenka has promised to renounce Dmitry and return to the Pole. Grushenka cheerfully contradicts Katya, insisting that she has promised no such thing, and the meeting ends with the two rivals grossly insulting each other, both using the most hurtful weapons they can summon up, in a scene that threatens to match the show-down between Nastasya and Aglaya. For a time Katerina has been able to hold sway over Dmitry with an aggressive generosity, which comes to a head when she deliberately puts temptation in his way by giving him the fatal three thousand roubles, asks him to send them to her sister in Moscow, and then makes no demand for the return of the money when he subsequently squanders it on an orgy with Grushenka. This attempt to control Dmitry backfires when his desperate quest to raise the funds he needs to repay Katya and clear his obligations to her creates all the damning circumstantial evidence that will be used against him in court.

By the time we get to Dmitry's trial, Katerina has lost control not only of other people, but of herself too, and is no longer able to act in either her own or Dmitry's best interests. She has almost certainly fallen in love with Ivan, which wasn't in her plan, but she still feels the need to try and save Dmitry by arranging for an expensive Moscow defence lawyer and an expensive Moscow doctor to testify at the trial, neither of whom turn out to be particularly helpful. She herself wavers between helping and hindering Dmitry, first creating a favourable view of the accused with a courageously edited version of their first meeting – a version that casts a considerable shadow over her own virtue. Later though, when she sees Ivan's terrible breakdown in the courtroom, she breaks court protocol and produces a piece of damning evidence against Dmitry that she had previously concealed. She does not understand that not even she, with her powers of manipulation, can save Ivan from the demons that torment him, and in her desire to redeem Ivan she has to sacrifice Dmitry – an action that she later regrets. Furthermore, because she expects to remain in control of everything, she is convinced that she alone is to blame for everything, even for Ivan's breakdown in court:

Oh, my rage is the cause of all this! And it was I who caused that damned scene at the trial. [Ivan] *wanted to show me his nobility of spirit, and that even if I did love his brother, he wouldn't destroy him out of revenge and jealousy. So that's why he came and spoke out at the trial. ... It was me, I'm the cause of everything, I alone am guilty.*[8]

After the trial she cares for the two brothers, arranging practical comforts and medical attention for both of them. The one thing she cannot bring herself to do is to confront Dmitry, until Alyosha forces her to visit him. Alyosha knows that Katya and Dmitry cannot start to rebuild their lives until they have forgiven each other, and in a scene that mirrors their first meeting, they are reconciled. *The Karamazov Brothers,* even more than any of Dostoevsky's other novels, is all about how we live together in the world, hurting each other, but also loving and forgiving each other. By the end of the novel Katerina is beginning to accept that she cannot control everything, even if she hasn't quite fully grasped the corollary that she is also not solely responsible for every catastrophe that she encounters. What she does finally learn though is that when things do get out of hand, forgiveness and reconciliation are possible, even from the basest Karamazov. Whilst Aglaya ends frozen in childishness, Katerina's encounter with the Dostoevskian world has left her sadder, wiser, but probably, in the end, happier, as we see yet another case of Dostoevsky revisiting themes from *The Idiot* and recasting them in a less pessimistic mould.

These clashes between the rational, ordinary characters and the chaotic side of Dostoevsky's universe can be usefully examined in the light of Friedrich Nietzsche's study of Greek drama, *The Birth of Tragedy from the Spirit of Music,* a work that, in combination with Dostoevsky's writing, played an extremely important role in influencing the next generation of Russian writers. Dostoevsky was greatly admired by the German philosopher, who wrote that Dostoevsky was the only psychologist from whom he had anything to learn, but it seems that Dostoevsky was never aware of the younger man's work, which is a pity because a dialogue between them would have been fascinating.

---

[8] *The Karamazov Brothers*, p 953 (Epilogue, Section 1)

In *The Birth of Tragedy,* Nietzsche wrote that the world is divided into two conflicting spheres, the Apollonian and the Dionysian, and he explains that it is the combination of these two elements that creates classical Greek tragedy. Apollo the sun god represents order, reason, and balance – he is the clear light of day, and these qualities are set against the chaos, darkness and intoxication that comes from the world of Dionysus. We associate Dostoevsky's work with disorder, with subjectivity, with bacchanalian chaos, but the rational, sensible people like Razumikhin and Dunya bring an important Apollonian balance to his disordered world.

For Nietzsche, the Dionysian element of Greek tragedy is also associated with role of the chorus, whilst the Apollonian desire to bring forth order from chaos is to be found in the dialogue and the actions of the tragic hero. The chorus element is very strong in Dostoevsky's novels, particularly in *The Idiot, The Devils* and *The Karamazov Brothers.* In the latter two novels, both of which are set in a small town in provincial Russia, the voices of the townspeople are frequently felt, either through the words of the narrator, himself an ordinary citizen (albeit implausibly omniscient and omnipresent), in the crowds at Dmitry's trial, and in the terrible events that follow the night of destruction in *The Devils. The Idiot* and *The Karamazov Brothers* make use of a further chorus feature that will be all too familiar to modern readers: grotesquely slanderous news reports, directed at Prince Myshkin and Mrs Khokhlakova, although like so many others who are seduced by their moment of fame, Mrs Khokhlakova seems more excited than angry about being pilloried in the national press.

The great Soviet critic Bakhtin described Dostoevsky's novels as being polyphonic, in that, like polyphonic music, they contain a multitude of equal and overlapping voices, each weaving their own way through the text, with no dominating point of view, and nowhere is the polyphony more strongly felt than in the babble of ordinary voices that judge and comment on the actions of the main characters. This public judgement is at its loudest during Dmitry Karamazov's trial when everyone in the courtroom has made up their mind in advance, basing their opinion on what they've heard of his character and behaviour; on whispered anecdotes and half-remembered stories.

Public trials were a relatively new concept in Russia: they had been introduced as part of Alexander II's reforms in 1864, and had thus been in place only for a couple of years at the time in which *The Karamazov Brothers* is set[9]. Whenever I read it I am stunned by how modern Dmitry's trial-by-public-opinion seems. The recent case of Amanda Knox, a young American girl studying in Italy, who was accused of murdering her British roommate, could have come straight from Dostoevsky's pen, and the world was judging Knox by her looks, by her alleged behaviour when she was arrested, and on whispered stories about her sexual history. Like Dmitry's case, the verdict seemed determined before she even entered the courtroom.

From the anonymous mass of the chorus Dostoevsky's narrators emerge; real, fallible human beings, who tell the story as eyewitnesses. Dostoevsky tries very hard, and not entirely successfully, to make the narrator of *The Devils* into an active character in the drama – he is a close friend of Stepan Verkhovensky, and a hanger-on of the clandestine political group; he is conveniently taken along to several of the secret night-time meetings, and witnesses other significant encounters, but he's not really a major player in the action, and by the time Dostoevsky gets to *The Karamazov Brothers,* he simply asks us to suspend disbelief and accept that the narrator is somehow privy to all sorts of private conversations. This technique of using an unreliable and subjective character as a narrator begins towards the end of *The Idiot* when the previously distant and apparently omniscient narrator steps forward and begins to cast doubt on what he's telling us:

---

[9] The novel was published in 1880, but we are told on the first page that the action took place "thirteen years ago".

We feel that we have to restrict ourselves to a simple exposition of the facts only, avoiding where possible all attempts at explaining, for the simple reason that in many instances we ourselves are at a loss to provide an explanation of what occurred. Such a reservation on our part must needs appear rather strange and puzzling, inasmuch as how can one continue recounting something of which one has neither a clear understanding nor a personal opinion? [10]

The ordinary narrators allow Dostoevsky to present his opinions to us through a filter that removes his own voice, and makes us think for ourselves instead of being preached at by an author who knows everything – I think this is the reason why Dostoevsky's fiction is so much better than his journalism, for it is in his journalistic writing that Dostoevsky does allow himself to get up into his pulpit to harangue us directly. Sometimes, the narrators are a little dense and fail to understand the finer subtleties of their stories, and at other times, they're asking us to accept things that they could only have heard second-hand or may even have invented. The result of all this narrative vagueness is that we as readers cannot lazily take anything at face value, but have to engage with the action and work out for ourselves what is going on.

Sometimes, Dostoevsky's characters step out from the polyphony to take a solo part, but they do this by setting their ideas out on cold paper, seeking strength and comfort in the introspection of the written word. Raskolnikov and Ivan Karamazov write articles; Ippolit and Stavrogin write out their confessions; and the life and sermons of Father Zossima are presented as a text written by Alyosha. These written documents allow Dostoevsky to sidestep his narrators and put across a big idea, but they also get their authors into difficulties because the solitary act of writing words on a page cuts them off from dialogue with other people. We live in a crowded, noisy world, and nowhere is that more vivid than in the pages of Dostoevsky, which are dominated by dialogue and by people's relationships with each other –

---

[10] *The Idiot* p603 (Part Four, Chapter 9)

we cannot, like the Underground Man, sit in a corner and rage impotently at the world – we have to go out and become a part of it.

Dostoevsky's personable, confiding narrators are as close as he himself can get as an author to overcoming the isolation of the written word. His narrators invite us into his world and introduce us personally to his characters, so that we can develop our own conversation with them. We are forced to think carefully about what the narrator is telling us, instead of just taking it at face value, then by choosing how we respond to it, we can build our own relationship with the characters and events, and become another voice in the glorious polyphony of Dostoevsky's writing.

This sense of being drawn into Dostoevsky's novels and actively playing a part in his imagined communities introduces us to one of his most important ideas, and one which will be explored more deeply during the next two chapters – that of collective responsibility and mutual love, whereby every individual is held morally and spiritually responsible for everyone else's sins and, just as importantly, for everyone else's happiness. This is not a politically imposed collectivist utopia, but a willing personal surrender by each individual ego. This is why Dostoevsky disliked socialism so much, for he saw in it an artificial attempt to force humanity into a brotherhood that should arise naturally and voluntarily. Western Europeans, he believed, were devoid of any natural sense of brotherhood, and were trying to create it artificially, but European individualism meant that socialism still came down to a question of individual rights, not collective responsibility. In his European travel memoir *Winter Notes on Summer Impressions* he writes:

But then what can a socialist do if the principle of brotherhood is absent from Western man, who recognises, on the contrary, the individual and personal principle which always insists on isolation and on demanding rights sword in hand? Because there is no brotherhood, he wants to create it, to build it up ... he determines the utility and cost of each individual, and works out in advance the balance of the world's blessings: how much each individual deserves them and how much each individual must voluntarily contribute to the community. ... But how can there possibly be any brotherhood if it is preceded by a distribution of shares and by determining how much each person has earned and what each must do?[11]

The most admirable of his ordinary good people, such as Razumikhin and Dunya, show how Dostoevsky's vision of brotherhood and mutual love can be achieved, not through pointless sacrifice, but by living a positive and loving life. In his *History of Russian Philosophy*, V.V. Zenkovsky writes:

It would be very one-sided not to draw attention to the profundity with which he reveals the luminous powers of the soul, its dialectic of the good. ... Dostoevsky exhibits not only the sin, corruption, egoism and, in general, the 'demonic' element in man with unprecedented force; he exhibits <u>no less profoundly</u> the impulses toward justice and good in the human soul, the 'angelic' principle in man.[12]

The fates of Aglaya and Katerina, on the other hand, vividly illustrate how easy it is to be driven off course by misunderstanding or weakness. Katerina attempts to impose a single-handed control over events, and when that fails, she attempts to take sole responsibility for the consequences, but this isn't the way that Dostoevsky sees the world. We have to recognise that alone, we are powerless, and although it's all too easy to become overwhelmed by the enormity of the suffering that we see around us, we cannot, should not, try to deal with it on our own.

---

[11] Winter Notes on Summer Impressions p70-71

[12] From an extract in *Dostoevsky. A collection of Critical Essays*, ed René Wellek, p133

> *How could God give up the most loved of his saints to Satan to play with, take his children from him, smite him with sore boils...and why? Just to be able to boast to Satan: "See how much my saint can suffer for my sake".*
>
> *(Father Zossima)*

SEVEN: FATHER ZOSSIMA

In his memoirs, Father Zossima describes how he first heard the Old Testament story of Job, at the age of eight. He was in church, and already deeply moved by the exquisite beauty of smoke from the incense dissolving into the bright sunshine that poured down from a window high above him. In this heightened spiritual state, he listened to a boy reading the story of Job; he felt a mixture of wonder, dismay and gladness, and became conscious, for the first time of God's words entering his own soul. It is quite possible that this passage came directly from Dostoevsky's own memories, for he too was deeply impressed by the Old Testament book of Job and its power remained with him throughout his life. Writing to his wife in 1875, he says:

I am reading the Book of Job and it transports me into a painful ecstasy; I leave off reading and walk about the room almost crying. ... This book Anya, it's strange, it was one of the first in my life that ever really struck me, when I was still almost a little child.[1]

---

[1] Letter to Anna Dostoevskaya, June 1875, *Collected Works* Vol 29, Bk 2, p43, my translation.

Job's is a scorching, difficult story, a testament of human suffering and endurance, rich in poetic imagery, and blood-curdling horror; it's deeply disturbing, right from the first chapter, when we see God and Satan calmly discussing the state of the world, like two old gentleman over tea, and making a silly bet on Job's virtue. Satan wagers that if all Job's blessings in life are taken away from him, then he'll lose his righteousness and curse his God; so that same God, who we are told, is so loving, coolly hands over Job and all his family to Satan, giving the devil free rein to blight Job's life and see what happens. Despite Job's puzzlement over why God appears to be punishing him when he has led a blameless life, he holds firm and refuses to curse his Lord, even as God allows Satan to push him further and further. Although Job is ultimately rewarded for his fortitude, he would probably rather have gone without the suffering that came first, and certainly without the loss of the innocent children who are destroyed as collateral damage in God's great game. Reading Job, we are forced to ask how we can possibly accept a God that does this sort of thing, but in our darker and more honest moments, we may also reverse the question: if God can inflict such bitter trials on the innocent, why does he apparently let the rest of us continue living in happiness, letting us get away with all our sins, great and small.

The dilemma posed by the story of Job is the same one that torments Ivan Karamazov, and which provokes him to his great rebellion against God – his insistence that, if paradise is founded on suffering, then he respectfully returns his ticket. And to answer Alyosha's gentle suggestion that the answer lies through faith in Christ's redeeming death, Ivan presents his majestic Grand Inquisitor story, in which he asserts that truly following the pure way of Christ is simply too difficult for mankind.

The immediate response to Ivan's challenge comes a few chapters later in the Father Zossima's sermons, but Dostoevsky later commented in a notebook that the whole book was an answer to the story of the Grand Inquisitor.[2] In this chapter I will discuss Dostoevsky's use of human suffering, and Father Zossima's response to it, and in the next chapter we will see how Father Zossima's idea of 'responsibility for all' is put into practice by one of the most unlikely people.

Ivan's struggle to comprehend why God allows suffering in the world is a culmination of Dostoevsky's own vast experience of the torments that life can inflict; experiences that lend a terrible moral weight to his fiction – for when Dostoevsky writes about human suffering, he does so with an authority that can only come from one who has seen too much of it himself. Ill-health, mental anxiety, mock execution, imprisonment in Siberia, a gambling addiction, the premature deaths of his parents, his first wife and his dearly-loved brother, poverty, exile, and, worst of all, the deaths of two of his children; it's a life that comes a good deal closer to Job's than many. We also know that Dostoevsky had an extraordinary sensitivity to the suffering of others, and a passionate hatred of the senseless cruelty that he saw around him, not just in the prison camp but in all the brutalities of daily life in Russia. In *Diary of a Writer* in 1876, he recalls an incident that occurred just as he was on the brink of adult life, and which made a great impression on him, probably for the context in which it occurred, rather than for it being out of the ordinary. The fifteen year-old Dostoevsky and his older brother Mikhail were en route from Moscow to St Petersburg, where they were to enrol in the military engineering school. The two boys were full of youthful idealism and excitement; they were discussing Pushkin, and dreaming of the poems and novels that they themselves planned to write. Whilst waiting at an inn during the journey, a government courier arrived at the inn to change carriages:

The courier came running down the staircase and seated himself on the carriage. The driver [a lad of about twenty] *stirred on,*

---

[2] *Collected Works*, Vol. 27 p48

but hardly had he started to move than the courier rose up and silently raised his hardy right fist, and, from above, painfully brought it down on the back of the driver's head. He jolted forward, lifted his whip, and with all his strength, lashed the wheel horse. The horses dashed forward but this in no way appeased the courier. Here there was method and not mere irritation – something preconceived and tested by long years of experience – and the dreadful fist soared again and again and struck blows on the back of the head. And then, again and again, and thus it continued until the troika disappeared out of sight. Of course, the driver, who could hardly keep his balance, incessantly, every second, like a madman, lashed the horses. ...This disgusting scene has remained in my memory all my life.[3]

The courier beats the driver, the driver lashes the horses, and Dostoevsky plausibly imagines that the driver then releases his pent-up rage and humiliation by beating his wife when he gets home, perpetuating the chain of violence and cruelty.

From this sensitivity comes Dostoevsky's eloquent compassion, which he uses to share with his readers the sufferings of others, getting away with deeply sentimental scenes that would be cloying and maudlin in the hands of lesser writers, or when taken out of context. When you're swept up in the whirlwind of a Dostoevsky novel, carried away by his passion, the heartbreaking tales of poverty, of frightened children, of grieving parents, cut right to the heart; as a reader you are there with the Marmeladovs, or the Snegiryovs, suffering alongside them. And when we read Raskolnikov's dream about the drunken peasants senselessly flogging a poor clapped-out old horse until she dies, we simultaneously feel deeply for the horse herself, for the anguish suffered by the sensitive little boy who has to watch the torture and doesn't understand it, for the adult Raskolnikov tormented by the memory, and for Dostoevsky himself who has taken on the burden of telling us all this. Ivan's utterly awful sto-

---

[3] *Diary of a Writer,* p185 (January 1876, Section Three, Chapter 1)

ries about the torture of children work in the same way, especially when we know that they all came from real cases. They're all there, in all their horror, in *Diary of a Writer*, although I have to confess that I find much of it too upsetting to read.

Perhaps unsurprisingly, in a country blighted with a brutal climate and a violent history, the suffering of innocents plays an important role in Russian spirituality, and martyrs in the Orthodox Church are revered for their pain, however pointless their sacrifice may have been. This emphasis perhaps explains why the young Dostoevsky was reading the book of Job in the first place – after all, in our sensitive times, when the wolf and the three little pigs are all allowed to live in friendship happily ever after, we would hardly consider it suitable reading material for children. The worship of innocents also expressed itself in the Orthodox Church's cult of the 'holy fool' – *yurodivy* in Russian; weird figures who lived life in a fervent religious passion, oblivious to the norms of the world around them, often behaving scandalously, or just strangely. *Yurodivy* were revered, particularly by the peasantry who believed they had clairvoyant, prophetic or other mystical powers.[4] The figures of the innocent martyrs and the *yurodivy* emerge in Dostoevsky's fiction in two fascinating minor characters, who each, in their own way, form the part of the background to Ivan's great rebellion – they are Raskolnikov's accidental second victim, Lizaveta Ivanovna, and Maria Lebyatkina, the virginal wife of Nikolai Stavrogin.

Lizaveta Ivanovna is the half-sister of the moneylender Alyona Ivanovna. We are told that she is simple-minded and shy, she's bullied and beaten by her older sister and is probably sexually abused too; the student overhard by Raskolnikov in the bar says that 'she acquiesces in everything' and claims that she is con-

---

[4] The most infamous of the *yurodivy* was Grigory Rasputin, whose malign influence on the Romanov family contributed to their downfall, and his.

stantly pregnant.[5] Yet this meek and humiliated woman unwittingly plays a vitally important part both in Raskolnikov's path into the darkness of crime and in his return journey to salvation. Maybe her role begins with the conversation in the bar, which gives Raskolnikov the first glimmerings of his mad idea, or perhaps it begins when he overhears Lizaveta in the Haymarket making arrangements to meet someone at seven o'clock that evening, for it this sudden knowledge that Alyona Ivanovna will be alone in her flat that pushes Raskolnikov over the precipice to his final decision. Lizaveta returns to the flat whilst Raskolnikov is still there, and in a panic, he hacks her down too. Having inadvertently created the circumstances for her own murder, Lizaveta, passive to the end, puts up very little resistance;

And so simple, crushed, and cowed was this unhappy Lizaveta that she did not even lift her hands to protect her face, though that was the most natural and inevitable gesture at that moment.[6]

Raskolnikov's journey to redemption begins when he discovers that Sonya was Lizaveta's friend, and on hearing that the two used to read the New Testament together, he commands Sonya to read him the story of Lazarus. Sonya reads from Lizaveta's own copy of the Gospels about the raising of the dead man, where we hear Christ's great promise: 'I am the resurrection and the life'.[7] It is the knowledge of Sonya's friendship with Lizaveta, and Sonya's simple confidence that Lizaveta will see God, because she was good, that gives Raskolnikov the impetus he needs to open up to Sonya. When he finally confesses to Sonya, her face mirrors Lizaveta's expression at the moment of his attack:

---

[5] In an early draft of *Crime and Punishment,* Lizaveta was in fact pregnant at the time of the murder (*The Notebooks for Crime and Punishment* edited and translated by Edward Wasiolek, University of Chicago Press, 1967 p96)

[6] *Crime and Punishment* p99 (Part One, Chapter 7)

[7] John, Chapter 11

As he said it another old and familiar sensation struck a chill in his heart: he looked at her, and suddenly he seemed to see Lizaveta's face in her face. He had a vivid recollection of the expression of Lizaveta's face when he was coming towards her with the hatchet that evening and she was slowly drawing back from him to the wall, thrusting out her hand, with her face full of child-like terror, looking exactly as little children do when they are suddenly scared by something and gaze motionless and in dismay at the object that frightens them. ... Almost the same thing happened to Sonya just now.[8]

Then he realises that the same expression of child-like terror is now reflected on his own face too; he has become like Lizaveta and Sonya as he faces up to what he has done. It is the simple, child-like suffering of the innocent Lizaveta that gives weight to all the moral arguments in the book, and we are left wondering whether Raskolnikov might actually have succeeded in his plan if he had only murdered the old woman, the 'louse'. Perhaps he could have conquered the world by crushing an insect, but spilling innocent blood is too much for him. Lizaveta brings salvation to the man who murdered her, just as the torments of the Orthodox saints brought salvation to the living,

Like Lizaveta Ivanovna, Maria Lebyatkina is not beautiful, and what looks she may once have had have been obliterated by poverty and hardship, but her soft, tender, grey eyes evoke pity and kindness, as the narrator tells us:

There was something dreamy and sincere in the gentle, almost joyful look she gave us. This gentle and unruffled joy, which also came out in her smile, surprised me, after all I had heard about the Cossack whip and the other brutalities of her precious brother. ... I almost took pleasure in looking at her, and it was pity rather than revulsion that I felt afterwards.[9]

---

[8] *Crime and Punishment* p424 (Part Five, Chapter 4)

[9] *The Devils* p151 (Part One, Chapter 4, section 5)

Maria's quiet serenity elicits an unexpected gentleness from her husband, Stavrogin, who has married her as a desperate act of self-glorification. He provides generously for her, is kind and solicitous when he visits her and when he encounters her in public, and he makes an effort to hide his contempt as he listens to her crazy babbling. The fact that she brings out kindness and sympathy even in such a monster as Stavrogin is testament in itself to the power of the innocent sufferer, but Maria has a symbolic role too, for she demonstrates the power of the simple Russian people over the false sophistication of Europe. She embodies traditional peasant beliefs – a mixture of simple Christianity and older folk-traditions, particularly the veneration of 'moist mother earth', a pagan deification of the Russian land. At the monastery where she lived for a while, a saintly hermit (perhaps not coincidentally named Lizaveta), gave her the idea that the Mother of God and the Russian earth mother were one and the same, and that by worshipping the earth and watering it with her tears she will find joy; but her meekness, her innocence and of course even her name, which she shares with the mother of Christ, suggest that she herself is this Russian mother-figure incarnate.

The pagan idea of moistening the soil has already been mentioned by Shatov, who furiously commanded Stavrogin to seek forgiveness by kissing the earth and drenching it with tears; and earlier, in *Crime and Punishment* Sonya instructs Raskolnikov to bow down and kiss the earth. Raskolnikov actually does this at the end of the novel, in a rather squalid way, bending down and kissing the filthy ground of the Haymarket amid the mockery of passers-by who can only assume that he's drunk. This act of surrendering oneself to the care of Mother Earth, or Mother Russia or the Mother of God comes to a glorious conclusion in *The Karamazov Brothers*. Father Zossima exhorts his followers to kiss the earth because the tears of the sufferer will then bring forth fruit, and at the moment of his death, he falls to the ground and kisses it with his last breath. Later, Alyosha, in the depths of despair after Zossima's death, throws himself to the ground and finally he finds peace and new inspiration:

He did not know why he was embracing the earth, he could not explain to himself why it was that he wanted to kiss it with such abandon, to kiss the whole of it, and yet he kept kissing it as wept and sobbed, drenching it with his tears, and passionately swearing to love it, to love it for ever and ever. "Drench the earth with the tears of thy joy and love these thy tears...", these words echoed in his soul. ... He fell to ground a weak adolescent, but when he rose to his feet he was a hardened warrior for life, and he felt and recognised this in a flash of ecstasy.[10]

Maria Lebyatkina imagines herself and Stavrogin in classic fairy-tale roles, so she dreams of her Prince, her falcon, who is great and good and who will look after her and protect her, just as the Russian people dreamed perpetually of their mythical good father Tsar. We can stretch further the metaphor of Maria as Russia in her first appearance in the novel – significantly it takes place in a church, and is the only time in Dostoevsky's major novels when we see people attending a regular Sunday morning service. Maria approaches Mrs Stavrogin during the service and is taken back to her house, where she exhibits a child-like awe and curiosity at the riches around her, and is ecstatically excited by the thought that she might hear French being spoken (she doesn't, it's just Mr Verkhovensky with his predilection for splattering his conversation with French phrases). At Mrs Stavrogin's, Maria is shown Russians aping European manners, and, as she says later, she sees that they are:

So rich and [they have] *so little gaiety – it all seems so revolting to me.*[11]

---

[10] *The Karamazov Brothers* p456-7 (Book Seven, Chapter 4)

[11] *The Devils* p280 (Part Two, Chapter 1, section 3)

While she is there, Nikolai himself arrives, and at the unexpected appearance of her Prince, Maria rapturously hopes that he has come to claim her and acknowledge her – here is Mother Russia hoping that the wanderer returned from Europe will put down roots into his native soil. And although Nikolai is kind, and helps to see her home, he denies that she is anything to him. Her grace could be his salvation, but he is blind to her Russian virtues, and sees only idiocy. Later, during Stavrogin's night-time visit, she accepts that he is not really her Prince at all, but a false pretender, and she rejects him, casting him out and pronouncing anathema on him – the strongest condemnation that the church can offer.

Lizaveta and Maria are completely passive, almost without personality; strange empty spirits floating through the pages of the novels, closer to Christ than others because they are already escaping the demands of the human ego. Sonya Marmeladova too is approaching this state of purity, and the apparent frailty of such characters is not a literary weakness, but a vitally important expression of Dostoevsky's belief in the need for a simple Christ-like love that will transform mankind. The reverse applies too: it should be no surprise that the stronger and more vivid a personality in a Dostoevsky novel, the further away that character is from salvation.

Salvation can only come about through genuinely innocent suffering, and Dostoevsky makes it quite clear that there is no short-cut to be found through self-inflicted pain, or by deliberately taking a path of misery and glorying in it. The quiet holiness of Father Zossima contrasts sharply with the ostentatious asceticism of his opponent, the ridiculous Father Ferapont, who is vain, rude and utterly unpleasant. In a horrible mockery of the torments inflicted on the inmates of the prison camp, he chooses to wear iron chains under his cassock – the sort of pointless exercise in self-mortification that achieves nothing and impresses only the credulous. It is telling, that his starvation-induced visions of devils hiding under the monks' cassocks are not so very far removed from Fyodor Karamazov's cartoonish ideas of devils dragging sinners down to hell with hooks, reminding us that overindulgence can come in spiritual as well as corporeal form. Lise Khokhlakova has similar visions of comic-book devils, and has her own fantasy obsession with grotesque cruelty. She works herself into a frenzy over her horrible story of the child with his fingers cut off, which in turn is her sick mind's exaggerated response to Alyosha's bitten finger. Lise seems to suffer from some illness that seems to be partly mental, and partly imagined by her mother, and her fascination with the suffering of others may stem from jealousy that they suffer genuine pain. In her own attempt to experience true suffering, she slams a door on her finger, and Dostoevsky's description of this act of self-harm is so vivid that it makes me wince to read it. After the finger-smashing, we hear no more of Lise and her hysterics, although I cannot help feeling that she would have been back with a vengeance if the sequel had been written, but for now, Dostoevsky has made his point – inflicting pain on yourself is a selfish rejection of the joys of living, and no good can come of it.

The same applies to mental or spiritual suffering, and Dostoevsky has little sympathy for characters who needlessly martyr themselves; in *Humiliated and Insulted,* Natasha Ikhmeneva, another hysterical teenager, is a case in point. She has broken the hearts of those who love her by leaving her family to live with Alyosha Valkovsky, who is callous, shallow and the son of her father's enemy. Refusing to face up to the damage she has inflicted on herself, on her parents and on Vanya (who is in love with her), she declares pathetically:

Somehow we've got to suffer our way through to our future happiness, purchase it by new ordeals. Suffering purifies everything. ... Oh Vanya, there's so much pain in life.[12]

---

[12] *Humiliated and Insulted* p81 (Part One, Chapter 15)

But for as long as she persists in pursuing happiness through the gratification of her own selfish desires, that happiness eludes her. Wallowing in her own misery, she is as much a prisoner of her ego as the hedonistic voluptuaries who we met in Chapter Five. In the same novel, the orphan girl Nelly exhibits a similar desire to prolong her own hurt, running away from her benefactor Vanya to beg on the streets. Vanya, who more than any other narrator speaks with Dostoevsky's voice, says:

She had been wronged, her wound could not have healed, and it was as if she were deliberately trying to aggravate her own pain and revelling in this selfish orgy of suffering, if I may put it that way. This rubbing of salt into the wound and taking pleasure in the act were familiar to me; it is the last refuge of the many who've been offended and humiliated, who've been oppressed by fate and are conscious of its unfairness.[13]

It is only when Natasha and her family are told the story of Nelly's terrible childhood and the genuine sufferings of her mother, who died in squalor in a Petersburg slum, that they are able to overcome their own self-inflicted injuries and reach reconciliation. Natasha is still deeply unhappy, but it's now a much healthier unhappiness that has come from the knowledge that she has done wrong and hurt others but can now make amends. Nelly's story has helped the Ikhmenev family to come through their own 'selfish orgy of suffering' to learn love and reconciliation. This is now suffering as a purifying force, like the refiner's fire – to use the Old Testament imagery. This possibility of a return to Christ's way of love through suffering is offered to other characters. Stavrogin rejects it, Raskolnikov is brought to it by Sonya, and Dmitry Karamazov embraces it wholeheartedly in his enthusiastic Karamazov style.

Unfortunately there are also evil human spirits who think that they can play god, who deliberately consign others to the refin-

---

[13] *Humiliated and Insulted* p282 (Part Four, Chapter 4)

er's fire for their own good. These evil spirits are egged on by Ivan Karamazov's Devil, who says that humans must suffer,

For without suffering, what pleasure would there be in life? Everything would turn into an endless Te Deum – holy but rather boring.[14]

Prince Valkovsky certainly believes this, and his account of how he treated Nelly's mother is unspeakably vile, one of those occasions when as a reader I feel frustrated at my powerlessness to reach inside the book and intervene:

I thought to myself, if I gave her the money, I might even make her unhappy. I'd have deprived her of the pleasure of being totally miserable <u>on my account</u> and of cursing me for it for the rest of her life. Believe you me, my friend, there is supreme pleasure to be derived from the kind of misery where one knows oneself to be quite blameless and generous. ... she probably went hungry later, but I'm sure she was happy. I didn't want to deprive her of this happiness... (and so it goes on).[15]

The natural response from Nelly's mother is stubborn pride, which she passes on to her daughter, thus prolonging the misery into the next generation. Prince Valkovsky comes out of it all very nicely for Nelly and her mother in fact possess the legal power to force Valkovsky to support them, but in their pride they refuse to use it. The pointless suffering of their squalid, miserable life in the filthy back streets of St Petersburg does not ennoble or purify them in the slightest, and it leaves Nelly further poisoned against anyone who tries to help her. Like Valkovsky, the Underground Man muses in a similar vein to justify his behaviour towards the prostitute Liza:

---

[14] *The Karamazov Brothers* p805 (Book Eleven, Chapter 9). Avsey's lovely pun on Te Deum/tedium only works in English but I think it's fully in keeping with the spirit of Ivan's Devil.

[15] *Humiliated and Insulted* p257 (Part Three, Chapter 10)

Isn't it better if she carries away with now an everlasting wound to her pride? Humiliation, after all, is purification; it is the acutest and most vivid consciousness! Tomorrow I should have polluted her mind and wearied her heart by my presence. But now the insult will never die within her, and however revolting the filth in store for her, her humiliation will elevate and purify her...through hate and... h'm, perhaps... forgiveness also. But will all this make things easier for her? And in fact: here, for my own benefit, I posed an empty question: which is better, a cheap happiness or lofty suffering? Tell me then, which is better?[16]

The Underground Man is beginning to show some doubt that is absent from Valkovsky's self-justification, and unlike Nelly's mother, Liza refuses to play along with it. There's a feeling that perhaps both of them could have found cheap happiness, or even exalted happiness, for the Underground Man has not yet sunk under his floorboards. Liza is his last chance, but casting her off so cruelly, he doesn't find lofty suffering, but cheap, squalid misery; loneliness, toothache, a sick liver and a wasted life. In Dostoevsky's eyes, wasting the great gift of life by self-destruction is a terrible crime and an infectious love for life that is incompatible with any deliberate search for suffering pours out of his pages. He shows us quite clearly that there is enough genuine pain in the world without taking on or creating extra burdens. His message is clear: if we can avoid either inflicting or receiving suffering, we should do so.

Ivan Karamazov deeply feels the beauty of life with all his being, but he is tormented and paralysed by the dilemma of how we can allow ourselves to enjoy the wonders of our lives, of God's earth and of a future paradise when we know that there is so much inexplicable suffering in the world and that our happiness may be founded directly on the pain of others. He even unwittingly demonstrates the impossibility of living without causing pain whilst he is telling Alyosha his awful stories:

---

[16] *Notes From Underground* p121-122 (Chapter Two, section 10)

"I'm making you suffer, Alyosha, you seem distressed. I'll stop if you like."
"It's all right. I'm happy to suffer too," muttered Alyosha.[17]

And with one more horrific story, Ivan tempts Alyosha into an outburst of anger, getting him to admit that the landowner who set a pack of dogs on a little child should be shot. It's impossible even to discuss such terrible things without causing more ripples of suffering, as the pain spreads out to Alyosha and to us, the readers. Ivan works himself up into a confused fever and his muddle is what happens to most of us when we try to think properly about suffering. Ivan wants to see retribution, but he also wants to see the victim rise up and embrace the murderer. There cannot ever be eternal harmony while a child's tears remain without atonement he says, but no-one has the right to forgive such sufferings, and without forgiveness, how can there be atonement and harmony? His acute sensitivity drives him in spirals of despair, culminating in his great rebellion:

I don't want harmony; for the love of humankind, I don't want it. I would rather that suffering were not avenged. I would prefer to keep my suffering unavenged and my abhorrence unplacated, <u>even at the risk of being wrong</u>. Besides, the price of harmony has been set too high, we can't afford the entrance fee. And that's why I hasten to return my entry ticket.[18]

Ivan himself acknowledges the confusion, for his Grand Inquisitor touches on it in his discourse on the first temptation, in which he accuses Christ of offering mankind too much in his gift of freedom:

They will cry out in the end that truth is not in You, for they could not have been left in worse confusion and torment than that

---

[17] *The Karamazov Brothers* p304 (Book Five, Chapter 4)
[18] *The Karamazov Brothers* p307 (Book Five, Chapter 4)

in which You left them, bequeathing them so many problems and unresolved questions.[19]

Dostoevsky, we remember, swore that he would stick with Christ even if it were proved that the truth was outside Christ and so I think these heartfelt words that Ivan has put into the mouth of the Grand Inquisitor might also be the thoughts of Dostoevsky himself, as he struggles to reconcile his love of Christ with his acute sensitivity to pain and suffering.

Consider too Dostoevsky's Pushkin speech, when he talks about Tatyana, the great heroine of Pushkin's poem *Eugene Onegin*. At the end of the poem, Tatyana rejects Onegin, in spite of her love for him, because she is bound by the sacrament of marriage. Even though she doesn't love the rich old general to whom she has been married, she sees it as her duty to remain loyal to him. Dostoevsky continues the theme by asking his listeners to imagine that they are building an edifice of human happiness, one that will bring peace to all, but that in its construction, one insignificant person must be tortured to death, just as the innocent old man would suffer if Tatyana were to betray him. Would we, he asks, consent to be the architects of such a building under this condition?

His use of the building image is particularly apt here, for both Dostoevsky and Pushkin are closely associated with St Petersburg – not just a house built on suffering, but an entire city. What greater symbol can there be of the utter impossibility of living a blameless life than that dazzlingly beautiful city, rising from the foetid northern swamps, and built, literally, on the bodies of tens of thousands of conscripted serfs, who died during its construction and whose bones form the city's foundations. Did they die so that I can stand on the Palace Bridge and marvel at the perfect view of glittering palaces and golden spires? How can we endure it? And what about the times when we consciously decide to do what is morally right, but we still cause suffering?

---

[19] *The Karamazov Brothers* p299 (Book Five, Chapter 5)

Tatyana chooses to stay with her husband, but what about Onegin, we all cry? Hasn't her choice made him suffer too? Dostoevsky doesn't answer the question, but he at least acknowledges the problem; sometimes, whatever we do will cause someone pain, even if it is the right thing to do.

So, how then can we live in a world of suffering? We cannot answer the question ourselves; the best that we can do is to seek shadows of the answer and find enough comfort to continue with that damned tricky business of living. Ivan's own personal answer to the question is that when he reaches thirty he will simply abandon everything, 'throw down the cup of life', and forget about both the beauties and the horrors of life. We assume when he first says this that is he is talking about suicide, but after the Grand Inquisitor poem we discover that what he really means is that he will give himself up to the Karamazov way of life – that he will simply stop caring about anything anymore, and numb his feelings by sinking himself in vice. We already know where that will lead, but Ivan fears that he will find no other solution, although he does leave the door open to redemption by promising to seek out Alyosha to talk to him one last time before giving up.

The Grand Inquisitor offers relief through organised religion – not through Christ's message, but by harnessing the powers of miracle, mystery and authority to create a society where people can live untroubled by the greater demands that Christ's freedom places on them. Alyosha's simple answer is the true essence of Christ, free from the distortions of the Grand Inquisitor. Christ can forgive all, he can atone for all suffering because of the sacrifice of his pure and perfect self. Dostoevsky's fuller response then begins in the pages of Father Zossima's hagiography, and continues on through the rest of the action in the novel.

The chapter *From the Life of Father Zossima* purports to be a collection of sermons and memoirs, taken down by Alyosha as the elder lay dying. We're reminded that it's a document that has been constructed by Alyosha, for the narrator knows that there were many people around the elder's death bed, conversation was fragmentary and it would have been impossible for Zossima to have dictated such a lengthy and fluent text. Therefore, as readers we have to remember that what we are given is as much Alyosha's creation as Zossima's, and this reinforces its position as an answer to Ivan's own poem.

Zossima relates the events from his own life that shaped his faith, beginning with an account of how the seeds of belief were planted in his soul by his elder brother, Markel, who died of consumption at the age of seventeen. Markel was an atheist intellectual, and could easily have become like Ippolit in *The Idiot*, furiously raging against his fate, but instead of leading to anger, Markel's illness brought him back to a message of faith and love which he passes onto his adoring younger brother, in the slanting light of the evening sun, Dostoevsky's usual setting for the deepest spiritual experiences. Zossima himself disregards his brother's message as he grows up, joins the army, and enjoys the typical carefree lifestyle of a wealthy officer. His conversion comes when he is about to fight a duel, and what brings him round is not the fear of death, but the way he lashes out in a temper at his servant Afanasy the night before, giving him a vicious beating. The next morning he is deeply ashamed of having spoiled what may be his last hours on earth by committing this act of senseless violence, and he remembers how his dying brother wished that he could serve the servants, for he considered himself unworthy to be waited on by any other person. Zossima remembers his brother's words that everyone is responsible for all, and that if people only realised that, there would be paradise on earth. At this thought, he suddenly comes to his senses, reflecting for the first time that he might be about to kill an honourable man, ruin his family and bring terrible misery to the woman he thought he loved. He attends the duel, allows his opponent to shoot, so that he cannot be accused of cowardice, and then announces, on the spot, that he intends to take the habit – of the many duels in Russian literature, surely this must be the strangest outcome.

In many ways, the night before the duel echoes the experience of the Ridiculous Man (see Chapter Five) – we see Dostoevsky building on the idea of the earlier story and working it through. Like the Ridiculous Man, Zossima has done something thoroughly mean, and is brought to his senses by his realisation that he still cares about what he did, even though he might be about to die. The Ridiculous Man dreams of paradise, and Zossima vividly recalls his brother's dying words, and as a result of their experiences, both men start their new life of Christian love by seeking forgiveness from the person they wronged. Through their suffering, the Ridiculous Man's little girl and Afanasy bring salvation to those who have hurt them, just as Lizaveta redeemed her murderer. Zossima's memoirs then elaborate the idea that the suffering that human beings inflict on each other would be lessened, or even eliminated, if people learned to live together in a commonwealth of love, and that the way this is to be achieved is by every single person taking upon themselves moral responsibility for the sins of others.

Dostoevsky's ideas about collective responsibility for sin are derived from the Russian village structures (see Chapter One), particularly the principle of *sobornost'*, the system of collective decision-making and mutual responsibility. He was not the first to elevate this to a guiding principle for a distinctively Russian way of life – the Slavophiles Alexey Khomyakov and Konstantin Aksakov had already identified *sobornost'* as the key to a spiritual renewal of European civilisation. In his sermons, Zossima says that the Russian monks should lead the way with their simple life of obedience, poverty and prayer, because they are free of the tyranny of material possessions, free of the desire to fulfil the ever-multiplying new needs that have been conjured up by technological and scientific advances. It's a very familiar lament:

So the idea of service to mankind, of brotherhood and human solidarity, grows ever weaker in the world, and truly it is now treated almost with derision, for how is one to shed one's habits, whither can the bondsman turn, if he has grown so accustomed to gratifying the multifarious needs which are of his own devising? He is isolated, and the world at large means nothing to him. We have reached a stage at which we have surrounded ourselves with more things, but have less joy.[20]

Father Zossima's mysterious visitor, Mikhail, talks about the isolating effects of contemporary life and the constant striving for individuality that keeps men apart from each other. Attacking socialism, he says that no scientific advance will enable men to share their property equally, for without love everyone will think he's been badly done by. The pride of self-sufficiency keeps people apart from each other and creates a dreadful isolation, instead of an understanding that true security comes from mutual support and solidarity. The idea of collective responsibility and brotherhood is one that Dostoevsky had been building on throughout his life, and, as we noted at the end of the previous chapter, it adds another dimension to his long aversion to Western European socialism, which prevailed despite his passionate hatred of suffering and injustice.

The final part of Zossima's sermons directly addresses the paralysis and despair that Ivan feels when he contemplates the evil in the world. He preaches that it is wrong to worry ourselves with things we cannot comprehend, or to use our incomprehension of sin and suffering as an excuse for not acting. God will not punish us for what our human natures cannot comprehend says Zossima, and his instruction to anyone who is overwhelmed by grief and indignation at the sins of others is that they should themselves seek suffering and penitence as if they had committed that sin themselves. We may never know, he says, how many times we ourselves have been an accomplice to someone else's sin. Perhaps, for example, you left an axe lying unattended in a kitchen instead of putting it away, or gossiped imprudently in a bar... We never know how our actions and choices will rebound, and so we must all live with the assumption that we are steeped

---

[20] *The Karamazov Brothers,* p393-394 (Book Six, Chapter 3)

in guilt. And just as people who are basically good and decent suffer immediately when they realise that they have inflicted pain on others, so the greater sinners will eventually realise that their actions have rendered them unable to love, and that is where they will find their hell, not in the comic book hell with its blazing fire and devils with hooks. Whether it comes to them in this life or the after-life, the spiritual agony that comes from the lack of love is a far greater torment than physical pain.

Much of Zossima's sermon is pretty straightforward Christian morality, with a good dash of Dostoevsky's Russian messianism thrown in, and as a literary work, it is a feebly spluttering candle when set against the mighty blaze of the Grand Inquisitor, notable only as a clever piece of ventriloquism. What is more interesting is how Dostoevsky then uses later events in the story to illuminate Zossima's responses to the problem of suffering and atonement, and in particular his idea of individuals taking on collective responsibility for suffering. Ivan and Dmitry, in their own way, attempt to accept the burden of guilt for their father's murder. Ivan torments himself with his inadvertent roles in the affair, from his initial philosophical conversations with Smerdyakov in which he expounds his idea that everything is permitted, and onwards to his departure for Moscow just before the murder; and in his confused courtroom appearance he attempts to plead guilty himself. The public prosecutor, on the other hand, in his summing up speech attributes exactly the same thoughts to Smerdyakov, saying that he must have hanged himself out of a morbid sense of guilt at leaving his master defenceless on the night of the murder. Grushenka too had her own part in it all, by being the agent of the rivalry between father and son, and she unwittingly helps to build the case against Dmitry by blurting out at his arrest that it is all her fault, and that she will follow him to Siberia. Even Alyosha does his bit, by failing to seek out Dmitry and talk to him the day before the murder, for who knows what effect his words may have had on his impulsive and muddled brother.

And so, just as several people take on responsibility for Fyodor Karamazov's murder, whether or not they are guilty, so there is also collective responsibility for Dmitry's conviction. Katerina hired the fancy Moscow lawyer who defends Dmitry so disastrously, and she herself belatedly chose to produce damning evidence against him. Ivan bungled his own attempt at exonerating Dmitry, and Alyosha's ardent sympathy for his unhappy brother mistakenly gives the impression that he's overdoing it and trying too hard to defend the indefensible. Even the general public must take their share of the guilt: consider the witnesses who allowed their preconceptions about Dmitry to colour their evidence, and the peasants on the jury who were determined to stand up for themselves. Today when society is more dispersed and nothing is local, the same sort of speculation goes on but it's dispersed across the wider news media, and we all become guilty by association just for consuming that media, no better than the townspeople who indulged in malicious gossip.

Dmitry wants to accept his punishment in an attempt to find relief for his own conscience but Alyosha understands that actually going to Siberia would be too much for him; imprisoning Dmitry would be senseless because the sufferings to be endured there would not heal Dmitry but break his spirit irreparably. Alyosha (who, note, has carefully ensured that no-one will be likely to suffer punishment for the planned escape) says:

The fact that you refused to carry that heavy cross will serve simply to arouse an even greater feeling of responsibility in you, and from then on, all your life, that feeling will help to resurrect your soul even more – more, perhaps, than if you had actually gone <u>there</u>. Because you wouldn't last out there, you'd rail against it, and in the end perhaps you'd say "I give up"... It's not given to everyone to bear the heaviest burden; for some it's impossible.[21]

---

[21] *The Karamazov Brothers* p959 (Epilogue, Chapter 2)

This is Dostoevsky's final word on the idea of salvation through suffering. It's not a definitive answer, but it's a very humanitarian way to close the debate. As we have seen, the theme of suffering innocence is one that Dostoevsky explored throughout his literary career, from the self-indulgent, egoistic suffering depicted in *Humiliated and Insulted,* to the strange and abused holy fool characters of Lizaveta Ivanovna and Maria Lebyatkina, and culminating in the shocking images and the message of collective guilt and responsibility in *The Karamazov Brothers.*

To return, however, to the starting point of this chapter, and the story of Job, Dostoevsky, for all his discussions and analysis of suffering never really attempts to answer the question of how a loving and merciful God can possibly inflict such cruelty on one of his people. His own memories of reading Job as a child find their way into Father Zossima's memoirs, but all Zossima can do is reflect on the suffering and note that Job was eventually rewarded by God with the peace and wisdom of old age, as his sorrows faded into a 'quiet tender joy', a bittersweet joy that is made all the more precious by the memory of the pain that was once there.

Where he is more active in proposing a response to the problems of Job is in his suggestions of ways in which people, individually, and as a society, can avoid creating unnecessary suffering themselves, and taking inspiration from Job's acceptance of his suffering and his refusal to curse God, Dostoevsky shows how and when suffering can be an opportunity for personal redemption and, just as importantly, when it can't. With this in mind, we can now look in more detail at how brotherhood and responsibility for all are manifested in that most unlikely example: Dmitry Karamazov.

An honourable young man at heart, but one who, alas, has been carried away to a rather excessive extent by certain passions.

(Nikolai Parfenovich, Examining Magistrate)

EIGHT: DMITRY KARAMAZOV

Art not thou too, O Rus, rushing onwards like a spirited troika that none can overtake? Smoking like smoke under you is the road, thundering are the bridges, all falls back and is left behind ... on rushes the troika, all-inspired by God! Rus, whither art thou racing? Give an answer. She gives no answer. The bells set up a wondrous jingling: rent to shreds, the air thunders and is transformed into wind: all that exists on earth flies by, and, looking askance, other peoples and nations step aside and make way for her.[1]

Nikolai Gogol, one of Dostoevsky's literary predecessors, ended the first part of his novel Dead Souls with this wonderful image of Russia as a runaway carriage, charging blindly into the future, with no regard for anything that might get in its way. Characters like Dmitry Karamazov and Parfyon Rogozhin are firmly in the driving seat of the troika, and as soon as I start reading a Dostoevsky novel, I find myself leaping back on board as a passenger, letting myself be swept along in the chaotic excitement. This comes partly from the energetic pace of the plots;

---

[1] Nikolai Gogol, *Dead Souls* p 282-3 (translated by Robert A. Maguire, Penguin Books 2004)

Dostoevsky is a master storyteller who keeps his reader permanently in suspense, knowing just how much to give away, and when to throw in a surprising twist. Characters or events that, to begin with, seem to have no relevance are all eventually drawn into a satisfying whole, and his dialogue has such dramatic intensity that I'm not reading words on a page, I'm watching a movie in my mind.

Dostoevsky's distinctive prose style makes its own contribution to the giddy excitement. His Russian lacks the polished elegance of some writers; the words tumble out in a frenetic rush, and this is exactly what the best translators, such as Magarshack and Avsey capture so well, perhaps because they are both native Russian speakers. The conclusion that I cheerfully draw from this is that it's perfectly acceptable to read Dostoevsky in translation, with no need to feel guilty: in fact one academic friend has suggested to me that in fact Dostoevsky reads better in translation because the Slavophile nonsense loses some of its force. Certainly the size and complexity of his novels means that, in any case, reading them in Russian is not practical for most of us. It's also worth noting that Dostoevsky's massive impact on the world of literature has come mainly through translations, and his influence transcends linguistic barriers. I read *Crime and Punishment* in Russian when I lived in Moscow, but I don't think I gained anything extra from it, other than a colossal sense of achievement, and picking over each page slowly and carefully, with frequent trips to the dictionary, meant that I lost the galloping sense of urgency and Dostoevsky's torrent of words slowed to a mere trickle. Some writers are held captive by their supreme mastery of their native tongue: for example, although Dostoevsky extolled Pushkin as a great universal writer, it is really only possible to understand why Pushkin is held in such reverence if you can read him in Russian. His Russian is beautiful and elegant; he whips all those harsh consonant clusters into order and exploits the language's grammatical structures to the full, and thus is almost impossible to translate. But the whole world is welcome at Dostoevsky's party; all that is needed is a translator to open the door; someone who can convey Dostoevsky's passionate urgency and keep the reader turning the pages as fast as the ink flowed from his pen.

Gogol's troika image still holds true, as anyone who has been to Russia will recognise, for it's a country that doesn't do things by halves. Consider the five-year plans and the madcap industrialisation of the late 1920s, or the Wild East capitalism of the post-perestroika years, both times in which the desire for advancement has lead to mindless destruction of the past, with a blatant disregard for anyone who stands in the way or can't keep up. This tendency is perhaps best illustrated by the story of the Cathedral of Christ the Saviour in Moscow, built by Alexander I in thanksgiving for the Russian victory over Napoleon. Stalin had it blown up, and he planned to erect in its place a massive People's Palace, to be topped by a gigantic statue of Lenin. This crazy act of hubris never came off, partly because the site on the bank of the Moscow River kept flooding (divine retribution, said the ever-superstitious Russian people), and eventually it was turned into an outdoor swimming pool. In the 1990s, the much-loved pools were drained, and the cathedral was rebuilt at breakneck speed. Nowadays, the extravagant brashness of its massive golden dome symbolises the resurgent Russian nationalism and the money culture of the new Russia as much as the glitzy Moscow office blocks and the tasteless neo-gothic 'cottages' that now encircle the city.

Living in Russia in my mid-twenties, I was quite happy to leap on board the troika and see what happened. Daily life in Moscow seemed more urgent, more intense, than it did among the staid comforts of Western Europe. Friendships were made faster and more deeply, business meetings were more tempestuous, parties were wilder. True to the cliché, long winter nights really were spent in intense discussions round kitchen tables, or smoking in gloomy stairwells; come summer and I passed my evenings perched on park benches with Russian girlfriends, swigging bottles of beer bought from kiosks. During my time there, I found myself doing silly things that make my cautious English self look back with some alarm. Did I really spend a train journey successfully pretending to be Bulgarian to avoid unnecessary attention from my fellow-passengers – mostly drunks and newly released convicts? Did I really win a contract by chatting up a stranger in the bar at Sheremetyevo airport? Did I really stroll through town with thousands of dollars in cash tucked in the pockets of my jeans? Did I really...? Surely not...

The ability of Russians to party extravagantly never ceases to amaze and delight me, and like many other Western visitors I've suffered from trying to keep up. In late 1990s Moscow, it seemed at times as if Dmitry Karamazov had taken over the city and turned it all into the village of Mokroye. I heard countless tales about the notorious Hungry Duck nightclub,[2] where drunken girls would cheerfully shed their clothes and dance on the bar, or have sex on the dance-floor (for the record, my own recklessness never extended to going there myself, although my friend Olga frequently tried to persuade me). Simple events had a habit of getting out of hand – my Moscow landlord dropped round once to fix something, it was the first time I'd met him, and I had a couple of friends over. Several hours later he was apologetically phoning his wife before going out to fetch more supplies of beer. And actual celebrations – birthdays, summer picnics, and best of all, New Year's Eve – were extravagant banquets that went on for hours, tables laden with *zakuski,* and countless toasts that got gradually more elaborate (one of my proudest moments was when I was brave enough to deliver one of these toasts myself at a friend's birthday party, to much kind applause).

But all of this is nothing, nothing at all, compared to the antics of Dostoevsky's wild boys, Dmitry Karamazov and Parfyon

---

[2] A retired ballerina who was on the directorate of the building where the club was housed was instrumental in having it closed down in 1999. In reference to her most famous role, the memorable headline in the English-language Moscow Times read 'Dying Swan finishes off Hungry Duck'.

Rogozhin, who surrender themselves to uninhibited pleasure-seeking on a grand scale. Dmitry squanders several thousand roubles on food, drink and gypsy girls in one night of wild partying at Mokroye with Grushenka – to put this sum into perspective, consider that Mr Marmeladov, as a low-level civil servant, receives a monthly salary of about twenty-five roubles. It would be bad enough if it were Dmitry's own money, but to make matters worse, it isn't even his, it belongs to his fiancée, Katya. As Dmitry puts it himself, he is:

A despicable debauchee, a vile creature, uncontrollable in his urges ... just like an animal, he couldn't control himself.[3]

Rogozhin goes even further, stealing ten thousand roubles from his father to buy a single pair of diamond earrings for Nastasya Filippovna after seeing her just once. We're not told what happened at the Yekaterinhof pleasure gardens after Rogozhin swept Nastasya off there from her infamous birthday party, other than that it was 'a terrible orgy', but it's probably along the same line as Dmitry's spree at Mokroye; reckless, unbridled excess, with no thought for the consequences.

Of course the dark side of these debauches is never far away. Dmitry's second trip to Mokroye begins with what else but a mad-dash troika ride, during the course of which his thoughts gallop away in a whirlwind, beyond any means of his to rein them in. The events of the night that follows spin further and further out of his control: so often we carefully imagine in advance how a particular encounter is going to play out, then the result is entirely different to what we originally expected, and this is exactly what happens to Dmitry. His great love, Grushenka, has unexpectedly run off to meet her officer, the man who seduced and ruined her five years previously, and who has suddenly returned and summoned her. Dmitry is full of noble thoughts about how this man is her 'first and rightful' love and

---

[3] *The Karamazov Brothers* p151 (Book Three, Chapter 5)

that he shouldn't come between them. However, in true Dostoevsky wild boy style, he can't do this quietly and just leave Grushenka and her officer to themselves; he dashes off after them, with hundreds of roubles' worth of food and drink, planning to relinquish first Grushenka and then his life in one final blast – not entirely unlike Svidrigaylov's last night on earth, although on a much grander scale. His words to Andrei the coachman on the way are telling:

Are you a driver? ... Then you know that you must make way. What sort of a driver is it who never makes way for anyone, who drives on regardless and runs over people. No, a driver must not run over people. One must not run over a man, one must not spoil people's lives, and if you've ruined someone's life, punish yourself and go away.

To which Andrei replies

Quite right, sir, you're quite right. One must not run over people or torture them, same as any other living creature, for every living creature, sir, is created by God ... Because you see, sir, some folks drives on regardless. Aye, sir, there's many a coachman who does that, too. There ain't no holding him, sir. He just goes dashing along regardless![4]

To hell, says Dmitry, to this, and of course hell is exactly where he thinks he's going himself. Despite his proclaimed intention to stand aside, he knows he's that driver who's about to run over someone, spoil their life and then go straight to on to his own death, with inevitable damnation to follow in the afterlife.

In the end though, Dmitry doesn't go to hell, and his tragedy plays out in a more complex way. Grushenka's gallant lover turns out to be a rather nasty little *customs* officer, and just to labour the point, Dostoevsky lets his awful nationalism show through, by making Grushenka's lover a Pole. What follows are

---

[4] *The Brothers Karamazov,* Magarshack p 484-5 (Book Eight, Chapter 6)

some painfully awkward and embarrassing scenes in which Dmitry tries to liven up the conversation and get the evening going, then loses at cards to the Pole and his friend (they cheat). Eventually, Dmitry picks a quarrel with them, and realising that the Pole is only after Grushenka's money attempts to buy him off. Grushenka is both touched that Dmitry has tried to buy her, and disgusted with her officer for apparently agreeing to the bargain, so to everyone's relief the Poles are sent packing. After another wild night of wine, women and song, an ecstatic Dmitry collapses into bed with Grushenka, who declares that she now loves only him. Their happiness, though, is tragically short-lived: they are woken by the police who have arrived to arrest Dmitry for the murder of his father.

Once again, we see a more positive reworking in *The Karamazov Brothers* of themes that Dostoevsky has already explored, in a darker ink, in *The Idiot,* and so Parfyon Rogozhin's story is much bleaker than that of his successor Dmitry. Rogozhin has spent his life acting on instinct, responding immediately to his passions with no sense of self-control, so that when he is finally faced with the potential loss of Nastasya Filippovna, he finds that he has no inner voice to restrain him. There is nothing to tell him what to do; he has no emotional or spiritual resources to support him; he is far beyond the reach of the saving powers of love, and so all he can do is go to hell, taking Nastasya and Myshkin with him. Like Dmitry, Rogozhin is driven by his all-consuming passion for a beautiful and dangerous woman, but if he hadn't met Nastasya, he would almost certainly have been possessed by some other compulsion – he himself quotes Nastasya's own vision of an alternative future for him:

You'd probably have ...worked up such a liking for money, you'd have finished with not just two but ten million roubles, and would have given up the ghost from hunger stretched across your sacks of gold, because hoarding would have turned into a passion with you. You can't help working yourself into a passion about everything.[5]

And if it hadn't been money or women, he could just as easily have become fervently religious, indeed it appears at times that, despite his demonic appearance, Rogozhin is aggressively attempting to save himself – a realisation that comes to Prince Myshkin in the moment of clarity that precedes his epileptic fit. However, Rogozhin's search for faith is doomed to failure, because his starting point is Holbein's painting of an all-too-dead Christ, the painting that causes others to lose their faith. Rogozhin's tragedy is that his passions are wholly misdirected: his love of beauty finds its outlet in Nastasya Filippovna, he is trying to find faith in a dead Christ, and he is trying to find brotherhood with a man who appears beautiful, but is really as dangerous as Nastasya herself.

Rogozhin and Myshkin are linked throughout the novel in one of Dostoevsky's greatest doublings. They meet on the first pages as they both return to Russia; they are inextricably bound together by their passion for Nastasya Filippovna; and, in the unforgettable horror of its final pages, the story ends with them lying in each other's arms, both out of their minds. Rogozhin asks Myshkin to exchange crosses, a deeply symbolic act in Russian Orthodox tradition, and one which binds them together in spiritual brotherhood, and he then takes Myshkin to his mother to receive her blessing, but both acts are something of a parody of true brotherhood. Myshkin has just recounted how he was tricked by a shameless drunkard into buying the cross that he now is giving to Rogozhin, and so Rogozhin is accepting someone else's cast-off faith, faith that was sold for a drop of vodka, and his mother is more or less senile and doesn't know what she is doing when Rogozhin lifts her hand to bless Myshkin. It's all indicative of Rogozhin's addiction to big dramatic gestures that are driven by an empty passion and devoid of any meaning.

---

[5] *The Idiot* p221-222 (Part Two, Chapter 3)

We've already seen how Prince Myshkin is a timeless figure, with no history, but his demonic opposite, his anti-Christ, is a man with no future. Rogozhin's impulsive actions are those of a man who lives only for the present moment, and he seeks immediate pleasure and destruction in equal measures, surrounding himself with a grotesque carnival of lowlifes who are unscrupulously enthusiastic in encouraging his excesses. Rowan Williams talks about the desire of the Devil to put a stop to history, and to strip human beings of their power to shape their own futures. Rogozhin embodies both of these elements in his absolute destruction of his own future and those of Prince Myshkin and Nastasya Filippovna, and we'll return to his demonic qualities in Chapter Eleven.

Dostoevsky understood reckless, destructive passion all too well. His own compulsive weakness was for gambling, a habit he acquired whilst travelling in Europe with his mistress, Polina Suslova, in the early 1860s, and which ensnared him hopelessly for the next decade. Whenever Dostoevsky was in Europe, he was drawn magnetically to the gaming tables. Like his own fictitious gambler, Alexey, he believed adamantly that it should be perfectly possible to beat the odds if only one could learn to suppress one's emotions fully and play like a machine. Writing to his wife's sister, during the time of his first marriage, he says:

I really do know the secret – it is terribly silly and simple, merely a matter of keeping oneself under constant control and never getting excited, no matter how the games shifts. That's all there is to it – you just can't lose that way and are sure to win. But the difficulty is not in finding this out, but in being able to put it into practice once you do. You may be as wise as serpent and have a will of iron, but you will still succumb.[6]

In 1867, Dostoevsky went to Germany with his new wife, Anna. It was only supposed to be a short holiday, but pursued by

---

[6] *Selected letters* p178 (1 September 1863, to V. D. Constant)

his creditors in Russia, Dostoevsky was forced to remain abroad to avoid debtors' prison, and he spent four miserable years exiled from his beloved homeland and shackled to the gambling tables. Time and again, with depressing predictability, he was forced to beg for money from his wife and her family, before confessing that he had lost it and pawning the family furniture yet again. Anna, in her youthful naivety and devotion, shared her husband's desperate belief that if he just possessed the necessary self-control, if he could shackle his will, he would make a fortune:

All of Fyodor Mikhailovich's rationalizations about the possibility of winning at roulette by using his gambling system were entirely correct. His success might have been complete – but only on condition that this system was applied by some cool-headed Englishman or German and not by such a nervous and impulsive person as my husband, who went to the outermost limits in everything.[7]

It seems hard to believe that this is Dostoevsky, the man who could write so powerfully about the real necessity of free will, and who understood so vividly that human beings simply cannot be reduced to automata. If nothing else, Dostoevsky the gambler is a living, breathing example of a man deluded into trying to stamp out his own humanity. He broke the habit in a final fling in 1871, just before the family were finally able to return to Russia, and he never gambled again, so it seems highly likely that the gambling was his way of coping with his exile, alienated as he was from the homeland that gave him his identity.

Alexey-the-Gambler plays roulette like Dostoevsky, with the same blind faith that human willpower can overcome the odds, but the characters we're discussing in this chapter have more in common with the novel's other serious gambler, the wonderful Grandmamma. She exuberantly gambles away her family's inheritance, at first winning eye-watering sums, but finally losing it all,

---

[7] Anna Dostoevskaya *Reminiscences* p130

and she doesn't care. I normally find the literary gambling addictions of nineteenth century literature rather tedious (although an exception has to be made for George Eliot's magnificent description of Gwendolen Harleth in the opening scene of *Daniel Deronda*), but Grandmamma's cheerful recklessness is a joy to behold. She is in thrall to the excitement of the play and nothing more, and seeing the horror of the odious General and his entourage, who hang on her every move as she gambles away the inheritance they are so desperate for, makes it all the more delicious. She's old enough that she doesn't have to care what anyone else thinks, and she stops before she loses her entire estate, sweeping gloriously off back to Russia, leaving chaos behind her.

We've had sex, we've had gambling, but the greatest scourge of Russia is, of course, alcohol. Vodka, Russia, the two are inseparable in the eyes of most (so much so that, bizarrely, I was given a bottle of vodka as part of my leaving present from my British colleagues before I moved to Moscow), although of course we in Britain are hardly immune to the curse of the bottle, and it's worth a wry note here that Dostoevsky was horrified by the public binge-drinking that he saw when he visited London in 1861:

On Saturday nights half a million working men and women and their children spread like the ocean all over town, clustering particularly in certain districts, and celebrate their Sabbath all night long until five o'clock in the morning, in other words guzzle and drink like beasts to make up for a whole week... Everyone is drunk, but drunk joylessly, gloomily and heavily.[8]

In 1865, Dostoevsky started making notes for a novel to be called *The Drunkards,* which would deal with the social problems caused by alcoholism, particularly its effect on family life and children. In the end it was never written, but some of these sketches found their way into *Crime and Punishment*, where the sordid streets of the Petersburg slums throng with drunks of all

---

[8] *Winter Notes on Summer Impressions* p52

ages, and the central characters of that unwritten story became the wretched Marmeladov family. It's perhaps a mercy that *The Drunkards* never materialised, for the passages in *Crime and Punishment* that describe the torments of the brave little Marmeladov children are heart-breaking almost beyond endurance; a whole novel would surely be too much. Mr Marmeladov is a caricature maudlin drunk, imprisoned in a bottle, burdening every passing stranger with his woes, and trapped in the vicious circle of drinking to escape from the misery that his drinking has caused. He's there today in every drunkard to be found staggering around the streets or comatose in a snowdrift, creating misery beyond endurance for his family and inconveniencing those he meets in public, and his death, as he falls under the wheels of a carriage, is a public nuisance.

In *The Idiot,* we meet a more complex and interesting victim of drink in Ganya's father, General Ivolgin. He is less obviously inebriated, but he is mentally weakened by drink and he succumbs to a loss of control over his own mind, indulging in fantasies of memory that affect his perception of the real world. Everyone he meets has to be found a fictitious place in his personal history: every pretty young girl was once dandled on his knee; he fought a duel over the mother of every young man he meets; he recasts anecdotes from newspapers as his own memories; and he tells ridiculous stories about meeting Napoleon and suchlike. General Ivolgin is adrift in a rapidly-changing materialist world, where new technologies dazzle and bewilder those who can't keep up – a world that is vividly portrayed through some of Dostoevsky's apparent digressions in the novel, and his fantasies allow him the chance to anchor himself in this new world, to create a space for his own personal history that links him to everyone else. In his habits, he's Rogozhin, or Dmitry, grown sad and old, diminished over time, but still hopelessly in thrall to his impulsive passions and struggling to carve out for himself something that feels like freedom.

In the end he is killed not directly by drink, but by his overwrought state of mind as he slides further and further into his fantasy world, consumed by his reckless lack of mental discipline. Lebedev cruelly mocks the General's inability to distinguish between fact and fantasy as he plays a prank involving a missing wallet, then later makes fun of his false memories by making even more ludicrous claims of his own. General Ivolgin eventually works himself up to such a state over Lebedev's teasing that he has a stroke, and it's as if his brain has exploded under the pressure of maintaining both fantasy and reality.

The actions of the wild boys, the gamblers and the drunks are another element in Dostoevsky's discussion of free will, and what it means to be human. At the time he was writing, advances in knowledge, the retreat of religion, and a growing tendency to apply rigorous new scientific techniques to social and moral problems were all sparking new debate about how much an individual can take responsibility for their own actions, and to what extent unsuitable behaviour can be linked to one's environment and upbringing. The radicals, naturally, believed firmly in the idea of moral determinism, asserting that we are formed by our environment, and that given the right social conditions, all crime and misery will magically vanish. But this brings us back again to the crystal palace, where people are forced into living neat and tidy lives that are governed according to some theoretical ideal of happiness. Succumbing to damaging and addictive behaviour is how people attempt to smash their way out of the confines of the crystal palace, so according to Dostoevsky, we cannot blame our behaviour on environmental conditions. If we would do silly things even when living in the supposed perfection of a crystal palace, then our actions must be attributable to our human nature, and we must take responsibility for them. In *Crime and Punishment* we see Razumikhin and Porfiry discussing this very topic, and their conversation neatly introduces Raskolnikov's own article on crime. The socialists are savagely attacked, with a speech that is pure Razumikhin in its passion and humour:

Environment is the root of all evil – and nothing else! A favourite phrase. And the direct consequence of it is that if society is organised on normal lines, all crimes will vanish at once, for there will be nothing to protest against, and all men will become righteous in the twinkling of an eye. Human nature isn't taken into account at all. Human nature is banished. Human nature isn't supposed to exist. ...They don't want a living soul! A living soul makes demands, a living soul scoffs at mechanics, a living soul is suspicious, a living soul is retrograde! The sort of soul they want may smell of carrion, and it may even be possible to make it of rubber, but at least it is not alive, at least it has not will, at least it is servile and can be guaranteed not to rebel! [9]

Whilst writing *The Karamazov Brothers*, Dostoevsky was reading the Emile Zola's *L'Assommoir*, a brutally realistic portrayal of poverty and alcoholism in the slums of Paris, and his approach to the problem of free will in his own novel stands in marked contrast to Zola's determinism.[10] Rakitin, the cynical young seminarian turned would-be critic, visits Dmitry in prison because he hopes to make a name for himself by writing an analysis of the case and demonstrating that Dmitry couldn't help committing a murder because he was a victim of his environment. In a wonderfully confused musing on the nature of consciousness, Dmitry says that he acted because of the quivering nerves with little tails in his brain and not at all because he has a soul, and for this reason he feels sorry for God who clearly has no place in this. (Dostoevsky makes it deliciously unclear as to

---

[9] *Crime and Punishment* p273 (Part Three, Chapter 5)

[10] Dostoevsky takes indirect pot-shots at Zola with Dmitry's clownish references to Claude Bernard, the French physiologist who informed much of Zola's thinking. Bernard developed a very strict methodological approach to scientific experiment, and Zola applied the same approach, using the novel as a laboratory in which to test and observe human behaviour.

whether the little tails are Rakitin's invention or Dmitry's muddled interpretation of a clearer explanation). But without God, asks Dmitry, doesn't that mean we can do whatever we like? After all, this is the superficial conclusion to be drawn from the arguments of his brother, Ivan, and in a faint echo of Raskolnikov, Rakitin replies that yes, we can do what we like, but that the cleverness lies in not getting caught.

Dostoevsky uses Dmitry's useless defence team to expose the falsity of the deterministic argument. Their case attempts to relieve Dmitry of any responsibility whatsoever for the murder, built as it is on the twin pillars of environmental influence and temporary insanity. Dostoevsky casts all his scorn on this line of defence in Mrs Khokhlakova's explanation to Alyosha, in which she seems to think that temporary insanity can be caught like a common cold. After a sensible refutation of the material evidence against Dmitry, the defence lawyer, Fetyukovich, undermines his entire case by essentially saying that even if Dmitry did do it, he can hardly be blamed for his actions, because his father abandoned him when he was a small child, and he was left to run around in rags until Grigory looked after him. Furthermore, continues the impeccable logic, as you can hardly therefore call Fyodor Karamazov a father, you can't accuse his son of parricide, and he suggests that Dmitry killed Fyodor in a moment of insanity occasioned by his justified hatred of the man who begot him. By using environmental factors to construct such a pathetically weak defence case, Dostoevsky is signalling his own disapproval of attempts to blame bad behaviour on environment. If it's all down to environmental factors, then Razumikhin's jest would be true and we would be able to get rid of crime and misery by creating a perfect society, but, just like the simple Russian peasants on the jury who reject Fetyukovich's argument, we all know in our hearts that this isn't possible: because we are all human, we must all take responsibility for our actions.

All too often we deliberately choose to act in a way that's going to hurt, so freedom is always going to mean that human beings do stupid, damaging things, in full consciousness of the consequences of their actions. And it's not just Dostoevsky's wild boys: as ever they are just the shock troops. We know that to some extent we all abuse our freedom with behaviour that damages either ourselves or other people, and just because we're not killing ourselves with drugs or alcohol, or gambling away our savings, or humiliating ourselves with an addictively degrading relationship, it doesn't mean that we're in the clear. Having that second drink on a work night, buying those shoes that you really can't afford; you keep telling yourself that you shouldn't do it, right up to the moment when you reach for the bottle or the credit card, and suddenly, regretfully, the deed is done. It's no wonder that there are those who, with the best of intentions, think that this freedom is too much for us to bear.

This brings to the Grand Inquisitor. This majestic 'poem', composed by Ivan Karamazov, and which he recites to Alyosha, must be the most famous passage in all of Dostoevsky's work. It has written about at length by literary critics and theologians alike, with the eloquence and subtlety that it deserves. I make no claim to add to their insights, but nor can I avoid it all together, so I humbly present my own reactions to it here, and in the two final chapters, and refer my readers promptly to the bibliography for further reading! The Grand Inquisitor is a magnificent piece of writing; it's powerful and disturbing, and pulsates with vivid imagery. The wizened old man is terrifying in his intensity, both in his public grandeur and in the midnight privacy of Christ's cell. We tremble at his invocation of:

The terrible and clever spirit, the spirit of self-destruction and annihilation.[11]

And we are awed by the silent power of Christ, who speaks but two words during his entire visit and then departs with a truly unforgettable kiss. More than anything Dostoevsky wrote, it

---

[11] *The Karamazov Brothers,* p315, (Book Five, Chapter 5)

bears repeated reading – there is always a surprising new thought, or a burning phrase that previously escaped notice.

The Grand Inquisitor rebukes Christ for having allowed mankind the terrible gift of free will, a gift that Christ renews in his rejection of the first temptation. By turning stones into bread and conquering hunger forever, he could have ensured for himself the unquestioning obedience of all mankind.

"And do You see these stones in this barren white-hot desert? [says the tempter] Turn them into bread, and mankind will come running after You, a grateful and obedient flock, although they will always tremble in fear that You may withdraw Your hand and stop their supply of bread" But You did not want to deprive man of his freedom, so You rejected the suggestion, for what sort of freedom would it be, You judged, if obedience were bought with bread?[12]

The Grand Inquisitor thinks that this freedom is too much for ordinary men to bear and that we should be deprived of it for our own good,

Because [we] *are weak, depraved, worthless and rebellious.*[13]

The antics of the wild boys, of the monsters we've already considered in Chapter Five, and indeed our own petty weaknesses, all make a strong case for the Grand Inquisitor's argument. Take away the freedom of Christ, runs the argument – it's too much for these little children! But, Dostoevsky's Christ cannot deny us the freedom to do stupid or evil things, because to do so would be to take away our very humanity. The mistake that we make is to confuse true freedom with the selfish satisfaction of our own desires, so in thinking that we have escaped, either from our conscience or from the conventions of the society we live in, we instead become slaves to our own egos, and we are deceived

---

[12] *The Karamazov Brothers* p 316-317 (Book Five, Chapter 5)
[13] *The Karamazov Brothers* p 317 (Book Five, Chapter 5)

into thinking we're happy, at least temporarily. This is the mistake that Dostoevsky's hedonists make, but unlike their wild behaviour, true freedom is never accompanied by shame and regret. As Frank puts it:

For Dostoevsky, freedom meant mastery and suppression of one's desires, not liberation from all constraints on their satisfaction.[14]

This then is what Dostoevsky's Christ is really offering us, the true freedom that gives us the chance to learn and grow and to cleanse ourselves of the lingering dirt that still clings to us as we wallow in our human desires.

Christ himself is given no opportunity to answer the Grand Inquisitor. It's not hard to see why, for it is impossible to imagine Dostoevsky daring to put words into the mouth of his Saviour. Instead, we are given the opportunity to see how we can be freed from the slavery of our selfish desires by living a life of love in which we take responsibility not only for our own actions but those of everyone around us. The beauty of this message is that we don't have to rely on the luck of predestination, or wait for a capricious god to decide whether or not to bestow his grace upon us. We all have it within ourselves to conquer our sinful weaknesses and live a new life of freedom, and what better ambassador for this new way of life could there be than Dmitry Karamazov, the irrepressible, irresponsible wild boy. Dmitry doesn't necessarily get it right because his impetuous, emotional spirit charges in with too much impractical enthusiasm; the important point here lies not in the outward consequences, but in the inner change that comes about in Dmitry, and the strength and comfort that comes with his discovery of a better way of living and thinking.

Dmitry's journey to redemption begins on the night of Fyodor's murder; a night that has seen him at his wildest and most reckless; a night that he thought would be his last on earth.

---

[14] Frank p883

The first step comes in his change of relations with Grushenka, as the two of them move beyond basic carnal lust, and open their hearts to a genuine love for each other. Grushenka is experiencing her own spiritual awakening, a process that began earlier on that eventful night in her conversation with Alyosha about the onion, but the moment of revelation and mutual joy that they share is shattered by Dmitry's arrest. His subsequent interrogation by the examining magistrate is recounted in the three chapters that are grouped together under the headings of *A Soul's Journey Through Torments*. These chapter headings would have had an immediate resonance for Dostoevsky's Russian readers, recalling as they do the journey that the Orthodox believe every soul makes after death. And Dmitry certainly is tormented, for in the course of the interrogation, he has had his words, deeds and relationships exposed to painful scrutiny and he has to undergo the physical humiliation of a full strip-search and the confiscation of his clothes.

After the rigours of his interrogation, Dmitry falls asleep, and dreams a terrible dream of desolation and destruction in which he sees a burned village in an empty steppe, starving peasants, and a baby, crying with cold and hunger, reaching out for its mother's dried up breasts. In his dream, Dmitry is at a complete loss to understand why the baby is cold and hungry and why the people don't wrap it up and feed it:

He felt a totally unprecedented wave of emotion well up in his soul which brought him to the verge of tears and made him want to do something for everyone, something that would make the bairn stop crying ... something that, from that moment on, would put an end to all tears once and for all, and he wanted to do it then, immediately, without brooking the least delay and with truly Karamazovian impetuosity.[15]

---

[15] *The Karamazov Brothers* p596 (Book Nine, Chapter 8)

To cement his new-found feelings, he then hears in his dream the voice of Grushenka telling him that she will remain with him always. And when he wakes up, he is deeply moved by the fact that some kind soul has put a pillow under his head while he slept.

The very fact that the dreaming Dmitry has frantically asked the question about why no-one is looking after the baby indicates the change in his thinking – it's not that he is able to do anything about it, but that suddenly he cares, and this is the practical effect of Dostoevsky's doctrine of responsibility for all, as set out earlier by Father Zossima. We aren't always in a position where we can do anything to help, but an earnest desire to make things better will make itself felt in all our thoughts and actions. We see the first signs of this new attitude when Dmitry wakes from his dream – he becomes more co-operative towards his interrogators, apologising for his earlier anger and vowing to change. He is still protesting that he is innocent, and is determined to clear his name, but he now accepts that he deserves the suffering that has come to him. He even begs the peasants for forgiveness as he leaves the inn: it's as if he's mysteriously imbibed every word of Father Zossima's exhortations and is immediately and literally putting it all into practice, albeit with the same wholehearted zest that previously went into his debauches.

In his book *The Varieties of Religious Experience* the great psychologist of religion, William James, wrote about conversion experiences, and his work has been discussed by, among others, Joseph Frank and Robin Feuer Miller in their analyses of Dostoevsky's own return to faith in the darkness of the prison camp, but it seems to me that Dmitry Karamazov is a textbook example of what James is describing. James emphasises that conversion can take on many forms, and is not necessarily limited to a straightforward passage from religious unbelief to belief. It is more likely to occur in people whose mental systems are open to being worked upon by the subconscious, and Dmitry, with his tendency to respond impulsively to events, certainly fits the bill here. One type of spontaneous conversion that James describes will come when the conscious brain is so overwhelmed with oppressive thoughts that it just gives in with emotional exhaustion and allows the subconscious to take over, resulting in a sudden feeling of joyfulness and of being at one with the universe, an ecstasy of happiness. Remember that Dmitry set off for Mokroye assuming that he would be killing himself in the morning: he's gone storming from suicidal despair, to ecstatic happiness, he's found life and love when he was expecting only death – then suddenly, he's lost everything. When he falls asleep, his subconscious does indeed take over, serving him up with a dream that points the way forward for him.

Having undergone this conversion experience, Dmitry (who is still the same enthusiastic, passionate Karamazov) attempts to be as excessive in his desire to take on suffering as he was in his wild behaviour. He is determined that he must go to Siberia for the sake of the baby in his dream, and his arrest is in fact just what he needs; in his conversations with Alyosha before the murder, he showed signs of anxious to cast off his sinfulness, but hasn't had the ability to do it – in the Jamesian model, he's not had the opportunity to let his better subconscious nature rise up and take over. Suddenly, with the crisis of his arrest and the prospect of spending twenty years in Siberia for a crime of which he maintains his innocence, here is Dmitry's time for suffering and for taking on responsibility.

In his cell, awaiting trial, Dmitry launches into a wild and defiant speech about how, since his arrest and the dream about the baby, a new man has arisen in him, a man who desperately wants to love and suffer for all. With the zeal of the convert, he says that he wants to go to Siberia on behalf of all the babies and children who suffer, but although it's a noble sentiment that shows he's thinking in the right way, there is no practical way in which going to prison would really help anyone, not even Dmitry Karamazov. Dmitry naively thinks that in the camp, he would be entirely liberated from his evil, selfish desires, and become free to love God, indeed that loving and serving God wholeheartedly would be necessary there. Dostoevsky knows the realities of prison life of course, and reading *Notes from the House of the Dead,* it's easy to imagine Dmitry getting thoroughly ensnared in all the vices of prison camp life – and his disappointment would be overwhelming. Dmitry is a tough man who would well withstand the bodily torments of prison, but he would not be able to bear the crushing disappointment and spiritual suffering that would come with the inevitable slide back into bad behaviour, and this is why Alyosha sensibly agrees to the escape plan. Far better that Dmitry settles quietly in exile with his beloved Grushenka, both of them there to support and nurture each other, creating something good.

At his trial, Dmitry has to be reprimanded for repeatedly interrupting proceedings and breaching court protocol. He freely admits his guilt in attacking Grigory, and violently curses Smerdyakov and his father. It's as if he wants to be convicted, because he still thinks that prison is the only solution for him. We are reminded again of the old Dmitry by public prosecutor who, in his speech, paints a picture of Dmitry's wild passions, his lack of self-restraint, and his habit of living for the moment, and he uses this psychological portrait to undermine some of Dmitry's claims about the events of the night and the source of his money for the second Mokroye trip. He then closes his speech with his own reference to Gogol, telling the jury that they have the opportunity to put a halt to the terrible troika:

The fateful troika is galloping at full pelt, maybe to its doom. Many hands have long reached out throughout the whole of Russia in an attempt to stop its wild lurching course. And even if other nations step aside to make way for its breakneck progress, then, in all likelihood, this is not out of respect, as the poet would have wished, but out of sheer terror – note this well! Out of terror or perhaps out of disgust, and we should thank our lucky stars that they do step aside, for in order to save themselves and their enlightened civilization, they might fail to step aside, and instead form a solid wall across the path of the charging apparition, thus putting an end to our galloping depravity! We have already heard these threatening voices from Europe. Do not tempt them, do not augment their ever-increasing hatred by passing a verdict acquitting a son of murdering his own father. [16]

Fetyukovich, the defence lawyer, attempts to turn the image around, transforming the troika into a majestic chariot that is seen arriving calmly at its destination of justice, but it seems fair to say that this is just a grotesque attempt at wishful thinking, for the horses still gallop tirelessly onward and no nation has yet halted the frenzied gallop of the mad Russian troika. However, Dostoevsky has found an alternative vision, with Christ at the reins of the troika. The ride is still a journey of exhilarating freedom, but no-one is crushed under the wheels, and the passengers all help to gather everyone they pass on the road lovingly into the troika, as it continues on its exciting path.

---

[16] *The Karamazov Brothers* p908, (Book Twelve, Chapter 9)

> *Dear me! We are freaks, all of us – we ought to be put on show under glass – and I first of all – at twopence a peep.*
>
> *(Lizaveta Prokofyevna)*

NINE: LIZAVETA PROKOFYEVNA

Tolstoy opens *Anna Karenina* with his famous statement that all happy families are alike, but an unhappy family is unhappy after its own fashion. Tolstoy's interest lies mostly in the difficulties of married life, and the conventional family structure of married parents with children drives the actions of Tolstoy's characters, whether they are striving to achieve it, or doing battle against its constraints. By contrast, Dostoevsky's families are fragmented, incomplete, and rarely happy. Parents are dead, or absent; children are left to be brought up by distant relatives, and many families include a confusing mixture of half-siblings and step-parents. In the case of *Crime and Punishment*, for example, Sonya Marmeladova is prostituting herself to support her father's second wife, Katerina Ivanovna, and Katerina's children from a previous marriage, to whom Sonya has no blood relationship at all, and in *The Adolescent* things get so confusing that at times, I'm grateful for the Russian use of patronymics, just to keep track of family relationships.[1]

Many of the characters who emerge from these jumbled-up and fragmented families find themselves forced to seek in others the close bonds that they should have been able to forge with

---

[1] See the Appendix section *Russian Names* for a brief explanation.

their parents, their children or their siblings, while others develop intensely close relationships with the remaining members of their immediate family. Unlike Tolstoy, Dostoevsky stays away from delving into the peculiar intimacies and dynamics of marriage – the closest he comes to this is in *The Devils,* the first part of which is dominated by the claustrophobic, sterile relationship between Stepan Verkhovensky and Varvara Stavrogina, and is but a hideous distortion of married life. He is not particularly interested in the people who at one point have made the decision to love each other and live together, but turns instead to the relationships between people who share the same blood. He probes deeply into the intense and often contradictory emotions that exist within families – the mad mixture of burning love and bewilderment, exasperation and devotion, jealousy and despair, and those close bonds that you can't choose and can't escape – the bond between parents and children, or between siblings.

In *Diary of a Writer*, Dostoevsky regularly returns to what he calls 'accidental families'; haphazard mixtures of stepparents, unwanted children and families where love has been banished or overtaken by other worries, and he investigates the associated problems of abandoned children and delinquent youth: the *Diary* includes, for example, a fascinating account of Dostoevsky's visit to a rehabilitation camp for criminal boys. Dostoevsky was particularly concerned with what he saw as the collapse of family life in industrialising Russia, and the consequences for society of all these broken homes. He writes too about the importance for children 'sacred memories', and he stresses that even the most hopeless, dissolute father will not have been entirely neglectful if he can bequeath such a memory on his child. The saddest, most hopeless, cases are those children who do not have even one single beautiful memory to which they can cling for spiritual sustenance. He talks about the casual upbringing of so many children, both rich and poor, and observes that the importance of faith in generating beautiful memories in children's minds has been disregarded by many. This idea of sacred memories finds its way into Alyosha's speech to his young friends, in the closing pages of Dostoevsky's last novel:

Remember that nothing is nobler, stronger, more vital, or more useful in future life than some happy memory, especially one from your very childhood, from your family home. A lot is said about upbringing, but the very best upbringing, perhaps, is some lovely, holy memory preserved from one's childhood. If a man carries many such memories with him, they will keep him safe throughout his life. And even if only one such memory stays in our hearts, it may prove to be our salvation one day.[2]

Many of the ideas about families and children that Dostoevsky explores in *Diary of a Writer* found their way into *The Karamazov Brothers* – as we've already noted, the incidents of child torture all have their origins in real cases that Dostoevsky reported on for the *Diary,* and Mochulsky calls it a laboratory for the Karamazovs.[3] In Dostoevsky's earlier St Petersburg novels too, there are throngs of miserable children; we see them begging on the streets, living in squalor and dying of cold and hunger, a reminder of the horrors of 19th century urbanisation. All these unhappy children find their voice in the pathetic story published in the first edition of the *Diary,* in January 1876 called *A Little Boy at Christ's Christmas Tree,* in which a young child, all alone after his mother's death, wanders the streets of St Petersburg. He watches through a window and sees luckier children enjoying the festivities round their tree, then he huddles up in a snowdrift and quietly freezes to death. His soul is taken up to heaven by angels, where he is invited enjoy Christ's own Christmas tree with all the other children who have suffered. It's a shamelessly sentimental tear-jerker, but it shows Dostoevsky's passionate concern for the horrors he saw around him. Arriving in heaven, the little boy learned:

---

[2] *The Karamazov Brothers* p972 (Epilogue, Chapter 3)
[3] Mochulsky p557

That these little boys and girls were all once children like himself, but some of them have frozen to death in those baskets in which they had been left at the doors of Petersburg officials; others had perished in miserable hospital wards; still others had died at the dried-up breasts of their famine-stricken mothers. ... These, again, had choked to death from stench in third-class railroad cars.[4]

And for the children who do survive, Dostoevsky worries about the effects on them of a city upbringing, particularly on those forced into backbreaking, soul-destroying factory work and prematurely exposed to the vices of adulthood. In this respect he is no different to so many other nineteenth century intellectuals, but Dostoevsky is concerned not only with the material and physical miseries of urban poverty. Socialists such as Engels saw urban poverty as alienating people from their true humanity, thus causing them to sink into animal-like degradation, but for Dostoevsky this alienation has an additional spiritual dimension, in the way that city-dwellers are cut off from the soil and thus from their true Russian way of life.

Dostoevsky's own wealth of sacred childhood memories came from the times he spent at the family's small country estate in Darovoe, acquired by his father to complete their transition to a gentry lifestyle. Like many Russian children today, the Dostoevskys spent long summers living in the country – running wild, playing with the peasant children, and for Fyodor, life at Darovoe marked the beginning of his passionate relationship with the Russian soil and the Russian people. It's something I find quite familiar, for even today, urban Russians have a far greater affinity with the land than many Britons, even those of us who grew up in the countryside. Almost every family owns or rents a dacha – a country cottage that can be anything from a small hut on an allotment, to a neo-gothic monstrosity, and just as in Dostoevsky's day, grandparents and children spend most of the summer there, with the working generation visiting at the week-

---

[4] *Diary of a Writer* p171 (January 1876, Chapter 2, section 2)

ends to lend a hand in the vegetable garden. For all but the very rich, the family dacha is an invaluable source of fresh produce (one of the engineers I worked with in Moscow would always go down with a mysterious illness when the time came for sowing potatoes), and of delicious pickles and jams to see the family through the winter; and everyone knows which mushrooms in the forest are edible, and where they can be found. Some of my own happiest times in Russia were spent with friends at their dachas, where I was treated to a little glimpse of what it feels like to love the Russian countryside, and where I formed my own most sacred memories of Russia.

Happy childhood life in the Russian village is occasionally evoked in Dostoevsky's early work, and there is a distinct contrast in Dostoevsky's between the sense of deep-rooted happiness in the country, and the misery, chaos and abandonment of the city. Varvara Petrovna, one of the epistolary narrators of his first novel, *Poor People,* recalls happy days in the country until poverty drove her family to the city; and in *Humiliated and Insulted*, Natasha Ikhmeneva and Ivan Petrovich enjoy an innocently blissful rural existence until the Valkovskys contrive to ruin both bliss and innocence, and the Ikhmenevs too are driven away to St Petersburg. It may seem strange that a writer who is so attached to the Russian landscape doesn't do more to evoke it in his novels, and I think this is partly due to Dostoevsky's own perceived limitations on his descriptive skills – he admired in Tolstoy and Turgenev an artistry that he felt was missing in his own make-up. But I think it's also because the Russian countryside is such a sacred haven for Dostoevsky that he cannot evoke it, because he's not really in the business of writing about peace and happiness. He's more concerned showing us what happens when people are torn away from the moist earth of their Russian land. He achieves an interesting compromise in *The Devils* and *The Karamazov Brothers* by setting them in a half-way house, a small provincial town, (the setting for *The Karamazov Brothers* is based on the old town of Staraya Russa, where Dostoevsky had a summer house). This allows Dostoevsky to write about people who he thought of as being real Russians, living in the ancient heartland of their country, but still in an urban setting, away from the village itself.

Despite the overwhelming presence of chaotic families in his novels, Dostoevsky's own experiences of family life were mostly positive, and this gives added authority to his writing. He knew from first-hand experience how even just one happy childhood memory can return to sustain the wounded spirit in the depths of despair – in his case the memory of the kind peasant, Marey. Dostoevsky was brought up in a stable, loving family, with several brothers and sisters and was particularly close to his older brother Mikhail, whose loving support sustained him through many trials. After Mikhail's death at the age of just forty-four, Fyodor wrote to their younger brother Andrei:

I shall not try to tell you how much I have lost with him. That man loved me more than anyone in the world, more even than his wife and children whom he adored. ... It is as though my life has been shattered.[5]

It is also clear that Dostoevsky took his own family commitments extremely seriously, and the financial problems that led to his flight to Europe seem to have arisen in part from his willingness to support Mikhail's widow and children – in her memoirs Anna Dostoevskaya has many angry words about the demands that Mikhail's family placed on her husband, and the impression she gives, which may, admittedly, require a pinch or two of salt, is that they were willing to exploit his generosity quite unscrupulously. After the unhappy interlude of his first marriage to Maria Isaeva (when he acquired yet another sponging hanger-on in the form of her son Pavel), Dostoevsky found his own happy family in his marriage to Anna, and he was an attentive and loving fa-

---

[5] *Selected Letters* p203 (29 July, 1864, to A.M. Dostoevsky)

ther who took great pleasure in being fully involved in the care and upbringing of his children.

His own father, Mikhail Andreevich Dostoevsky, was strict, but probably no worse than many 19th century fathers, and letters between his parents, quoted by Frank, suggest that their marriage was happy. Mikhail Andreevich was a hard-working military doctor, who had succeeded in liberating himself from the priestly caste into which he had been born. By his own efforts and determination, he managed to obtain the rank of collegiate assessor in the complicated hierarchy of the Russian civil service. This position permitted him to enter the register of nobility, which he himself considered to be nothing less than the rightful restoration of his family's ancient title, for his ancestors had been landowners in Lithuania. The Dostoevsky children were constantly being made aware of their noble background, despite the fact that they lived in a cramped apartment in a Moscow hospital, and Dr Dostoevsky was fiercely determined that his sons should continue the task of restoring the family's position and fortune. The boys were made to study hard, and, under their father's instructions, applied for places at the prestigious Academy of Engineers in St Petersburg.[6] Mikhail Andreevich's aspirations to a gentry lifestyle were such that, despite his limited means, he maintained a staff of six servants, and their janitor was required to put on livery and accompany Dr Dostoevsky's wife whenever she went out in public – a situation that his son was later to mock in *The Double* in the pretensions of Mr Golyadkin.

From the descriptions that have come down to us of Mikhail Andreevich Dostoevsky, certain traits emerge that are quite recognisable to anyone familiar with his son's life or his books. He was morbidly proud, prone to explosive anger, frequently depressed, and despite his achievements, was bitter with his lot in life. It was rumoured that he met his end at the hands of his own

---

[6] Fyodor Mikhailovich was accepted, but his older brother Mikhail was rejected for medical reasons and was sent to an engineering school in the provinces.

serfs when he attacked one of them in a drunken rage, but the official version is that he died of an apoplectic fit. The truth probably lies somewhere in between, but the family covered up the matter and did not press charges against the serfs,[7] leaving it to become one of those stories that are left to fester, giving off a miasma of myth. The figure of Fyodor Karamazov, widowed, living alone in the country, drinking and allegedly fathering children on the servant girls, clearly bears a superficial resemblance to Mikhail Andreevich Dostoevsky, and this similarity no doubt helped to fuel the rumours.

In his essay *Dostoevsky and Parricide*,[8] Freud certainly links the death of Mikhail Andreevich to the murder of Fyodor Karamazov. He also suggests that Dostoevsky experienced such a sense of parricidal guilt when his father died that it brought on his epilepsy, and that he endured his unjust imprisonment in Siberia because he was accepting punishment at the hands of the Father Tsar for causing his own father's death. Freud takes the story of the Karamazovs as evidence of Dostoevsky's own sense of guilt, and he places particular importance on the scene in which Father Zossima bows down to Dmitry, who will eventually take on the guilt of all parricides – not just for his brothers, but for Dostoevsky too. It is possible that Dostoevsky's constant requests for more money had been driving his father to treat his peasants so harshly that they turned on him, either murdering him or bringing on the apoplexy, whichever story one believes, but there is no indication that Dostoevsky suffered any agonies beyond a normal degree of grief over the news, and his epileptic fits did not begin until he was in Siberia. Indeed when his father died, he was now released from any obligation to continue with the army career that Mikhail Andreevich desired for him, and

---

[7] Frank points out that this was not necessarily done from altruism – in those days before the emancipation of the serfs, the value of an estate was tied to the number of its serfs, so charging a large number of them with murder would have devalued the estate.

[8] In *Dostoevsky: A collection of Critical Essays*, ed René Wellek, p98 - 111

was free to devote himself fully to writing. If he blamed himself at any point for his father's death, he may have drawn on the experience when writing *The Karamazov Brothers*, but I think Freud over-eggs the pudding in suggesting that Dostoevsky felt any excessive guilt in the matter.

Whatever the relationship with his own father, there are few positive examples of fatherhood in Dostoevsky's fiction; fathers are either absent or dead, and those who are still around are often drinkers, debauchers, or just neglectful of their responsibilities. There are however, two men who stand out as devoted, loving fathers, desperate to do their best for their families despite all the misery and suffering that the world throws at them. They are Nikolai Ikhmenev in *Humiliated and Insulted* and Snegiryov, father of poor, brave little Ilyusha in *The Karamazov Brothers*. The tender scenes that Dostoevsky describes between Snegiryov and Ilyusha, their quiet walks to the stone, Ilyusha's passionate defence of his father when he is publicly humiliated, and the absolutely heart-breaking moment when the doctor pronounces Ilyusha's illness to be incurable, speak of a deep father-son relationship that is all the more notable for its uniqueness in Dostoevsky's pages.

The side-story of the Snegiryov family is there to give us a stark contrast to the rancorous Karamazovs, for here is a family who stand firmly together, even though they are desperately poor and humiliated (to add to their woes, their mother is sunk in senility, and one daughter is crippled). They are a motley collection of broken people, but still nonetheless a family, bound together not just by biology but by love. The point about unnecessary suffering and vainglorious pride is made again here: Snegiryov initially refuses Katerina's offer of charity, but when Ilyusha falls ill, his love for his son is stronger than his pride and he accepts her support. Even Varvara, the permanently bad-tempered eldest daughter, is fiercely protective of her family's dignity, and although her father's tomfoolery infuriates her, her anger comes from love. Varvara is an intriguing figure, for, despite the family's humble origins, she is studying in Petersburg, and I'd love to know how she got there and what she did with her life – I wonder if she was destined to be developed in the unwritten sequel, for she has the makings of a feisty Dostoevskian heroine.

In his defence of Dmitry, the lawyer Fetyukovich makes the point that Fyodor Karamazov was never really a father to Dmitry and he defines a father as:

[The man] *who begat me, who loved me, who for my sake did not spare himself, who felt for me when I suffered all my childhood illnesses, who struggled for my happiness all his life, and who lived his life only through my joys and triumphs.*[9]

His speech eventually builds up into an exhortation to all fathers that they must earn their children's love – it doesn't come automatically with conception, particularly if the child was created in a moment of drunkenness or lust, with no thought for the eventual consequences. A father, we are told, must be able to tell his children why they should love him, and if he can't, then the children are released from any obligation, the bonds of the family are shattered, and there is nothing to hold together its component parts. Fetyukovich reinforces his argument by throwing in a few more examples of parental cruelty, and asks whether the servant girl who was found to have murdered three babies at birth can ever be called a mother. Fetyukovich knows that he is addressing not just the crowded courtroom, but all of Russia, for the case is being followed avidly by the public across the country, and similarly Dostoevsky himself is taking the opportunity to hector his readers, just as he did in the pages of *Diary of a Writer*.

We get the rhetoric from Fetyukovich, but then almost immediately afterwards, Dostoevsky shows us the reality of true paternal love, the unfathomable grief of Snegiryov at his son's funeral, impossible to paraphrase, and impossible to read without crying. Snegiryov himself, lost for words to express his grief

---

[9] *The Karamazov Brothers* p933 (Book Twelve, Chapter 13)

when he realises that his son is dying, turns to the Bible for that heartrending lament from Psalm 137:

If I forget thee, O Jerusalem, may my right hand forget her cunning. If I do not remember thee, let my tongue cleave to the roof of my mouth.[10]

None of the Karamazov sons suffered in this way when they lost their father.

The stark contrast between the accidental families and those governed by steadfast love goes right back to Dostoevsky's earliest works. One only has to think of the drifting lost souls of his first novel, *Poor People* – Varvara and Devushkin, distantly related and struggling in vain to give each other care and guidance through the horrors of life in the Petersburg slums, or the contrast in *Humiliated and Insulted* between the Ikhmenevs and the Valkovskys, the latter being an early, but typical case of an accidental family. The tender love between Nikolai Ikhmenev, and his only child, Natasha is put sorely to the test when she abandons her family to live with Alexey Valkovsky, whose father has ruined the Ikhmenevs and is Nikolai's bitterest enemy. The broken-hearted father tries to convince himself that he has rejected Natasha, and thrown her off for good, but beneath his show of stubborn pride, it's quite clear all along that he still loves her deeply and longs for her to come back. It is only by the insertion of the orphan Nelly into the Ikhmenev household that Nikolai begins to relax the iron-grip that he has placed on his feelings, and when he learns the full story of Nelly's past and sees the parallels with his own life, he finally admits his error and learns how to be a loving father again, welcoming Natasha back. Nelly herself has the means that will force her own father to acknowledge her, but she refuses to make any contact with him at all for she understands that he is no more of a father to her than Fyodor Karamazov will be to his sons, and she searches instead for sub-

---

[10] Psalm 137 v5-6.

stitutes in Ivan Petrovich, in Masloboyev the detective, and in the elderly doctor. In *Humiliated and Insulted,* Dostoevsky has not yet reached his full stride; the moralising is decidedly unsubtle, and the plot dénouement is no great surprise; but it's an entertaining read. It's an experimental novel, in which, although many ideas remain undeveloped, we can see Dostoevsky embarking on his exploration of what it really means to be a parent, and, conversely, what it means to be someone's child.

In a grotesque distortion of the fatherly duty to pass on wisdom and sense to the next generation, Prince Valkovsky seems determined to teach his son his own vices: he heartlessly makes fun of Alexey's rather feeble ideals, encourages his dissipation and womanising, and propels him towards a cynical marriage of convenience with Katerina. This idea of unhealthy relationships between fathers and sons that began with the Valkovskys then lies strangely dormant until after Dostoevsky himself had become a father – it's as if he doesn't really want to criticise until he has experienced both sides of the father-son relationship for himself, but the searches for substitute father-figures loom large again in his last three novels: *The Devils, The Adolescent* and *The Karamazov Brothers*, and run in parallel to his studies of the Russian family in his journalism.

Nikolai Stavrogin's father abandoned the family when the boy was still young, and Nikolai's entire intellectual development was entrusted to Stepan Verkhovensky, who, in his employment as the boy's tutor, acts as a substitute father. He provides Stavrogin with an education based on the liberal and romantic individualism of Western Europe, but neglects to teach him the virtues of his native land. He also tries to treat the little boy as his equal, sharing adult emotions with him, without ever teaching him how to understand them. As Verkhovensky's emotional life is centred on Nikolai's own mother, it is particularly inappropriate that he should share his feelings about her with her own child, and he probably does much to damage the relationship between mother and son. Meanwhile, Stepan neglects his own son, Pyotr who, in turn, grows up to become one of Dostoevsky's most disturbingly self-reliant characters, appearing to survive quite happily without any intimate ties to other people. He has no-one who he can call his father – tellingly he disdainfully addresses his own father with the Latin *pater* – and this huge absence has left him with no capacity for love. Verkhovensky's spiritual and biological sons, Nikolai and Pyotr grow up to infect the town with their devils, and Stepan Trofimovich realises too late that it is all his fault.

In his next novel, *The Adolescent,* Dostoevsky takes the mixture of substitute and natural fathers even further. The narrator, Arkady Makarovich Dolgoruky is the illegitimate son of Andrei Versilov, an impoverished aristocrat. Then it gets complicated. Arkady's mother, Sofya Andreevna, separates from her husband, Makar Dolgoruky, to live with Versilov, but as anyone familiar with Russian names will have noticed, Arkady retains the patronymic and surname of Makar, who is to all intents and purposes his legal father. Makar comes to some sort of amicable arrangement with Versilov concerning Sofya and her children, then leaves to become a religious mystic, wandering the length of Russia and only occasionally visiting his family. Arkady is deposited in a boarding school, and when he emerges from school at the beginning of the story, he finds himself floundering in an adult world for which no-one has prepared him. He is torn between hatred for Versilov and a touching desire to earn his respect, but it is also clear that Versilov, a spendthrift womaniser who is sunk in his own spiritual confusion, is in no way a suitable role model for the young man. Eventually, just like the Karamazovs, Fyodor and Dmitry, they end up in that most poisonous of rivalries where both men are competing for the love of the same woman. There's a hint of this situation between the Valkovskys too, and another echo of it in Varvara Stavrogina's attempts to marry off Stepan Verkhovensky to Nikolai Stavrogin's mistress Dasha. All these instances of sexual rivalry highlight the alienation between the fathers and their sons and the failures to keep a suitable distance between the generations; it would be grotesque to imagine such a situation occurring in a loving father and son relationship in which both men are sensitive to what is appropriate.

The only person who might have been able to offer Arkady the love and moral guidance that he has missed is his legal father, Makar, but he is mostly absent, and having given up his family to Versilov, he takes his immense capacity for love to the people of Russia. He returns to his wife and her family in Petersburg when he is dying, and arrives just in time to rescue Arkady from the moral and spiritual abyss into which the boy has sunk. The plot is incredibly complicated, and it's worthy of the best Victorian potboilers or even of an opera, for it involves secret documents, a gang of fraudsters, fallen women and philandering men galore, lust, betrayal, several suicides, a mad gambling scene, a wicked French whore, and plenty of hiding behind doors. Arkady is at the heart of it all, and he simply cannot cope, physically or mentally. When Makar arrives, Arkady has lain unconscious for nine days as a result of a calamitous night, and he is plunged into a deep depression. At this dark moment, Arkady meets in Makar, probably for the first time in his life, a person who lives by the example of loving self-sacrifice and responsibility for all, and importantly, Arkady recognises what he identifies as Makar's 'seemliness', meaning his natural and undisputable moral rectitude. Makar tells long, gently rambling stories that make a deep impression on both Arkady and Versilov, and he appears to bring reconciliation and proper family relations between Versilov, Sofya Andreevna and their children. It doesn't last, and the terrible intrigues and scandalous behaviour rumble on, but Arkady re-emerges into this world with a new inner strength. It is now only fitting that Arkady should be known as Arkady Makarovich Dolgoruky, for he bears of the man who has eventually become a true father to him.

Of the Karamazov brothers, only Alyosha has been able to find positive substitute father-figures, firstly in Father Zossima, and following his death, Father Paissy, both of whom give him the spiritual and moral guidance that he lacked in his own father. This is why, of all the brothers, Alyosha suffers the least from the guilt of parricide – he has found a new father, and is properly mourning his death, rather than concerning himself with imagined guilt for the man who happened to beget him. Zossima has insisted that when he dies, Alyosha go back to the secular world; and so the monastery becomes for Alyosha a second chance of childhood, in the sense of childhood being a time for learning and of preparation for the inevitable moment when we have to make our own way in life. Alyosha's actual childhood did not prepare him for much, but in the monastery, he is now able to repeat the experience of learning and growing under the firm guidance of a loving father-figure, and when he returns to live in the world he is now much better prepared to face its challenges.

The father-child relationships that Dostoevsky portrays are there because he wants to make a point concerning the responsibilities and duties of individual parents, and to make a wider statement about how society as a whole brings up its children. It's important to reiterate here the traditional Russian view of the Tsar's role: that the Tsar was to be first and foremost a father to his people, a firm but loving father, who always does what is best for his children (an image that Vladimir Putin has also tried to cultivate). Dostoevsky deeply believed in this vision of the Russian monarchy, so every time we see a neglectful, cruel or selfish father, we can assume that this is a message that Dostoevsky would like the Tsar to consider just as much as the ordinary parents. He hammers home his message with fathers who are mostly black-or-white: Marmeladov allowing his daughter to sell her body; Fyodor Karamazov neglecting his children; and in contrast to such failures, the tender love of Snegiryov and the torments of Nikolai Ikhmenev as he struggles to do the right thing.

During the trial, Ivan Karamazov asks 'Who doesn't wish his father dead?' – and, as ever in Dostoevsky, there are many different levels at which this can be read. In the context of the story of a parricide, Ivan is adding his contribution to the collective guilt of the brothers, who all played their own part in the death of Fyodor. He was a vile old man, he neglected them cruelly, they each stood to gain a useful inheritance, and they probably all wished him dead at some point, even Alyosha. In the sociological context, touched on again by Fetyukovich, is it any surprise that the generation of children who have grown up without true parental love should want to turn on that generation and destroy it – a desire that extends to politics too, as we will see in the next chapter, and which hints at the wish of so many young Russians to destroy the father-Tsar. And then, on top of everything else, there is God, the father of all; and when Ivan the great spiritual rebel asks 'Who doesn't wish his father dead?' he could easily be thinking of God as much as Fyodor.

This brings us back again to Fetyukovich's words in his speech for the defence:

Let the son stand before his father and ask him: "Father, tell me, why should I love you? Father, prove to me that I should love you!" And if the father is willing and able to answer him and give him proof, there you have a truly proper family. ... On the other hand, if the father fails to prove that he is worthy of love, that's the end of that family: he is not a father to him, and from then on the son is free ... to regard his father as a stranger, and even as his enemy.[11]

Ivan cannot see any reason to love a God who has brought so much suffering to the people who are supposed to be his children, and so there are two parricide trials going on here: the trial of Dmitry accused of murdering his father Fyodor, and of Ivan who is undergoing such terrible mental punishment as a consequence of his attempt to destroy God.

Mother-and-child relationships in Dostoevsky's novels receive quite a different treatment, for Dostoevsky uses them to reflect on the more private, intimate side of family life. He considers the

---

[11] *The Karamazov Brothers* p938 (Book Twelve, Chapter 13)

close bond and sacrificial love that should exist between parent and child, and what happens when that love is misguided or distorted. They also provide the setting for some sharp social comedy, as Dostoevsky turns his keenly observant eye on that most fraught of family relationships – the mother and adolescent daughter.

The most touching portrayal of motherhood is Raskolnikov's mother, Pulkheria Alexandrovna, a woman who worships her son, who has devoted her life to him, but who has absolutely no understanding of his life or his thoughts. It was on reading the passages in *Crime and Punishment* about Raskolnikov and his mother recently that made me realise that Dostoevsky has something to say to everyone, of every age. During my first fervent teenage reading, my eyes were on Sonya, and her love for Raskolnikov, but returning to the novel a few years after becoming a mother myself, Pulkheria Alexandrovna suddenly grabbed my attention. Many of the scenes between mother and son are painfully awkward; she flounders about, desperately wanting to talk to him, but in complete awe of him and not having the first idea what to say, creating moments of unwitting comedy as she attempts to flog the dying conversation back to life. She can see that her son is going through some terrible crisis, and as we feel her anguish, she brings to mind that same awful desolation felt by Mary, the mother of Jesus, who stands at the foot of the cross, not understanding why her son is suffering so much, absolutely powerless to do anything about it, but knowing that she must never, can never, abandon him. Pulkheria Alexandrovna and Mary both understand that all they can do is offer that all-consuming maternal love and hope desperately that their suffering sons are able to feel its power and draw comfort from it.

Eventually, Pulkheria Alexandrovna's quiet love wins through, and although their parting is filled with grief, you can't help thinking that she must also feel a great relief when Raskolnikov has the courage to throw aside all his cynicism, and suddenly becomes a frightened, lost little boy, who desperately needs his mother:

"Mother, whatever happens, whatever you hear about me, and whatever people tell you about me, will you go on loving me as you do now?" he asked suddenly from the fullness of his heart, as though not thinking of his words or weighing them. "I've come to tell you frankly that though you will be unhappy, I want you to know that your son loves you now more than himself, and that all you thought about me – that I was cruel and didn't love you – is not true. I shall never stop loving you".[12]

It is in this poignant, intimate moment, when Raskolnikov acknowledges his love for his mother, no matter what may come after, that we realise he really has found his way back from the darkness. Here is that first human emotion, the love for one's mother that every child must surely experience, even though it may be tragically brief for the least fortunate; a love which we must preserve forever, at all costs; a love which, in its purest form, goes beyond the demands of the ego, and which is too strong to be subjected to the tests of nihilism; so it's when Raskolnikov accepts and returns to his mother's love that we can finally be certain that he is ready to confess his crime.

Mother and child relationships become more intense and claustrophobic as the novels progress. Pulkheria Alexandrovna is all too aware of her helplessness in the face of her son's anguish, and keeps a respectful distance, perhaps confident that the bond with her child is strong enough that it will eventually overcome anything. Varvara Stavrogina and, in *The Karamazov Brothers*, Lise Khokhlakova's mother, are both far too anxious about their offspring to give them any sort of distance at all, and their motherly love crosses a boundary to become something rather more selfish. Both women are afflicted with the desire that so many parents battle with – the desire to live vicariously through their

---

[12] *Crime and Punishment* p525-6 (Part Six, Chapter 7)

child by controlling and directing their life. Mrs Khokhlakova apparently wants to keep her daughter totally dependent on her; it's easy to suspect that she is exaggerating Lise's illness, enjoying the fuss of having doctors around, relishing the role of worried mother; and it is little wonder that her bored daughter is spiteful and capricious, like a caged animal. One can easily imagine Mrs Khokhlakova summoning up every half-remembered pseudo-scientific theory she can think of in order to explain her daughter's character without ever accepting the fact that she has made her that way.

The opposite danger of course is the parent who is too lax, whose indulgent mothering gives us people like Liza Tushina of *The Devils*, a girl who is so accustomed to doing exactly what she likes that she is going completely off the rails. Praskovya Drozhdova, Liza's mother,[13] is another one of those characters who is frozen in childishness – she occupies herself picking quarrels or reminiscing with her old school-friend Varvara Stavrogina, and allows herself to be bossed around by her wayward daughter. Liza was also educated by Stepan Verkhovensky, and is in many ways Nikolai Stavrogin's spiritual sister. She wants to be a liberated European woman, but she only manages a feeble imitation of true freedom, and her attempts at emancipation lead her into dubious sexual behaviour and youthful riotousness around the town. She had turned her back on her Russian mother, who is unable to tame her, but European habits give her no viable alternative. Her attempt at a relationship with that European devil, Nikolai Stavrogin, is a terrible failure, and her ridiculously melodramatic death is Dostoevsky's crude attempt to let the Russian people punish the younger generation for their betrayal of their native land.

The only really normal, stable families to feature in the major novels are to be found in *The Idiot,* these being the Yepanchins,

---

[13] Another fragment of a family: Liza's father has died, and Mrs Drozhdova remarried, hence the difference surname, but she is a widow again.

and to a lesser extent, the Ivolgins. Both families are still together as a complete unit – married parents, with their own children, and no other complications. The Ivolgins are certainly not a happy family, and they live under the strain of Ganya's nervous collapse and General Ivolgin's infidelity, alcoholism and a spell in debtors' prison, but they stick together, albeit with a good dose of very realistic squabbling between the three siblings. They probably wouldn't choose to live together if they weren't related, but Mrs Ivolgin and the children at least understand the importance and obligations of the family unit.

The Yepanchins form a bastion of bourgeois respectability at the heart of the chaotic relationships surrounding Prince Myshkin and Nastasya Filippovna. They're materially comfortable, and are settled in the sort of fond despotism that comes only after many years of marriage. They have a trio of happy, pretty daughters who all seem set to make suitable matches themselves, and their marriages will enhance the family's social standing and enable them to continue their comfortable Petersburg life (for one or two more generations anyway – thinking of the turmoil that will soon hit them, I can't help but feel sorry for people like the Yepanchins).

Despite the Yepanchin family's respectable comfort, the General's wife, Lizaveta Prokofyevna is wracked with doubts and insecurities. She knows she's a bit eccentric and worries terribly about whether her own faults are hindering her daughters' marriage prospects. She reminds me a lot of Mrs Bennett from Jane Austen's *Pride and Prejudice*, and has the same tragic-comic air about her, whilst still being wholly Russian, and somewhat more self-aware than her English equivalent:

Lately, Lizaveta Prokofyevna had begun to lay all the blame on herself and her 'unfortunate' character, which only served to augment her anxiety. She constantly castigated herself as a 'stupid, unseemly misfit'; she tormented herself for her apprehensiveness, and was always daunted and forever sorely tried by the most trivial problems, which amounted to turning molehills into mountains.[14]

Her natural propensity is to mother everyone she encounters, in a way that is kind-hearted, overbearing and enormously bossy, and which must be immediately recognisable to anyone who has spent time in Russia, particularly in Russian families. It is women just like her who stuff you full of delicious pies, who tell you off for not buttoning up your coat, who fiercely question any stupidity and who generally keep the country running, and it is in their honour that I have chosen to name this chapter after Lizaveta Prokofyevna.

I have always found Lizaveta Prokofyevna to be a wonderful comic creation, but my appreciation of this aspect reached an entirely new level when I saw the wonderful portrayal of her by Vera Pashennaya in the 1959 Mosfilm version of *The Idiot*, which captures her spirit perfectly. It seems apt that she should have the final words of the novel, the great Russian mother figure giving the entire country a good telling-off:

At least I have had a good Russian cry over this poor fellow. We've had enough of being carried away by enthusiasms. It's high time we grew sensible. And all this, all this life abroad, and all this Europe of yours is just a delusion, and all of us abroad are a delusion. Mark my words, you'll see it for yourself![15]

Lizaveta Prokofyevna's relationship with her youngest daughter Aglaya is particularly well drawn, and again I can't help but marvel at Dostoevsky's insightfulness as he deftly sketches out the tensions between a mother and daughter who are fond of each other but disconcerted by their similarities. Lizaveta Prokofyevna fears that her daughter will become like her, and Aglaya is shocked and alarmed that her mother seems to understand her with such unerring accuracy. The pair are locked in an intense

---

[14] *The Idiot* p341 (Part Three, Chapter 1)

[15] *The Idiot,* Magarshack p618 (Part Four, Chapter 12)

debate that is superficially about whether or not Aglaya should marry Prince Myshkin, but which is really about the whole mother-daughter relationship and how it shifts as the girl becomes a woman, and the woman becomes an old woman, and I defy any woman to read about Lizaveta Prokofyevna and Aglaya without a shiver of recognition for one or both sides. As Lizaveta Prokofyevna's own family grow up and leave home, she is reluctant to relinquish her maternal role, for this is what has defined her for most of her life, and so she takes it upon herself to play mother to the orphaned, lonely Prince, and (when they let her) to the wayward boys, Kolya and Ippolit, giving her a chance to prolong the feeling of motherhood and responsibility for someone else.

The culmination of the worst sorts of parenting undoubtedly lies in the tangled Verkhovensky-Stavrogin quartet, where parent and child roles are thoroughly mixed up. Stepan Verkhovensky and Varvara Stavrogina exist in a hideous relationship that appears to contain all the worst elements of married life and absolutely none of the benefits, not even sex. At other times their relationship resembles that of a mother and child as Varvara chooses Stepan's clothes, issues him with an allowance and pays his bills, and this is how the narrator sees it:

He had at last become her son, her creation, one might say almost her invention. He had become flesh of her flesh.[16]

We've already noted that the written word cuts Dostoevsky's characters off from proper dialogue, and this is taken to its ridiculous extreme as Stepan Verkhovensky and Varvara Stavrogina avoid dialogue by continually writing letters to each other instead of speaking, with frequent misunderstandings that arise because of the limitations of the written word. Their obsessive daily correspondence must have seemed dated for recent generations of readers, but in the world of emails, texts and social-

---

[16] *The Devils* p29 (Part One, Chapter 1, section 3)

networking, where everything is written down again, it suddenly has a surprising freshness. I'm sure I'm not the only person who has had to pick up the phone to resolve a situation that has become horribly messy after protracted and misunderstood email correspondence; and when I do so, Stepan and Varvara often come to mind.

As these two cannot manage to maintain a healthy adult relationship, it is hardly surprising that their relationships with their sons are equally disastrous. Unlike Pulkheria Raskolnikova, Varvara Stavrogina is unable to maintain a healthy distance, and in her blind adoration, she cannot see the disordered state of her son's mind. She creates a fantasy figure of the perfect young man; dashingly handsome, socially successful, making a brilliant army career, and she clings to that fantasy, even though his beauty is a grotesque mask, his choice of company is a gang of dropouts, he has married an impoverished simpleton, and his career has been dropped in favour of an impotent dabbling in politics. After allowing his mother to project her fantasies onto him, it is no surprise that Nikolai should effortlessly achieve the same effect with everyone else, including his psychological brother, Pyotr Verkhovensky. It seems to make no difference to how the two boys have been brought up – one rejected and foisted on distant relatives, the other smothered with love – they both inflict unbearable cruelty on their parents. Pyotr systematically destroys his father, step by calculating step, and Nikolai doesn't even mention his mother in what is, effectively, his suicide note. These four people are adrift in the world, each, in their own unhappy way, completely incapable of love.

Stepan Verkhovensky and Varvara Stavrogina both get in a mess with their sons because they attempt to blur the boundaries between the generations – adults treating other adults as children, adults treating children as adults, and failing to recognise that each generation has its place. Lizaveta Prokofyevna, on the other hand, worries like a mother hen about her daughters, but she realises that all she can do is chide them and hope for their happiness, for she seems to accept that they are a new generation and will do things differently. For all her faults and self-doubts, this archetypal Russian mother seems to be the one who has got things right. But what of that younger generation, who puzzle her so much and are subjected to her scolding? We've looked at the fathers – now it is the turn of the sons.

> *Let us all be ... intelligent, brave and generous like Kolya,*
> *who, I'm sure, will be much cleverer when he grows up.*
>
> *(Alyosha Karamazov)*

TEN: KOLYA

Just as the action in *The Karamazov Brothers* seems to be reaching a climax, with the murder of Fyodor, the declaration of love between Dmitry and Grushenka, the death of Father Zossima, and Dmitry's arrest, Dostoevsky suddenly breaks off the story to introduce one of his most entertaining and delightful characters, the precocious thirteen year-old ('fourteen in a fortnight') Kolya Krasotkin. Kolya himself is a development of his namesake, the equally charming Kolya Ivolgin of *The Idiot*. The two Kolyas are spirited, idealistic, and not yet seriously afflicted with any of the cynicism of age, however much they may affect it. They are also an acute reminder that the best of Dostoevsky's intellectuals – Raskolnikov, Razumikhin, Kirilov and Ivan Karamazov – probably grew out of boys just like them.

It's easy to imagine too that perhaps Dostoevsky is creating an idealised version of his own younger self, with the same burning intellectual passion and curiosity, and that hugely irritating mixture of conceit and insecurity with which all clever teenaged boys seem to be afflicted. Both of the Kolyas are redeemed, however, by their cheeky charm, which I suspect they possess in a greater degree than Dostoevsky himself ever did – he was reportedly morose, and painfully shy all his life. I've marvelled at Dostoevsky's brilliant ability to get inside the head of a middle-aged mother, or a besotted young girl, so the precocious boys should have posed him no difficulties at all, and I have no doubt that I will re-read the Kolyas with new flashes of recognition as my own clever, cheeky little boy grows up.

The Kolyas are important because they are both at the age when their characters can be moulded by the people around them: we've seen already how Nikolai Stavrogin has been shaped by the dubious influence of Stepan Verkhovensky (incidentally, Kolya is the diminutive form of Nikolai). Kolya Ivolgin is resourceful, street-wise and quite happy to involve himself in adult affairs by running messages for everyone. He is attracted by the band of young nihilists, and Lizaveta Prokofyevna fears for his morals, but the Prince, whom he immediately befriends, provides a counterweight. His innate goodness is revealed when Lizaveta Prokofyevna forces him to read aloud the horrible, libellous, newspaper article, and with all the passion of youth, he suffers from the article far more than the Prince himself. When he finishes the reading he has to turns his face to the wall in abject shame at being forced to play such a part in the public humiliation of his friend.

Kolya also shows patience and sympathy for his father, in a way that is touching and mature beyond his years, and he sticks with the old drunkard right to the end. We are given a small hint about Kolya's future in the epilogue, when we learn that it is Kolya who makes sure that the Prince is properly cared for – he knows what needs doing and who to ask. His mother fears that he is too thoughtful for his years but the narrator states that he will grow up to be a good man. Kolya ends the novel in regular correspondence with Radomsky, who, of all the men around him is probably the best role-model for the boy, so perhaps Dostoevsky sees in Kolya, in the end, a small glimmer of hope for Russia's future.

Kolya Krasotkin is another young boy in desperate need of calm adult guidance. He has already learned for himself, by way of his wild escapade on the railway line, the big lesson that initially eludes Dostoevsky's great heroes – that 'everything is permitted' does not work, that there are limits to what we can do because we live in a social world where our actions affect other people. When he realises how much his silliness has distressed his beloved mother, he calms down, and although, of course, as an adolescent boy he can't possibly show any emotion, he becomes:

Less talkative, more modest, more mature, and more thoughtful.[1]

He has a great deal of influence over the other boys and is obviously a natural leader – he's assertive but still liked for it. He's susceptible to all the latest ideas, of course, so he knocks the medical profession and claims to be an atheist and a socialist – and who can fail to smile at his naïve explanation of socialism to one of his younger friends, which shows that he has only a general grasp of the idea but wants to look knowledgeable and blasé all at the same time:

It's when everyone's equal, all goods are owned in common, there's no marriage, and religion and all the laws are whatever anyone fancies, and so on and so forth. You're still too young for that...[2]

At this stage in his life, the positive example of Alyosha Karamazov becomes crucial for Kolya. Even before Kolya meets Alyosha, he's terribly anxious about making a good impression, although again, according to 'the rules and regulations' of boy behaviour, he has to act cool. For all his act though, when he is confronted with the terrifying reality of Ilyusha's illness, he is completely undone, but attempts to hide his distress by bluffing through the cruel trick and great surprise that he has prepared for Ilyusha. The whole episode with the dog has really been planned for the glory of Kolya Krasotkin: he revels in the affection he has earned, and becomes more and more of a show-off,

---

[1] *The Karamazov Brothers* p651 (Book Ten, Chapter 1)
[2] *The Karamazov Brothers* p662 (Book Ten, Chapter 3)

but he is now acutely aware that Alyosha is watching him. In his subsequent conversation with Alyosha, he flaunts his knowledge and his opinions, most of which have been acquired secondhand from Rakitin, but Alyosha is neither impressed or shocked, and instead gently offers him guidance, without reproach.

The spiritual shock that Kolya experiences at Ilyusha's bedside is comparable to the shocks that rocked Alyosha after the death of Father Zossima. The death of the elder could have sent Alyosha on a path of anger and rebellion, especially with Rakitin there, ready to prod him in that direction. Kolya could also, at this point, have let his own despair and anger about Ilyusha manifest themselves as atheism and socialism (again, with malicious help from the devilish Rakitin), but instead he becomes Alyosha's first opportunity to fulfil the role that Father Zossima intended for him. Alyosha is able to pass on to Kolya the same comfort and guidance that he has just received from Father Paissy and Grushenka, and he gently helps Kolya to recognise and acknowledge how badly he has behaved towards Ilyusha although like Raskolnikov, but at a far younger age, Kolya cannot be forced; he must look into his heart and discover the lesson for himself. By the time we reach the novel's optimistic ending, Kolya is losing his cynicism and even joyfully accepts Alyosha's vision of the resurrection of the dead.

And always, all our lives, we'll walk hand in hand! Hurrah for Karamazov![3]

proclaims Kolya, who has to have the final word of the book. I'd love to know what happened to him.

By looking at the history of intellectual life in Russia, and using a bit of imagination, we can get some ideas about what Kolya Krasotkin might have grown up to be. Remembering that the events of *The Karamazov Brothers* happened, according to the narrator, thirteen years previously, Kolya Krasotkin himself

---

[3] *The Karamazov Brothers* p974 (Epilogue, Chapter 3)

would have been twenty-six by the time Dostoevsky was writing the book in the late 1870s, and thus belongs to the generation of young people who held Dostoevsky in deep reverence as a teacher and prophet. In her *Reminiscences,* Anna Dostoevskaya notes the large numbers of students, men and women, who turned out for Dostoevsky's vast and spontaneous funeral procession, many of whom then stayed in the church to recite psalms over his coffin. But the history of his relationship with that younger generation, with the Kolyas (both of whom, I am sure, would have been participating enthusiastically in that funeral procession), is somewhat surprising, particularly given his condemnation in *Crime and Punishment* and, more angrily, in *The Devils,* of the ideas that inspired the radical youth of the 1860s.

In the topsy-turvy, carnival world of *The Devils*, the younger generation – Nikolai Stavrogin, Pyotr Verkhovensky and Liza Tushina – bully and manipulate their parents, who, for their part, are mostly unable to understand that they themselves are responsible for unleashing the demons that possess their offspring. The diabolical behaviour spreads outwards from Nikolai and Pyotr, and a kind of collective madness takes over as the youngsters rampage around showing casual disrespect for the church, for authority and for the dignity of life itself, to the horror and bewilderment of their elders. Only Stepan Verkhovensky is beginning to grasp his ideological responsibility, and just before the final showdown and rupture between father and son, we find the older man preparing himself for one last battle with the younger generation by reading one of the core nihilist textbooks: Chernyshevsky's novel *What is to be Done?* Speaking to the narrator, he says:

I agree that the author's fundamental idea is right ... but that makes it more awful! It's just our idea – yes, ours! We were the first to plant it, to nurture it, to get it ready – and what new thing could they say after us? But, good Lord, how they have expressed it all, distorted, mutilated it! ...Were those the conclusions we wanted to draw? Who can recognise the original idea here?[4]

This short passage neatly sums up Dostoevsky's original political motivation for writing the novel. He was overcome by disgust at what he thought his generation had done, and he was planning to express this in a cautionary short story, a satirical pamphlet. This plan went astray when Nikolai Stavrogin marched out of the notes of another project, to be called *The Life of a Great Sinner* and onto the stage of *The Devils* to steal the show, but the original political satire is still there.

The catalyst for the story lay in events that took place just before Dostoevsky's return from Germany, when a young nihilist called Nechaev was put on trial for instigating student unrest in St Petersburg, and for his alleged involvement in the murder of a student who apparently objected to Nechaev's control over the members of his revolutionary cell. Reports of the Nechaev affair in the Russian press captured Dostoevsky's imagination and, although he was still living in Germany, he gathered as much information from the papers as he could, for he saw with horror that in Nechaev and the revolutionary students the excesses that he had imagined when he created Raskolnikov were actually beginning to be realised. Even worse, it dawned on Dostoevsky that it was the great Westernising intellectuals of his younger years, the 1840s liberals, among them Belinsky, Herzen, Granovsky and Turgenev, who were responsible for inciting the youth of the late 1860s and early 70s to such horrifying extremes.

Living in their comfortable, aristocratic surroundings and suffused with the spirit of German Romanticism,[5] the 1840s liberals retained an appreciation of the beautiful things in the world, and

---

[4] *The Devils* p 308 (Part Two, Chapter 4, section 2)

[5] The Tsarist authorities were so afraid of the revolutionary influences in France, that they prevented young Russians from going to France study, and sent them to Germany instead, where, in the end, the prevalent Romantic ideals turned out to be just as troublesome.

understood the important role that art and beauty play in enriching our lives, but for the next generation, these things were lumped in with all the other values of the old world that the liberals had taught them to despise, so art and beauty got thrown out along with tradition, religion, serfdom and all other forms of oppression, while the rationalism of the Enlightenment metamorphosed into bleak utilitarianism. This rejection of the beautiful was indiscriminate, there was nothing to put a check on the doctrine of destruction, so everything had to go. The liberals had planted the seeds of socialism and atheism; the nihilists of the next generation had stripped away the romanticism; and now the younger nihilists were putting the these ideas into violent practice – but it was the liberals who started the process. Presenting the novel to the Crown Prince Alexander Alexandrovich Romanov, the future Tsar Alexander III, Dostoevsky wrote:

Our Belinskys and Granovskys would never have believed it if they had been told that they were the direct spiritual fathers of the Nechaev band. And it is this kinship of ideas and their transmission from fathers to sons that I have tried to show in my work.[6]

The older generation is represented in *The Devils* by Stepan Verkhovensky and the writer Karmazinov who, as we have already noted, is a malicious portrait of Turgenev. Dostoevsky's friend Maikov described the novel as 'Turgenev's heroes grown old',[7] which pleased Dostoevsky immensely, and is a great one-sentence summary of the book. Dostoevsky was particularly disgusted by Turgenev's opportunistic claim that he himself had become a nihilist, and, like Turgenev, Karmazinov attempts to win the affections of the younger generation:

The great writer was most painfully afraid of the advanced Russian revolutionary youth, and imagining, in his ignorance, the

---

[6] *Selected Letters* p370 (10 February 1873, to A. A. Romanov)
[7] *Selected Letters* p348-9 (2/14 March 1871, to A.N. Maikov)

keys to Russia's future were in their hands, he ingratiated himself with them in a most humiliating way, mainly because they paid no attention to him whatever.[8]

Stepan Verkhovensky, on the other hand, sticks firmly to the convictions that he has held all his life. His character is a general sketch of the liberal intellectuals of the 1840s, but there were two representatives of that generation who Dostoevsky particularly had in mind when he was writing: Alexander Herzen, who died in January 1870, just as Dostoevsky was starting work on *The Devils*, and the Moscow historian T.N. Granovsky (Stepan Verkhovensky is, in fact, called 'Granovsky' in the notebooks until his own personality had properly emerged). In his introduction to the novel, the narrator puts Stepan Verkhovensky immediately into context for his readers by saying that his name was, for a time, mentioned in the same breath as those of Granovsky, Chaadayev, Belinsky and Herzen.

The name of Herzen is one of those that crops up all over the Russian 19th century. Despite his importance and stature, he is relatively unknown in the West, although his extensive memoirs *My Past and Thoughts* are greatly praised – Isaiah Berlin puts them firmly on the same level as the great novels of Turgenev, Tolstoy and Dostoevsky.[9] Herzen is regarded as the father of Russian Socialism, but his particular brand of socialism owed more to the utopian dreams of French thinkers like Saint-Simon than the grim practicalities of Marxism that eventually triumphed in Russia. Like the anarchists who followed him, he dreamed of workers' communes, free of any state control, where everyone existed in a happy equality, and he was not interested in abstract political programmes or slogans that could be used in their turn as weapons of oppression. His guiding principle was the supreme importance of individual freedom, and his socialism

---

[8] *The Devils* p219 (Part Two, Chapter 1, section 1)
[9] Isaiah Berlin *The Great Amateur* – New York Review of Books 14 March 1968 http://bit.ly/SHS6Z1

sprang from the awareness that freedom throughout Russia, for everyone from the humblest serf to the highest aristocrat, was ruthlessly quashed – absolutely everyone had their place and had to conform to the strictures laid down by the autocracy, but Herzen dreamed of true freedom, in which men and women are enslaved to neither rulers nor ideas. It's the romantic dreaming of a man who cared greatly about the good of humanity, but who himself led a privileged life and was able to indulge in the luxury of impossible dreams. His work then influenced Russian anarchists such as Bakunin and Nechaev who were more concerned with putting those dreams into practice, adding violent struggle and resistance to Herzen's romantically pacifist line of thought.

The other model for Stepan Trofimovich, T.N. Granovsky, was described by Dostoevsky's friend Strakhov as 'a pure Westerniser' and it was Strakhov's review of a biography of Granovsky, published in 1869, that helped Dostoevsky to muster his thoughts about the relationship between the 1840s liberals and the nihilists who followed them. Granovsky shared the liberal Westernising outlook of Belinsky and Herzen, perceiving the Russian people to be backward and primitive, but differed from his fellow-liberals in that he was unable to accept their militant atheism, and remained clinging to hopes of immortality. It is this uncertainty and fear of making the final, decisive intellectual step that is such a defining feature of Stepan Verkhovensky, who claims initially that he believes in God, but in a pagan, naturalist sort of way – a nice easy get-out that requires no spiritual commitment in either direction.

For all his anger and his disgust at what his generation had created, Dostoevsky's portrayal of Stepan Verkhovensky is not the cruel satire that he unleashes through Karmazinov, but a kindly picture of a rather foolish man, full of silly pretensions, blinded by a misguided, romantic urge to put the beautiful above all else, but ultimately well-intentioned. Several years after the book was published, Dostoevsky wrote a piece in *Diary of a*

Writer about Granovsky which gives us the key to Stepan Trofimovich's character:

Granovsky was the purest of all men of those days; he was irreproachable and beautiful. An idealist of the Forties – in the loftiest sense – he possessed the most individually peculiar and original nuance among our progressives of a certain pattern of his time. He was one of the most honest Stepan Trofimovichs ... and I love Stepan Trofimovich and profoundly respect him.[10]

One of the peculiar strengths of Dostoevsky's writing lies in the fact that his strongest characters, those iconic figures such as Raskolnikov or Ivan Karamazov, who everyone remembers, are those who reject Dostoevsky's own world-view, while his deepest convictions find their way into the mouths of fools. Dostoevsky has such confidence in the strength of his own beliefs that he is able to send them out into the world in this fragile packaging, because he knows that they will withstand any buffeting they receive. Stepan Verkhovensky's ludicrous speech at the fete, for example, is accompanied by jeering, and degenerates into a farce, but actually, when we look at it out of context, it is a deeply moving tribute to the power of art and beauty, a great lament for the errors of the younger generation:

The enthusiasm of our modern youth is as bright and pure as it was in our time. ...The whole misunderstanding has arisen only round the question what is more beautiful: Shakespeare or a pair of boots, Raphael or petroleum! [Shakespeare and Raphael] *are the fruit of all mankind, and perhaps the highest fruition that can possibly exist. ...*[mankind] *can get on without science, without bread, but without beauty it cannot carry on, for then there will be nothing more to do in the world!*[11]

---

[10] *Diary of a Writer* p379 (July-August 1876 Chapter 2, section 1)
[11] *The Devils* p483-484 (Part Three, Chapter 1, section 4). The arch-nihilist Pisarev claimed that 'boots are better Shakespeare'.

The mention of Raphael here is deeply personal, for Raphael's *Sistine Madonna*, above all others, was Dostoevsky's favourite painting.[12] Leonid Grossman explains that Dostoevsky was enthralled not just by the visual beauty of Renaissance art, but by the philosophical ideas that it represented; a cult of the morally beautiful individual mingled with humanism, a deep love of nature, and an understanding of the enlightening power of reason.[13] We're so accustomed to seeing only that pair of kitsch and cheeky cherubs, reproduced to the point of cliché on tea-towels, coffee mugs and greetings cards, that it's easy to forget the rest of the painting, and even easier to forget how amazing the warm humanity that radiates from the Madonna's face must have seemed to a Russian brought up on the cold austerity of Orthodox iconography. The *Sistine Madonna* is the positive side of Holbein's portrait of Christ's body, and for Dostoevsky, it's the touchstone of everything that is beautiful in European culture, but he bravely uses the painting in *The Devils* to symbolise all that the younger generation resent in their elders. Mrs von Lembke attempts to show off her progressive ideas to Varvara Stavrogina by dismissing the painting, saying she was disillusioned by it, and that her great oracle Karmazinov said it was difficult to understand. Only the old men like it, she says. Varvara Stavrogina then stores up these words to hurt Stepan Trofimovich, echoing the ideas of Dobrolyubov and Chernyshevsky on the utility of art:

It's of no use whatever. This jug is useful because one can pour water into it; this pencil is useful because you can write anything with it, but that Madonna is just a woman's face which is inferior to any face in nature. Try drawing an apple and put a real apple beside it – which would you take? You wouldn't hesitate, would

---

[12] Anna Dostoevskaya tells a lovely story of how she obtained a reproduction of the painting and smuggled it into Dostoevsky's study as a birthday surprise for him. It can still be seen in his house-museum.

[13] *Dostoevsky: A Biography,* p408 Leonid Grossman, translated by Mary Mackler, Allen Lane, 1974.

you? That's what all our theories boil down to now that the first light of free investigation has fallen on them.[14]

Stepan Verkhovensky and Dostoevsky give their answer to Varvara Stavrogina, and the youngsters whom she is aping, in the speech at the fete. Stepan ends in hysterics, reminding his audience that he is speaking as 'a crushed and insulted father' and begging for the friendship of the younger generation. The surprising juxtaposition of such heartfelt words and a farcical situation is a good example of Dostoevsky's sense of carnival, of turning things upside down – an idea discussed at length by the critic Bakhtin. We're set up to believe that the fete is a comic interlude that is going to demolish Karmazinov and Stepan Verkhovensky once and for all, but suddenly we're made to sit up and take notice, as this passionate defence of beauty leaps out of the page and grabs us with all the force of the unexpected. Ivan Karamazov explains to his younger brother that clarity comes through absurdity, and so when Dostoevsky gives intelligent men words that he considers to be lies, and puts his deeply held truths into the mouths of fools, he makes us stop and think, just as he does with his flawed narrators; we as readers have to do the work, instead of accepting unquestioningly what we're given by the author.

The reference to Stepan Verkhovensky reading Chernyshevsky comes just before the final show-down between father and son, and, in fact, it mirrors the exchange that had been going on in real life between Herzen and the younger generation of nihilists. Pyotr is unforgivably rude to his father, and then to top it all, he alleges that he's not actually Verkhovensky's biological son anyway, provoking his father to curse him and throw him out of the house. Pyotr's attempt to deny his parentage works as a political metaphor, a refusal on the part of the younger generation to acknowledge the original source of their own ideas, just as Stepan's slowly dawning realisation of what a monstrosity he has

---

[14] *The Devils* p343 (Part Two, Chapter 5, section 3)

created reflects the varying degree of recognition on the part of the older generation of their role in creating the nihilists.

Herzen had tried to make peace with the younger generation, insisting that they had the same goals, and he called for both sides to find common ground. For his pains, he received a vicious reply from Alexander Serno-Solovievich, one of the key members of the émigré revolutionary circle, who wrote to Herzen informing him that he was yesterday's man who flaps his wings impotently, failing to see that he has been left behind, and Herzen responded dejectedly that:

The majority of young Russians are the same and we're the ones who have contributed to make them like this.[15]

As he lies dying, Stepan Verkhovensky finally recognises what he has done, and the meaning of the novel's epigraph is explained as he muses on the strange parable in the gospels[16] about the devils entering a herd of pigs. Jesus has cast the devils out of a possessed man, and they beg him not to cast them back into the depths but to allow them to possess a nearby herd of swine. The insane pigs promptly rush headlong down the hill into a lake and are all drowned. Verkhovensky likens the sick man to Russia, and he, Pyotr and Nikolai are the swine into which the devils have been driven:

The devils who go out of the sick man and enter the swine – those are all the sores, all the poisonous exhalations, all the impurities, all the big and little devils, that have accumulated in our great and beloved invalid, in our Russia, for centuries, for centuries! ... and all those devils, all those impurities, all those abominations that were festering on the surface – all of them will themselves ask to enter into swine. And, indeed, they may have entered into them already! They are we, we and them, and Peter – et les au-

---

[15] See Frank p640-641

[16] The story is told by Matthew, Mark and Luke, but Dostoevsky uses Luke's version (Luke, chapter 8 v26-36)

tres avec lui, and perhaps I at the head of them all, and we shall cast ourselves down, the raving and the possessed, from the cliff into the sea and shall all be drowned, and serves us right, for that is all we are good for. But the sick man will be healed and 'will sit at the foot of Jesus', and all will look at him and be amazed.[17]

And so, after a life of pathetic ineffectuality, Stephan Verkhovensky has finally done something: through his offspring he has infected Russia with atheism, anarchism and egoism. Writing to another friend, Apollon Maikov, just after the completion of the first chapters of *The Devils*, Dostoevsky set out his intentions:

It is true that the facts have also proved to us that the disease that afflicted cultured Russians was much more virulent than we ourselves had imagined, and that it did not end with the Belinskys and the Kraevskys and their ilk. [after explaining the parable of the swine, he continues] *Exactly the same thing happened in our country: the devils went out of the Russian man and entered into a herd of swine, that is, into the Nechaevs and Serno-Solovieviches et al.*[18]

In keeping with the parable, the devils should all perish, but Dostoevsky doesn't destroy them completely. Pyotr, the worst of them all, is allowed to survive – a vividly clear warning that in fact the disease has not been eradicated; it is merely dormant, slumbering in a safe haven in Europe, awaiting its opportunity to infect Russia all over again.

Within a few years of *The Devils* being published, an incredible change took place. Dostoevsky, venomous critic of all things radical, was serialising his next novel, *The Adolescent,* in the pages of *Notes of the Fatherland*, one of the radical journals with which Dostoevsky had engaged in bitter polemics throughout the 1860s, and which was now edited by the poet Nekrasov, another of his one-time friends from the early days, but with whom

---

[17] *The Devils* p647-8 (Part Three, Chapter 7, section 2)

[18] *Selected Letters* p343 (9/21 October 1870, to A.N. Maikov)

he had quarrelled, and drifted away from ideologically. It was Nekrasov who had rushed enthusiastically to Belinsky with the manuscript of *Poor People,* thus launching Dostoevsky's career, but their friendship was brief, due, recalled Dostoevsky to:

Misunderstandings, external circumstances and the meddling of good people.[19]

They found themselves engaged in political polemics, but never lost respect for each other's literary work. Nonetheless, the move to *Notes of the Fatherland* surprised everyone, and dismayed many of Dostoevsky's oldest friends, particularly Strakhov and Maikov; it was also a real sign of how the intellectual world was re-aligning itself, following the outrages of the Nechaev affair.

The true horrors of nihilism, particularly its complete disregard for the sanctity of life, had become apparent to many during Nechaev's trial, and the radical students who thronged the courtroom began to reconsider their own ethical position. Whilst their political aims remained firmly socialist, the extreme scientific utilitarianism of the nihilists was abandoned in favour of a more moral approach, which eventually became known as *narodnichestvo,* or Populism. The elitist attitude of the nihilists, with their contempt for the little people was called into question, and the Populists tried to re-establish connections with the peasantry in a movement that became known as 'going to the people'. Young men and women began travelling out to the countryside to live in the villages, hoping to improve the lot of the peasants through education, but also intent on learning from them, in the hope of finding a purer, simpler life, free of the corruption of the modern world. From all this came a realisation that the human spirit cannot after all be discounted, or reduced to a scientific phenomenon, and this reawakening of the intangible was matched with a renewed respect for religion, and a particular interest in the moral side of Christ's teachings. It is not

---

[19] *Diary of a Writer* p937 (December 1877 Chapter 2, section 1)

difficult to see how Dostoevsky would eventually align himself with this student movement, but it didn't happen immediately.

The Devils was, unsurprisingly, bitterly criticised by all parties. The older generation were angry at the mockery doled out to them, whilst the students saw it as harshly reactionary. It tends to be read today as a 'grim prophecy of the Russian revolution', (to quote the blurb on my Penguin Classics copy), but in truth, there was nothing particularly prophetic about it – with some allowance for exaggeration on the part of both Dostoevsky and the Russian press, he was writing about exactly what was going on in Russia at the time. The chaos into which the town temporarily sinks is a warning of the consequences of immoral, undirected social upheaval, but primarily the novel deals with the tendencies prevalent in Dostoevsky's Russia. Neither the young nor the old escaped his harsh criticism, and their reactions were equally damning. A young member of the intelligentsia recalled that:

In liberal literal circles ... and among the student youth ... he was unceremoniously called someone 'off his rocker', or – more delicately – a 'mystic' or 'abnormal'. ... Dostoevsky's novel seemed to us then a monstrous caricature, a nightmare of mystical ecstasies and psychopathology.[20]

Dostoevsky, retreating from the wrath engendered by *The Devils,* and urgently in need of money, ended up as editor-in-chief of *The Citizen,* an ultra-reactionary journal, which included on its board Konstantin Pobedonostsev, tutor to the future Alexander III and, later, the hand behind the severe political oppressiveness of Alexander's regime. Editing *The Citizen* alienated Dostoevsky still further from many of his friends, but it was also, ironically, one of the sources of his eventual rehabilitation. The link was a young woman called Varvara Timofeyevna, who wrote for the radical journal *The Spark,* and although that was clearly where her sympathies lay, she also supported herself by

---

[20] Quoted Frank, p671

working as a proof-reader for *The Citizen*. She was initially very wary of Dostoevsky, who was demanding, gloomy, and unapproachable, and it is her words that I quoted above. However, she gradually got to know him as they discussed the content of the journal, and she particularly recalled discussing with Dostoevsky an article he had written about N.N. Ge's painting of the Last Supper. In common with her contemporaries, Timofeyevna was gradually discovering the moral values of Christian teaching, and she was deeply moved by Dostoevsky's passionate devotion to Christ as he explained his response to the painting to her. Dostoevsky, for his part, discovered by talking to Timofeyevna that he and the current generation of students were spiritually more akin to each other than he had realised.

Timofeyevna's friendship with Dostoevsky, and the crystallisation and publication of Populist ideas, led to a gradual thawing of relations between the older writer and the new generation of radicals. The great philosopher of the Russian Silver Age, Vladimir Solovyov, then in his early twenties, met Dostoevsky at about this time, and he claimed that Dostoevsky's novels had cured him of his youthful nihilism; the two became close friends and Dostoevsky's influence is clear in the younger man's work. It was as a consequence of Dostoevsky's friendship with Timofeyevna, combined with the fact that he and Nekrasov had not entirely burnt their boats, that his penultimate novel, *The Adolescent* ended up in the home of his old detractors, the socialist journal *Notes of the Fatherland*.

There was now a great deal of sympathy on both sides, and the young Populists came to revere the formidable old man who had suffered so much. They enjoyed a shared belief in Russia's destiny, and the virulent atheism of the nihilist had given way to, at the very least, an interest in what the teachings of Christ could offer, but the Populists were still socialists, and Dostoevsky seems to have viewed them as wayward children, who could perhaps be brought back to what he saw as the correct path. His paternal feelings for the populists are expressed in *The Karamazov*

Brothers in Alyosha, in the band of young boys who become his friends, and also in the young intellectual Ivan Karamazov.

Dostoevsky intended that *The Karamazov Brothers* would be followed by a sequel, entitled *Children,* which was to follow the lives of Alyosha and his friends. This was not Dostoevsky's first attempt at creating a band of children: in his notebooks for *The Idiot*, we can see that he wanted to include a sort of children's club, run by Prince Myshkin, the idea being that it should be a vision of the kingdom of heaven on earth, and a contrast to the hell of grown-up society, and the that the children would play a part in influencing Rogozhin, Nastasya Filippovna and Aglaya, for example by bringing Rogozhin to confess his crime.[21] It's a vision inspired by the image of Christ calling the little children to come to him, but Mochulsky suggests that Dostoevsky abandoned the idea because it would have made Myshkin not a Christ-like figure, but Christ himself.[22] In the end, the closest we come to the children's club is Kolya running messages for the adults and Prince Myshkin's account of his friendship with the village children in Switzerland, in which he primarily comes across as a sad lonely man who seeks the society of children because he is uncomfortable with adults. This comes out too in his relationship with Kolya, where he is relaxed and cheerful and enjoys the boy's good natured questioning and banter in a way that is absent in his interactions with adults. There's also a hint that Kolya is actually his closest friend, for right at the end, as the disaster unfolds, the narrator tells us that 'even Kolya' didn't know what the Prince planned to do. Alexey Karamazov's friendship with the boys is more wholesome, but like the Swiss children in *The Idiot,* the group coalesces around someone who is initially an outcast, and both groups of children are brought together by men who teach them kindness and love.

---

[21] *The Notebooks for The Idiot* p191 (ed Edward Wasiolek, University of Chicago Press 1967)

[22] Mochulsky p350

Dostoevsky apparently told Alexey Suvorin, a journalist, that in the sequel to *The Karamazov Brothers* he wanted create a truly Russian socialist, in the form of Alyosha, with his ideas originating from, and nourished by, the Russian soil, rather than any external influence. Suvorin also claimed that Alyosha would end up assassinating the Tsar, but this seems incompatible with Dostoevsky's own idiosyncratic views as to what Russian Socialism would consist of. For whilst the views of Dostoevsky and the Populist youth had their common origins in a faith in the Russian people, and in socialist principles flavoured by Christ's teaching, their ultimate visions were poles apart. The Populists imagined a communist society, based on equality and common ownership, developed from the peasant village structure. What Dostoevsky dreamt of was nothing less than Christ's kingdom on earth, with all people living a life of love and peace, with shared responsibility, but under the rule of a benign Tsar. Just a few days before his death, he set out his hopelessly utopian vision of Russian Socialism in *Diary of a Writer*:

To the people the Tsar is the incarnation of themselves, their whole ideology, their hopes and beliefs. ... The fact that in Russia all fundamentals are different from anything in Europe may be demonstrated by the following example: Civil liberty may be established in Russia on an integral scale, more complete than anywhere in the world. ... It will be based not upon a written sheet of paper, but upon the children's affection of the people for the Tsar, as their father. ... They may be entrusted with much that has nowhere been encountered, since children will not betray their father, and, being children, they will lovingly accept from him any correction of their errors.[23]

This explains Ivan Karamazov's curious article on ecclesiastical courts that marks the first appearance of this most fascinating of Dostoevsky's characters. Ivan is asked by the monks to explain

---

[23] *Diary of a Writer* January 1881 p1032-1034 (January 1881, Chapter 1, section 5)

his article, and although Alyosha fears that his older brother will be condescending, Ivan discusses his article in a modest, restrained way, with, as we are told, great courtesy; and the conversation that follows neatly introduces the novel's main themes – love, crime, redemption and faith. In brief, Ivan explains that the existing relationship of Church and State is unsatisfactory and inconsistent. When the Roman Empire accepted Christianity, he says, it absorbed the church into the structures of the pagan state, wherein the church gradually carved out a niche for itself. The Catholic church since that time has attempted to fill itself out to become the State itself – this, in Dostoevsky's eyes, is Catholicism's great failing, and he returns to it again in the Grand Inquisitor. What Ivan is advocating is subtly different – it is the State that needs to grow and raise itself up so that it becomes the Church. Once the State has become the Church, and is therefore as close as possible to being the establishment of Christ's kingdom on earth, punishing criminals becomes simple. Rather than physical punishment, all that will be required is excommunication, for then the criminal is placed entirely outside society, forced to renounce the companionship of men and Christ, and only spiritual redemption and true repentance will bring him back into the fold. Ivan and the more intelligent monks – Zossima and Father Paissy, discuss and develop this idea, but they are mocked by Miusov, who is a thoroughly old fashioned European liberal, firmly in the camp of the atheist socialists. Miusov is another case of Dostoevsky having a bit of fun once the serious business of tackling a big idea is over and done with, and thus Miusov is the comic coda to Stepan Trofimovich – a case of history repeating itself as farce. The discussion ends when Miusov quotes a detective he once met in Paris, who maintained that Christian socialists were far more dangerous than the atheists. Father Paissy immediately asks whether Miusov thinks that the monks are socialists, but they are interrupted by Dmitry's arrival, and we are left to think about the answer as we read the rest of the novel.

Ivan Karamazov is the climax of Dostoevsky's work, and we will have much more to say about him in the remaining chapters. At first glance, his views on the ecclesiastical courts, and his vision for the role of the church are puzzling, for it doesn't seem to make sense that an intelligent young atheist should be advocating the dissolution of the State into the Church. It's partly, I think, Ivan expressing a desire for intellectual consistency, for taking an idea to its final conclusion and seeing what happens, but what we're also getting here is a first hint of the great schism that Dostoevsky sees in Ivan's mind, and that he thinks should exist in the minds of all members of the Populist intelligentsia. Their natural tendency, given their education and background and the influence of their elders, is to atheism and secularism, but for Dostoevsky this is entirely incompatible with the love of the Russian people that the Populists also profess. If you really want the Russian people to fulfil their destiny to save mankind, says Dostoevsky, this is the path that they have to be taking, and whatever the Populists may tell themselves, they have to reconcile themselves to this vision.

The serialisation of *The Karamazov Brothers* came at a time of increasing tension and political unrest; there had been several attempts on the Tsar's life by Populist extremists, and these created a self-reinforcing cycle of terror and restrictions that we would easily recognise today. What was different then was that many people found themselves sympathising with the aims of the terrorists – the removal of a repressive regime – despite being appalled by their methods. Dostoevsky's fable of youthful rebellion against God, the murder of a loathsome old man and a message that human society must be built on the basis of mutual responsibility gave his readers something to latch onto during these frightening and confusing times, a vision of love that went beyond mere partisan politics. It is this universal message, that transcends the time and place where it was written, that explains some of Dostoevsky's enduring appeal, for, like the first readers of *The Karamazov Brothers,* we can find within its pages the same challenges to our complacent views, the same sense of a once solid world being violently shaken, but also the same optimism and comfort.

The public expression of this new-found devotion to Dostoevsky reached a climax at the unveiling of the Pushkin statue. Dostoevsky ended his speech, as we have seen, by calling Pushkin a prophet, and the crowd reacted with hysterical enthusiasm: students invaded the platform with a huge wreath, the audience sobbed, embraced each other, and cried out that Dostoevsky was their new prophet. To make the point, Dostoevsky was asked to read Pushkin's poem *The Prophet* at the close of the celebrations. It was a poem he had already made his own, and his recitals of it were famous, for, somewhat surprisingly, given what we know about his shyness and touchy pride, Dostoevsky was apparently a marvellous public speaker. Pushkin's poem speaks of the poet's mission and duty towards society, and is worth quoting in full, for it vividly illustrates how Dostoevsky saw himself, and how, eventually the people of Russia came to regard him:

Parched with the spirit's thirst, I crossed
An endless desert sunk in gloom,
And a six-winged seraph came
Where the tracks met and I stood lost.
Fingers light as dream he laid
Upon my lids; I opened wide
My eagle eyes, and gazed around.
He laid his fingers on my ears
And they were filled with roaring sound:
I heard the music of the spheres,
The flight of angels through the skies,
The beasts that crept beneath the sea,
The heady uprush of the vine;
And, like a lover kissing me,
He rooted out this tongue of mine
Fluent in lies and vanity;
He tore my fainting lips apart

And, with his right hand steeped in blood,
He armed me with a serpent's dart;
With his bright sword he split my breast;
My heart leapt to him with a bound;
A glowing livid coal he pressed
Into the hollow of the wound.
There in the desert I lay dead.
And God called out to me and said:
"Rise, prophet, rise, and hear, and see,
And let my words be seen and heard
By all who turn aside from me.
And burn them with my fiery word". (Trans D.M Thomas)[24]

But, rather like William Blake's *Jerusalem*, I think there's a sting in this poem. Look at the imagery – the serpent's forked tongue, the blazing heart of coal. The poet as prophet has a decidedly demonic aspect.

---

[24] *Alexander Pushkin, The Bronze Horseman and Other Poems* Translated D.M. Thomas (Penguin 1983)

If everything on earth were rational, nothing would happen ... there would be no events

(Ivan's Devil).

ELEVEN: PYOTR VERKHOVENSKY

In the course of his conversation with Ivan Karamazov, the Devil claims that his role in the world is negation and the destruction of rationalism. He has been put on earth to create events, because without events, nothing can happen and history would come to an end; without him, there would be nothing but 'an endless hosanna' – and where would be the life in that, he asks. Similarly, in *The Devils,* Kirilov remarks that when all mankind achieves happiness, there will be no more time, because there is no longer any need for it. This devil doesn't have any overall guiding plan or any goal, and he doesn't create any coherent narrative; he just meddles, interferes and works to destroy happiness, then resorts to the eternal defence of the coward, whining that he's just following orders. The events that keep history moving are, in the main, driven by the baser elements of human nature, by ambition, hatred, rivalry, greed and lust, so the Devil's work is not difficult – in fact, he hardly needs to do anything at all. He simply seeks out fertile ground where he can sow his evil seeds and then he carefully nourishes the plants that shoot up, but there is no beauty or order to his garden, it's just a tangled mess of weeds.

Devils abound in Dostoevsky's fiction, on varying levels of reality and metaphor. There are visitations, demonic characters, and those who appear possessed. Sometimes the Devil is a rational, argumentative creature, and at other times, most notably in the character of Pyotr Verkhovensky, he appears as the trickster, sowing the seeds of chaos, but the common thread that links the demonic elements in Dostoevsky's fiction is this ability by the Devil to exploit the weaknesses inherent in human free will.

The Western view of the Devil is strongly coloured by the art and literature of the Middle Ages: here the Devil is Lucifer, fallen angel, cast out from the kingdom of God and left to rule over the tormented souls of the sinners in hell. He is a millennial Devil, who will return in glory at the end of time to engage in a final great battle with the forces of good. The idea of the Devil as King of the Underworld grew out of the efforts of early Christian thinkers to fuse the new teachings of Christ with the old Hellenistic beliefs of the Roman Empire, and so Pluto ruling over Hades becomes our modern Satan, with the lurid trappings of the Book of Revelations thrown in for good measure. This colourful and frightening way of seeing the Devil gained strength in Europe in the mid-14th century in response to the ravages of the Black Death, as men attempted to explain why such horror had been unleashed on the world, and then later when the perceived menace of witchcraft gripped Europe in mass hysteria the Devil was again seen to be behind it all, for this is a Devil who actively participates in worldly life by taking possession of human souls.

For Dostoevsky, a man who has seen hell on earth, this European view of the Devil is superfluous; for him the lakes of fire and instruments of torture are just fairy tales – like Sartre, he knows that human beings are perfectly capable of devising their own torments without the added extras of fire, sulphur and gridirons. Dostoevsky's use of cartoonish devils with horns and tails can be seen as a marker of a European way of thinking: the monk Father Ferapont and Fyodor Karamazov both, in their own way, think that this is how the Devil manifests himself. Ferapont sees horned demons hiding in corners and crawling over people, like little spiders, and talks about catching one by trapping his tail in a door – echoed when Lise Khokhlakova, the 'little she-devil' slams her finger in a door. Fyodor Karamazov on the other hand, tries to play the sophisticated, worldly unbeliever, believing himself to be a child of the European enlightenment, and he attempts to satirise hell in the manner of Voltaire. He muses on the physical tortures of the underworld, and asserts that if there were no actual hooks dangling from the ceiling of hell, 'il faudrait l'inventer'. He also misquotes, in French, a description of hell from a poem by Charles Perrault:

J'ai vu l'ombre d'un cocher, qui avec l'ombre d'une brosse frottait l'ombre d'une carrosse.[1]

The original line comes from Perrault's own parody of Virgil's *Aeneid,* so we now have, in Fyodor, several layers of mockery and parody, and quite a clear indication that this European hell is far removed from what Dostoevsky believes it to be. Laughing at the Devil by dressing him up like a fairy-tale monster is dangerous, as Lebedev warns us in *The Idiot* when he says that the hoofs and horns are just a human invention, and that the real devil is a 'great and ruthless spirit' who shouldn't be mocked.

Lebedev's description gives us the clue to uncovering the origins of Dostoevsky's demonic characters, sending us back to the Jewish Satan of the Old Testament and his Islamic counterpart.[2] Satan here is not the proud ruler of the underworld, but a trickster creature who still remains under God's power, and has to do his will; he's the spirit who tormented Job, and he's the Iblis of the Koran, who spends his time leading men astray and tempting them to sin. The name Satan derives from the Hebrew word *Ha-Satan*, translated sometimes as 'the adversary' and sometimes as

---

[1] I have seen the shadow of a coachman, beating the shadow of a carriage with the shadow of a brush.

[2] The Islamic Shaitan is also derived from the Jewish Ha-Satan, and we know from the list of books that he requested from his brother that Dostoevsky was reading the Koran during his Siberian exile, after he was released from prison.

'that which opposes', and it derives from the verb 'to obstruct'.[3] This *satan*, or adversary, may attempt to thwart God's will, but, as in the case of Job, he does it with God's permission; he is an officially sanctioned opposition, not an independent free spirit, and he remains answerable to God. Throughout the story of Job, Satan can only do what he is told – first he can only harm those around Job, then when that fails to sway Job's faith, Satan is given additional permission to hurt him, but without killing him. The Devil who tempts Jesus in the wilderness also appears to be acting with God's permission, for there there certainly seems to be a sense in the Gospel story that the encounter has been pre-arranged, with Jesus being led by God's Spirit into the desert.

The idea of the Devil as the driver of human action and the creator of meaningless events is always lurking in the background of Dostoevsky's fiction. His narratives are driven onwards by people doing such crazy, irrational things, damaging themselves and those they claim to love, that some sort of diabolical influence seems to be the only plausible explanation. The Underground Man accurately diagnoses this tendency in humans, identifying the desire for self-assertion and freedom which so often overrides our conscious knowledge of what is actually best for us. This gets straight to the essence of the Devil in Dostoevsky's fiction, for he is decidedly ambiguous. Sometimes he is shown as a manifestly external presence, acting on humans who are powerless to resist him, and at other times the demonic is something within us – not possession by demons, but a hidden part of our own nature, which surfaces and takes control, to terrible effect. Frequently, the boundaries between the internal and external Devil are deliberately blurred, so we are never quite sure whether a character's downfall comes from without or within, and in Ivan Karamazov's nightmare, there is a terrifying fusion that gives us no clues as to what is real. In the end, for Dostoev-

---

[3] Most literally in the story of Balaam's ass (Numbers 22), when a *satan*, usually translated as "an angel of the lord", stands in the way of the donkey, to hinder Balaam's journey.

sky, it doesn't matter what form the Devil takes: what is important is how we respond to his suggestions.

From time to time, people have been possessed with the urge to overcome the Devil by supressing human freedom and herding everyone into a crystal palace, a paradise on earth, where everyone would be happy if only they would do as they are told. Dostoevsky was concerned particularly with two of the strongest proposals mankind has ever come up with for creating utopia, and he uses his more overtly devilish characters to point out their weaknesses and ultimate failure. One of those systems was already losing its power by the time that Dostoevsky was writing, and the other was just beginning its ascendency – they are organised religion (particularly Roman Catholicism) and socialism. In fact the two were closely linked in Dostoevsky's mind, and he saw atheist socialism as an inevitable consequence of Western European Catholicism. If this seems strange, the parallels will become clear later, when we examine the visions of Shigalyov and the Grand Inquisitor.

Dostoevsky's early stories abound with mysterious demonic figures who exert a frightening control over others. Yefimov, the father of Netochka Nezvanova, in the uncompleted novel of the same name, lives an unremarkable life as a mediocre clarinettist in a provincial nobleman's orchestra, until he becomes friends with a strange Italian musician who lives a dissipated life and meets a violent end. It turns out that he has bequeathed his very valuable violin to Yefimov, who initially acquires a miraculous talent for playing the instrument. Yet the violin slowly exerts a strange force on Yefimov, and he too sinks into a life of degradation; he gives up actually playing his instrument, but is obsessed with a monomaniacal idea that he is the greatest violinist the world has ever known. He is eventually driven insane, and dies. This vivid tale of urban squalor, heartbreakingly told through the eyes of the child Netochka, could stand simply as a case study of human weakness, the descent of a man unable to resist the temptations of drink, and destined by the sensitivities of his own personality to struggle in his relationships with other people, but over it all hangs the idea of the violin and its malign influence. The violin is an instrument closely associated in folklore with the Devil, and its presence adds a terrifying dimension to the story, lifting it from social realism to a chilling case of Urban Gothic. Unfortunately, after Yefimov's death, we hear no more of the violin. The story continues with the life of Netochka and becomes much less interesting, until even Dostoevsky gives up on it, leaving it unfinished; but the tale of Yefimov gives us an indication of the heights that its author would eventually reach.

Before *Netochka Nezvanova*, in his second published work, *The Double,* Dostoevsky powerfully introduces the idea of the dualistic Devil, who appears as a palpably separate individual, but who seems to have emerged from the depths of his victim's soul. When it was published, *The Double* was received with incomprehension and derision, but it is in this work, not the social realism of his first novel, *Poor People,* that we get the first indications of the psychological and imaginative achievements of which Dostoevsky is capable. Mr Golyadkin Junior, the double of the title he possesses all the smooth Machiavellian charms that are needed for advancement in the civil service, and he gradually takes over Mr Golyadkin's life, scheming and wheedling his way ahead. Golyadkin Junior is an early version of Pyotr Verkhovensky; unprincipled, ruthless and always capable of getting his own way.

These early demons – the violin and its previous owner, and Golyadkin's double, are thinly sketched; more of a ghostly presence than fully-fleshed human beings and this type of demon reaches its pinnacle of destructive terror in the figure of Parfyon Rogozhin, the double and opposite to the Christ-like Prince Myshkin. Rogozhin's role is laden with demonic symbolism. He is the book's spirit of chaos and destruction; he rampages around St Petersburg with his hellish entourage, and repeatedly tempts Nastasya Filippovna away from Myshkin. He lives in a gloomy, deathly house that was previously inhabited by a sect of castrates

– and what greater symbol could there be for a life devoid of any future, lived entirely in the present. Inside the house, of course, hangs that painting, of Holbein's visibly, undeniably dead, human Christ, showing the very moment when the powers of death and hell briefly appeared to be triumphant.

One of the most powerful passages of the book describes the Prince's crazed meanderings around St Petersburg; he is on the verge of an epileptic fit, he is losing his mind, and keeps seeing Rogozhin's eyes, not Rogozhin himself, just his eyes, amongst the crowds; they are 'flashing fire' at him, and he feels as though he is possessed by a demon who is pushing him towards Nastasya. Opposing this feeling of demonic possession he has the strange sense of eternity and blissful happiness that accompanies his epileptic fits, and it's as if heaven and hell are waging battle in his soul. The chapter concludes with Rogozhin's attempt on Myshkin's life: the devilish eyes step out of an alcove, the knife is raised, and the Prince collapses under the full onset of the epileptic fit that has been building all afternoon. In a strange way, heaven has saved Myshkin, because, horrified by the sight of the epileptic fit, Rogozhin doesn't kill him.

Ippolit also feels the demonic influence of Rogozhin, and he recounts his experience in the extended suicide note that he calls his Testament. He has had brief business dealings with Rogozhin, and he longs to see him again, because he feels that Rogozhin understands him. Ippolit visits Rogozhin in his flat and he too sees the painting, which has a tremendous effect on him, as we'll see in the next chapter. Afterwards, as he lies in his room, delirious and sick with consumption, he has a truly horrible nightmare about a strange tarantula-like creature – the spider being Dostoevsky's own particular symbol of death. He thinks he has woken up, and Rogozhin appears in his room, but just as in Ivan Karamazov's encounter with his devil, the boundaries between fantasy and reality are confused, and Ippolit has no idea whether he's awake or dreaming. The figure sits in silence as Ippolit lies in bed watching him with terror:

The thought also kept flashing through my mind: if it was an apparition and I wasn't frightened, why did I not get up, approach him and verify for myself? Maybe I was frightened after all, and just couldn't pluck up the courage. But as soon as I realized I might be frightened, cold shivers ran down my spine, and my knees began to buckle. At that very instant, as though he'd realized I was terrified, Rogozhin ... began to open his mouth as though preparing to burst out laughing.[4]

The spider and Rogozhin's visit are too much for poor Ippolit's troubled soul. Overcome with disgust at the humiliation brought on by these nightmares, he decides he must bring his life to an end, and the Devil, taking the form of Rogozhin, appears to have won one little victory. He wins a similar victory over Nikolai Stavrogin, who tells us in his Confession that he suffers from demonic hallucinations, although, of course, he has a lot on his conscience, and it's tempting to say that his monstrous crime means that he deserves to be tormented, in this world and the next, and forever. Sometimes the visions come in the form of Masha, the little girl he raped and drove to suicide, but not always; he too sees spiders; and he feels the mockery of a malignant spirit. This shadowy devil drives him to action; first with his plan to make a public confession, and then, when Tikhon has guided him away from that path, the defeated devil pushes Stavrogin to suicide. The Devil treads a fine line in his confrontations with men, however, for Ippolit and Stavrogin could both have made different choices, with a better outcome, and had they done so, the results would have been attributed to the power of God's saving grace – Ivan's visitor moans that:

Somebody else takes all the credit for what is good, and all the dirty work is left to me[5].

---

[4] *The Idiot* p 429 (Part Three, Chapter 6)
[5] *The Brothers Karamazov,* Magarshack p762 (Book Eleven, Chapter 9)

And so, as *The Karamazov Brothers* reaches its climax, we get a real devil putting in an appearance, or rather, Ivan's vision of him. This, we must remember, is Dostoevsky, and however fantastical his characters, he is thoroughly grounded in realism, so logically, the Devil must be a figment of Ivan's extremely disturbed imagination, but we're drawn so much into Ivan's madness, and the visitor is so plausible, down to the last little details, that there is an element of doubt, however much we, and Ivan, try to convince ourselves that it's just a hallucination. William James's reaction to mysticism is worth remembering here, for he suggests that if a supernatural experience or vision appears real to the beholder, then we must treat it as such, for the impression left by such visions is itself real, and is so strong that no degree of scepticism on the part of anyone else can shake it. In that respect, Ivan's devil is real. And if that goes for the devil, then why shouldn't it be the same for God?

Ivan's devil is Dostoevsky at his funniest. The whole passage is a finely-tuned work of black comic genius, and Ivan's visitor takes his place in a wonderful gallery of imaginary comic devils who are highly amusing, but also disturbing and thought-provoking: think of C.S. Lewis's Screwtape, Bulgakov's Woland and Koroviev in *Master and Margarita* (Koroviev, like Ivan's devil, also wears check trousers) or even Andy Hamilton's wonderful BBC Radio Four creation, Old Harry. The humour in these devils comes from the way that they wreak their havoc by playing expertly on human weaknesses, and of course they don't have to work very hard; they just push the right buttons, make a few suggestions, dangle temptations and easily ensnare their victim. They come from within our own nature, and are all the more terrifying for it. Even their hells mimic human society, with bureaucracy, rules, rumours, gossip and complaints about how things aren't what they used to be. Ivan's devil understands this completely, as playing on a quotation from the Roman playwright Terence, he says:

Satan sum et nihil humanum a me alienum puto
I am Satan, therefore nothing human is strange to me.[6]

Part of the awfulness of Ivan's devil lies in his very banality. Even when imagining Satan himself, Dostoevsky cannot resist giving us a detailed physical and psychological description, so that this tawdry, shabby old man is conjured up in full detail for us. This is not the Grand Inquisitor's devil, the terrible, great and wise spirit, the burning fire of argument, and he even taunts Ivan with it, saying that he bets that Ivan is disappointed with the guise in which he's chosen to appear, without a red glow and scorched wings. He's whining and unhealthy; he moans that he's been appointed to the job of negation by decree (presumably from God – we're not told) and he performs it with a heavy heart. Amusingly, he likens himself to a critic on a journal, who has to stop everything from being just an 'endless hosanna', and says that without him and the suffering he causes, people would not live a real, fully human life. Left to his own devices, he'd rather come back as a the overweight wife of a Moscow merchant, living a comfortably dull bourgeois existence. (It's fun to imagine the lifestyle he would chose in our own time and place...). He claims that at the moment of Christ's ascension to heaven, when the cherubim and seraphim cried hosanna, he too wanted to join in, but that had he done so, life would have come to a stop and there would be no more events, so out of duty, he was obliged to suppress his own rejoicing.

This meddling, disruptive Devil, who uses human weaknesses as the fuel that keeps the engine of history turning, is vividly brought to life in Pyotr Verkhovensky, who must surely rank as one of the most evil creations anywhere in literature, and one who very definitely keeps the hosannas firmly at bay. He is preceded in Dostoevsky's fiction by the equally despicable Foma Fomich of *The Village of Stepanchikovo,* a farcical novella writ-

---

[6] The original quotation is *Homo sum et nihil humanum a me alienum puto* – I am a man therefore nothing human is strange to me,

ten in Siberia and published in 1859 (sometimes translated as *The Friend of the Family*). Foma Fomich is a petty tyrant, who has inveigled his way into a rural family and suborned everyone to his wishes. He insists on being addressed as 'Your Excellency', and his birthday regularly changes so that he can upstage the celebrations of other family members, even the little children. He is addicted to exerting control over others, even at his own expense (he turns down the offer of a large sum of money to leave the estate), and gets his own way by threats and histrionics, but somehow the family cannot do without him, and when they finally throw him out, it's not long before they're begging him to come back. Foma Fomich may be a devil, but like Ivan Karamazov's visitor, he knows that the world cannot keep going without him.

Like Foma Fomich, Pyotr Verkhovensky has absolutely no redeeming features at all, and yet what makes him so frightening is the fact that he isn't just a cartoon sketch of evil: just as he does when he creates Ivan's Devil, Dostoevsky pays great attention to the nasty details that make Pyotr all too plausible. I'm struck by his insatiable demand for tea,[7] his habit of helping himself to food at any opportunity, and the ill-mannered vulgarity that he uses to show his contempt. In case we're in any doubt about his diabolical tendencies, even his physical appearance puts us in mind of that first instrument of the Devil, the serpent. He has a sharp pointed face, small eyes and a strangely elongated, flattened head. Words drip from his mouth like venom, and:

You somehow could not help feeling that he must have a sort of peculiarly shaped tongue in his head, a sort of unusually long and thin one, very red and with an exceedingly sharp and incessantly and uncontrollably active tip.[8]

---

[7] Dostoevsky himself had quite an addiction to tea, as do most Russians; they surely rival the English for their tea consumption.

[8] *The Devils* p188 (Part One, Chapter 5, section 5)

Pyotr Verkhovensky exerts a diabolical force over the events of the novel; every single death can be traced back to Pyotr's actions, including that of his own father, and it just takes a gentle tug on any thread of his nasty little schemes for it to become clear that everything is tangled up in one messy cats cradle. He controls events through his mastery of intrigue, specialising in accidentally letting slip facts that he knows perfectly well are going to cause trouble, then wriggling his way out with feigned innocence. He charms and flatters whilst simultaneously sowing doubt and insecurity; he makes plans with one hand and schemes to undermine those same plans with the other. He plays off against each other the town authorities and his secret cell of revolutionaries; he promises to von Lembke, the governor, that he will give him proof that Shatov is behind the revolutionary activities going on in the town, whilst at the same time convincing the group of five that they must murder Shatov before he informs on them. His general meddling and instigation of all sorts of disturbances among the town's spoilt youth and among the factory workers drives von Lembke to insanity. He urges Mrs von Lembke to organise and attend the disastrous fete at which everything comes to a head, whilst at the same time arranging for it to be sabotaged. And crucially, like T.S. Eliot's Mystery Cat, Macavity, he's never there himself at the scene of the crime – why should the Devil ever do anything himself when it's so easy to get humans to do his dirty work for him.

Pyotr's skills are displayed at their cruellest in his destruction of his own father. First he breaks up his father's long standing friendship with Varvara Stavrogina: this is a deep and long lasting platonic attachment, and despite periodic disagreements, it is clear that they are completely reliant on each other, and apparently inseparable, until Pyotr spreads his poison. He boasts to his father:

She herself keeps repeating every minute that she is only just beginning to "see things in their true light". I told her in so many words that all this friendship of yours is nothing but a mutual outpouring of slops.[9]

And poor Stepan Verkhovensky sees for himself just a few pages later just how well Varvara Stavrogina has learnt her lesson from his son:

You're awfully fond of pathetic exclamations, Mr Verkhovensky. It's no longer the fashion. People to-day talk rudely but plainly. ... Every letter you wrote to me was not written for me but for posterity. You're a stylist and not a friend. Friendship is merely a glorified expression. In reality it is nothing but a reciprocal outpouring of slops"
"Heavens, how many words you've picked up from others! Lessons learnt by heart! And they've already put their uniform on you! You, you too are rejoicing."[10]

And unlike Job, or Jesus, the people of the town comprehensively fail the test and fall prey to their devil, either individually, as in the case of Shatov's murderers, or collectively, as seen in the whole town's descent into chaos. The normal laws of civilised social behaviour are overturned, and Pyotr is always there, hovering in the background, his mere words enough to unleash the devilry. The townspeople are no more wicked than any of us, they're just ordinary, weak human beings, who are unable to see that they are being tested, let alone resist it.

The character of Pyotr Verkhovensky and the events that he orchestrates were, as we have seen, loosely modelled on the Nechaev affair, but Dostoevsky was also able to draw from his own experience of his brief dabbling in revolutionary activity. In *Diary of a Writer* in 1873, he admitted that he could have been a Nechaevist (but not actually a Nechaev) in his youth. In his biography of Dostoevsky, Mochulsky draws parallels between the activities of the inner-circle of the Petrashevsky group, and the core

---

[9] *The Devils* p309 (Part Two, Chapter 4, section 2)
[10] *The Devils* p341-342 (Part Two, Chapter 5, section 3)

group of the plotters in the Devils. It's all standard secret-society stuff – a clandestine printing press, members sworn to kill any traitor, but it is worth remembering when reading *The Devils* that Dostoevsky had once taken the first steps along the path followed by the likes of Virginsky or Liputin. Nechaev convinced the members of his secret society that they were part of a nationwide network of revolutionary cells and built a web of myths around himself, convincing veteran revolutionaries in Switzerland, such as Bakunin and Ogarev, to fund his activities whilst unscrupulously stirring up fear and personal intrigues amongst those who were helping him. In a final touch, the poem printed in the political leaflets that appear in the town is a parody of a poem called *The Student* that was written by Ogarev to commemorate Nechaev's exploits.

Pyotr Verkhovensky doesn't appear to have any true political convictions. He is nominally a socialist, but when challenged by Stavrogin, he cheerfully admits that he's merely a rogue. Socialism provides a useful entrée into the right political circles where a plentiful supply of enthusiastic idealists can be found; similarly Nechaev, although he may have had a genuine desire to bring about a better society, was clearly more excited by the mechanics of revolution than its actual results, and like so many protestors and revolutionaries, he does not pay a great deal of attention to the boring technocratic details of what should actually happen once the existing social order has been destroyed. Bakunin, who was also thought to be a model for Stavrogin, is a similar figure and Isaiah Berlin's description of Bakunin captures all of them:

There are no coherent ideas to be extracted from his writings of any period, only fire and imagination, violence and poetry, and an ungovernable desire for strong sensations, for life at a high tension, for the disintegration of all that is peaceful, secluded, tidy, orderly, small-scale, philistine, established, moderate, part of the monotonous prose of daily life. ... He wanted to set on fire as much as possible as swiftly as possible; the thought of any kind of chaos, violence, upheaval he found boundlessly exhilarating.[11]

Pyotr Verkhovensky is, even more than Nechaev, an opportunist, driven only by his diabolical urge to sow the seeds of chaos. As a side-line to his principal theme, Dostoevsky reminds us that revolutionary political circles are all too easily susceptible to manipulation by the Nechaevs and Verkhovenskys, as the deft political operators outmanoeuvre the idealists. *The Devils* is a perceptive diagnosis of what can so easily go wrong in any moment of political upheaval; the corruption of pure but ultimately impractical dreams by those who scent an opportunity for power has repeated itself over and over again, across the world, and continues to do so.

The true colours of Pyotr Verkhovensky are revealed in the chapter *Ivan the Crown Prince,* in which he outlines to Stavrogin his intentions to set the latter up as a long lost claimant to the Tsarist throne – playing on a persistent myth among the peasantry that the Tsar was a false pretender and that the true Tsar would appear and relieve the people of their suffering. There is no Socialism to be seen now, only a frighteningly naked lust for power, revealed in Pyotr's almost sexual adoration of Stavrogin and his momentary loss of self-control when Stavrogin refuses to play. He also knows how he intends go about seizing power, and how to hang on to it – he will follow the method outlined by Shigalyov, a member of the secret political group that meets in the town.

Shigalyov presents a terrifying vision that he claims is the only possible scientific way to organise society, offering a solution that, he says, eluded such great thinkers as Plato, Rousseau and Fourier. Unfortunately, despite starting from an idea of unlimited freedom, he arrives at unlimited despotism It's not what he expected, indeed he is dismayed by his results, but like any scientist in thrall to the enchantment of hard data, he is convinced

---

[11] Isaiah Berlin *Russian Thinkers* p126-7 (Penguin Books, 2008)

that however awful it is, the answer must, incontestably, be correct, because it all adds up.

Shigalyov's theory is an extension of Raskolnikov's ideas about dividing mankind into the ordinary people and the great men. Nine-tenths of humanity will become docile slaves, happy in their ignorance and condemned to a life of hard work, whilst the remaining tenth will rule over them with unlimited powers. Shigalyov wanted to achieve equality but came to the conclusion that the only way equality is possible is to remove everything exceptional; the closest mankind can get to paradise will be by reducing the bulk of humanity to a primeval, ignorant mass, deprived of their will, equal in their slavery. Education will be limited so that the masses are unable to rise above their station; we don't need anymore science or knowledge, says Pyotr, for we have enough to keep us going. Dostoevsky cannot resist throwing in a warning that the conditions in contemporary Russia are ripe for someone with ideas like Shigaylov's to start putting them into action, and he allows Pyotr to lists the people who are contributing to the process: atheist schoolteachers, judges who justify murder on the grounds of social inequality, and progressive-minded writers and bureaucrats. Meanwhile the vice and drunkenness prevalent in Russia are, he says, the perfect starting point, for such bad habits soften people, making them cowardly wretches.

It is a necessary warning as far as Dostoevsky is concerned, for Shigalyov's theory was not a complete fiction. Frank points out the connection between Shigalyov and the Social Darwinism of the populist writers Tkachev and Zaitsev (and Shigalyov is, at first, called Zaitsev in Dostoevsky's notes). Not much needs to be said about Zaitsev: it is enough to note that he defended slavery in America on the shockingly misguided basis that he thought the inferiority of the black races meant they could never survive without the 'protection' of slavery. Tkachev feared that the forces of natural selection and perpetual struggle could end up in nothing but endless injustice and inequality and that striving for equality through political or legal means was the wrong approach. What is needed, says Tkachev, is to ensure that all human beings live under exactly the same material conditions and be given the same education; this way, everyone will evolve to become physiologically the same. Pyotr Verkhovensky points out that under Shigalyov's system, Shakespeare, Copernicus and Cicero would be eliminated for rising above the common level – Pyotr's sinister term is 'levelling the mountain'.

Pyotr Verkhovensky also notes that, according to Shigalyov's book, 'Everyone belongs to all the others, and all belong to everyone'.[12] We may be forgiven for thinking that this has a familiar ring to it, because it's not so far removed from Dostoevsky's own cherished dream of responsibility for all, and again, echoes the ideas prevalent in Russian thinking at the time. The difference is that Dostoevsky's dream is founded on Christian love, and in a selfless and willing conquest of the human ego. Before he starts on his greatest exposition of this theme, in *The Karamazov Brothers,* he's giving us a warning of what might happen if humanity tries to go it alone, without the guidance of Christ. Mankind may strive for unlimited freedom, but if we try to do it by ourselves, the result will be unlimited despotism and misery. At this point, Shigalyov's society is a nightmare vision for the future, but when Dostoevsky returns to the subject in *The Karamazov Brothers,* he now examines an institution that, in his eyes, bears certain resemblances to the unlimited despotism of Shigalyov, and one which also began with one man's dream of unlimited freedom; the church.

The Grand Inquisitor analyses the Devil's three temptations of Christ in the wilderness,[13] and describes how, in rejecting the temptations, Christ has over-estimated the spiritual and moral strength of humanity and our capacity to cope with unlimited freedom. The Inquisitor, on the other hand, takes a very dim

---

[12] *The Devils* p418 (Part Two, Chapter 8)
[13] Matthew Chapter 4

view of the human race, and assumes that the vast majority of us have already become something like Shigalyov's dumb cattle. The role of the Church, says the Grand Inquisitor, has been to correct Christ's mistake, to give people the comfort and security that they crave, coupled with an illusion of freedom, but at the same time protecting them from their own weakness.

We recall that in the first temptation Satan suggests to Christ that he could turn stones into bread. Christ knows that if he were to accept this offer and feed people, he would then enjoy their unlimited devotion and obedience, but it would be merely the obedience of the enslaved, for men would eventually come to fear that without Christ, they would starve. In rejecting the temptation, Christ has given people the freedom to choose whether or not to follow him.

The second temptation concerns faith, and whether Christ should have given unquestionable proof of his divinity by throwing himself from the tallest pinnacle of the temple, knowing that if he did, the angels would save him. By refusing this, he gives us the freedom to believe, requiring from us the strength of faith instead of material proof – and I'll return to this in more detail in the final chapter, but again, it's a choice between 'love freely given or the slavish gratitude of the captive'.[14]

The church's solution to the problem of faith has been to wrap religion up in mystery, resulting in the tortuous riddles of medieval theology and the aesthetic mysteries of liturgy; and obedience to the mystery, says the Grand Inquisitor, is what has captured the hearts of the people. The pure message of Christ can only be endured by a few spiritual athletes – the one hundred and forty-four thousand saved souls of The Book of Revelations – but surely, says the Inquisitor, the weak should have their chance too, and by clothing Christ's message in a beautiful garb of mystery, the church has made it easier. Don't trouble yourselves with what it all means, says the church, we'll do that

---

[14] *The Karamazov Brothers* p321 (Book Five, Chapter 5)

for you, all you have to do is accept the heavenly bread from us. Just believe what we tell you, do what we say.

The Grand Inquisitor maintains that humans cannot bear the terrible gift of freedom offered by Christ's rejection of the temptations; we must have rules to tell us what is right and wrong, and like little children, we need a guiding hand to lead us. Recognising this, the Church, or specifically, the Roman Catholic Church to which the Inquisitor belongs, has provided that guiding hand and has taken on itself the burden of deciding the truth:

They will bring us their most tormenting problems of conscience – everything, they will bring everything to us and we shall resolve everything, and they will accept our judgement with joy, because it will spare them the great burden and terrible torment of personal and free choice that they suffer today. And everyone will be happy, all the millions of beings, except the hundred thousand who govern them. For only we, we who guard the mystery, only we shall be unhappy.[15]

The Inquisitor claims that he too began by desiring Christ's freedom before coming to the conclusion that it is madness. He wants mankind to return to an Eden where the knowledge of good and evil are guarded by a few unhappy chosen ones who are strong enough to carry the burden. Dostoevsky was thinking particularly of the Roman Catholic church, and the political power of the Popes, but religion invites the surrender of freedom all too easily, and in many ways. Biblical fundamentalism provides a release from the difficulties of hard science, lulling its adherents with easy fairy-stories about creation, shielding them from the need to understand the complicated beauties of the natural world. The doctrine of confession, as the Grand Inquisitor explains, allows people to feel unburdened of their sins, if only for a short time, but that blissful feeling of forgiveness only

---

[15] *The Karamazov Brothers* p325 (Book Five, Chapter 5)

lasts until the next sin, and the more sins that can be contrived, the sooner the need for confession comes round again. Enthusiastic evangelical preachers who urge their congregations to trust in God for all their decisions are advocating yet another form of slavery, teaching people that they cannot think for themselves. We all know that sometimes it can be very relaxing to let someone else make the decisions – Stella Gibbons puts it delightfully at the end of *Cold Comfort Farm,* when she says of Flora Poste:

Like all really strong-minded women, on whom everybody flops, she adored being bossed about. It was so restful.

But that's just the problem; it's restful and lazy, and by now we know enough about Dostoevsky's moral framework to realise that in his eyes, flopping onto the church and relinquishing all responsibility for our moral decisions diminishes our humanity.

The final temptation invites Christ to assume unlimited authority over the earth, but this requires Him to reject God, and bow down to worship Satan, and here the Inquisitor unveils his true self. Mankind, he says, desires peace and harmony, but we need the peace and harmony of the anthill, where all is ordered and mindless and freedom has been surrendered; we're back to the nightmare of the Underground Man. This is what the Inquisitor's church is striving for, and, he admits that eight centuries ago, they joined forces with Satan to try to achieve it, proclaiming themselves rulers of the world.[16] This is one version

---

[16] Dostoevsky is presumably referring here specifically to the assertion of temporal power by the medieval Popes, which began during the rule of Gregory VII in the 11th century. When the Inquisitor alleges that the church went over to the Devil 'eight hundred years ago', Dostoevsky has either forgotten that the Inquisitor is supposed to be speaking from the 16th century, not the 19th, or he's counting his eight hundred years from the date of the appearance of the Donation of Constantine – a medieval forgery which began circulating in the 8th century, and purported to be a letter from the Emperor Constantine bestowing earthly authority on the Pope. There are other suggestions as to which events Dostoevsky had in mind: the fact that there are so many possibilities rather backs up Dostoevsky's arguments!

of how history might end if the Devil stops his games. There will be nothing happening, just existence. Scientists tell us that the eventual end of the universe will be a state of entropy, when all energy has decayed to the form of heat, and nothing more can happen, no movement, no change, nothing. If the Devil can be said to have any goal at all, it is to nudge us towards a spiritual and social entropy, where all human expression has been eradicated, and we are just brute beasts, slaving away in our anthill, while he enjoys his happy retirement as an overweight Muscovite housewife.

They read and talk all their lives, filled with bookish sweetness, but they themselves dwell in perplexity and cannot resolve anything.

(Makar Dolgoruky)

TWELVE: IVAN KARAMAZOV

We've already encountered Ivan Karamazov several times, mostly through the voice of his own monumental creations, the Grand Inquisitor, and his devil, but now it is time to look behind Ivan's fictions to the man himself. He is, undoubtedly, Dostoevsky's greatest and most complex character, the culmination of his life's work – which is why he has to wait until the last chapter. But who is Ivan Karamazov, and what is it about him that leaves such a strong impression? I confess that I approached the job of writing about him with a great deal of trepidation. I was afraid of Ivan's grandeur, a little intimidated by everything else that has been written about him, and filled too with a fear of admitting to the conclusions that I was drawing for myself from this, Dostoevsky's last battle of faith and reason. In the end, though, there was nothing for it but to let myself go, follow my thoughts and write honestly about my own responses to Ivan. After all, it's only what I've been doing for the previous two-hundred and fifty pages, so there is no reason to stop now.

When we meet Ivan, he is on the verge of a successful career as a writer and thinker in St Petersburg, one of Russia's polymath intellectuals. We're told that he studied natural sciences, but he's also writing short stories and reviews, he's doing translation work, and he has published a controversial article about ecclesiastical courts which has brought him to wider public notice. He is proud and independent; he has paid for his university studies by his own hard work, leaving his inheritance untouched, and he is now making plans to use that money to fund a trip to Europe. At this point, he pays a surprise visit to his chaotic family in the provinces, possibly to mediate in the family quarrel between his father and his older brother Dmitry. He seems to be the only person who can exert any sort of influence over his disgustingly dissolute father, and to crown it all, Dmitry's rich, clever and beautiful fiancée, Katerina, is showing signs of being attracted to him. In short, we are given an admirable portrait of a clever, hardworking young man who is expected to do well for himself.

But somehow, the real Ivan, when we meet him in the flesh, doesn't quite match this glowing portrait. He's clearly troubled, and is moody, introspective and enigmatic. Much is made in the novel of the 'Karamazov' tendencies to excess, and early on, Rakitin insists that all the Karamazovs are incurably degraded sensualists, even saintly Alyosha. The point is not that the Karamazovs are automatically immoral, rather that they enjoy an abundant passion for life, and a desire to cram as much as possible into their allotted time; and this exaggerated capacity for living pushes them to extremes of behaviour. Dmitry and Fyodor Karamazov both go for straightforward hedonism, indulging in drink and women. Alyosha turns his passion to Christ and a zealous love for humanity, but Ivan's Karamazov traits manifest themselves in the extravagance of his thoughts. All his energies are poured into thinking and writing, for the sheer pleasure of using his brain and provoking debate, and therein lies his downfall. It is Ivan who has been unable to resist the temptation to fill Smerdyakov's mind with ideas that his half-brother later debunks by actually translating them into all-too gruesome action. Extravagant thoughts are all very well, but they become dangerous when let loose in the world, and Ivan's theories eventually come back to bite him, first as he sees Smerdyakov putting them into practice, and then when his pupil uses them to sow the seeds of tremendous guilt in Ivan's mind.

Ivan appears, initially, to be an atheist. With his intellectual background, it would be surprising if he were otherwise, and he states the fact quite candidly over an after-dinner brandy with his father and Alyosha. Both brothers are asked by Fyodor whether there is a God, and whether there is immortality. Yes, both exist, says Alyosha, quite simply. No, says Ivan, just as simply: there is no God and no immortality. Fyodor Karamazov's response to this stark statement is, to me, one of the saddest, bleakest lines ever written, for it evokes all the cold emptiness of our universe:

Who then is laughing at mankind, Ivan?[1]

Ivan shrugs off the question. He supposes that it must be the Devil, except of course he doesn't believe in the Devil either. But the fatalism of Fyodor's question, his assumption that somewhere, someone or something must be laughing at what Thomas Hardy calls our 'blighted star' is a warning of what we will have to confront in this mighty novel, a hint of the power that *The Karamazov Brothers* might have over its readers. Why, some people may lose their faith by reading this book.

The rise of atheism across Europe in the 18th and 19th centuries can be attributed to many factors. Scientific discoveries replaced superstition and provided new explanations for things that had previously been taken as biblical truths; an urbanising and better educated population became less susceptible to the control of priests; and the fall of kings destroyed the idea of a monarchy anointed by God. Underpinning all these developments was the growing freedom to think independently, without the fear of stigmatisation or, worse, persecution for heresy. Scientific advances, particularly in areas such as geology and evolution rocked the faith of many, and we have already seen the effect of books such as David Strauss's *Life of Jesus,* which examined Jesus

---

[1] *The Brothers Karamazov,* Magarshack p156 (Book Three, Chapter 8)

as a strictly historical figure and caused many to question their previously firm beliefs.

Mobile populations can be a boost for religion if churches rise to the challenge and provide comfort and stability to uprooted people and relief from the harsh realities of life in an alien city, but in Russia the Orthodox church, which was little more than a religious department of the Tsarist bureaucracy, let these opportunities drift by, leaving the urban masses spiritually adrift. One of my former teachers observed to me that the Russian church exists in its own separate geological stratum, operating on a different timescale and oblivious to changes going on around it, and one only needs to step into an Orthodox service, with its beautiful liturgy frozen in time, to see that this is still true. By Dostoevsky's time, this timelessness and separateness of the Orthodox church had already lost it many of the aristocratic elite – Turgenev, for example was brought up as an atheist – and now it was losing its grip on ordinary people too.

Atheists in 19th century Russia were still met with suspicion and disapproval, if not worse – Raskolnikov is beaten up by his fellow prisoners for being an atheist. Lizaveta Prokofyevna scolds Ippolit for corrupting Kolya by leading him down the path of atheism, and the narrator of *The Karamazov Brothers* refers to atheists in slightly squeamish tones. Prince Myshkin blames the spread of atheism on the Roman Catholics, and Makar Dolgoruky puts it down to too many books. In his letters and essays, atheism frequently drives Dostoevsky to anger and distress, such as this passage, written in fury to his friend Maikov shortly after a huge row with Turgenev that marked the final severance of any friendship between the two men:

And these people, by the way, boast about their being <u>atheists</u>! ... But, my God, Deism gave us Christ, i.e. a concept of man so lofty that it cannot be understood without reverence, and it is impossible not to believe that this is the eternal ideal of mankind! And what have [they] *to offer us? Instead of the loftiest, divine beauty, on which they spit, all these people are so disgustingly vain,* *so shamelessly petulant, so shallowly proud, that one simply can't make out what they are hoping for or how anyone could follow them.*[2]

But as we delve deeper into Dostoevsky's own faith, and the way that he approaches questions of faith in his novels, everything becomes a bit more complicated. For one thing, much of his anger against the atheists arises from their failure to share his cherished vision of Christ's perfection, as can be seen from the passage quoted above. Furthermore, the letter goes on to criticise Turgenev and his circle of Europeanised exiles for their rejection and abuse of Russia itself. We must remember that Dostoevsky often uses atheism as a convenient shorthand, and even a term of abuse, for anyone who does not share his two greatest devotions: Christ and Russia.

Dostoevsky's violent reaction against atheism could be the zealousness of the convert, but I think it can also be attributed to uncertainties about his own fragile faith, and a desire to protect himself against his own doubts by protesting too much. He allows Prince Myshkin to tell us by way of his friend's experiences, that, when facing death by firing squad on Semenovsky Square, Dostoevsky had no certainties about what would follow and no particularly clear hope of immortality; he recalls thinking that perhaps he will merge into the rays of the sun suddenly breaking through a cloud – and this must surely explain the symbolic importance in the novels of the slanting rays of the evening sun that so often illuminate moments of spiritual crisis. Even after his release from prison, when he had returned to a life of faith, he still expresses doubts. In the letter to his friend N.D. Fonvizina, written shortly after his release from prison he writes:

At such a time, one thirsts for faith as 'the withered grass' thirsts for water, and one actually finds it, because in misfortune the truth shines through. I can tell you about myself that I am a child

---

[2] *Selected Letters* p254 (16/28 August, 1867, to A.N. Maikov)

of this century, a child of doubt and disbelief, I have always been and shall ever be (that I know), until they close the lid of my coffin. What terrible torment this thirst to believe has cost me and is still costing me, and the stronger it becomes in my soul, the stronger are the arguments against it.[3]

But this passage comes just before his famous assertion that if Christ is proven to be outside the truth, he would rather remain with Christ. It strikes me that in the simple hell of the prison camp, it was easy for Dostoevsky to believe, and to take the much needed comfort that faith can bring, but on his return to the complexities of the real world, he is afraid that his new-found faith will desert him.

In light of this, it's no wonder that Dostoevsky is remarkably kind to his suffering fictitious atheists, creating not monsters, but intelligent, thoughtful and unforgettable characters, such as Ippolit, Kirilov and Ivan, disturbing in their torments, but driven by a desire to do good. They exist in the murky borderlands between faith and reason, and Dostoevsky tests them by putting them into situations where they are forced to confront the God that they think they have denied. Atheists also command a degree of respect for the fact that they have at least made some effort to think about spiritual matters. Father Tikhon, echoing the angel in the Book of Revelations who condemns the "lukewarm", remarks to Nikolai Stavrogin that complete atheism is better than lazy indifference, and he is certain that the confirmed atheist is only one step below the most ardent believer; and Father Zossima (perhaps unhelpfully) tells Ivan that he should give thanks that God has given him a questioning soul.

Like Ivan, Ippolit (*The Idiot*) and Kirilov (*The Devils*) are young, clever, rootless young men, not wealthy, but unencumbered by the constraints of land or family, and they are typical of a Russian social group that has been given the label *raznochintsy*. The word literally means 'different ranks' and has had various

---

[3] *Selected Letters* p68 (15 February-2 March, 1854, to N.D. Fonvizina)

definitions since it was first coined in the time of Peter the Great, but has generally been used as a term for lumping together people who didn't fit clearly into any other category. By the 19th century, it was being used to describe people of non-noble origin who weren't serfs, and it took on a socio-political meaning as the strict legal definitions of earlier times fell into disuse. Typically the *raznochintsy* were the sons of the petty-bourgeoisie, such as lower-ranking bureaucrats, freed serfs or priests; men at the lower end of the social ladder, but, crucially, who had acquired an education far beyond what might be expected of them. Lacking any official rank in what was still a rigidly hierarchical society, the *raznochintsy* intellectuals naturally clustered together and tended towards radical politics and thought; the best-known living member of this group was the critic Vessarion Belinsky, whilst in literature they are represented by Turgenev's Bazarov, by the characters of Chernyshevsky's novel *What is to be Done,* and, of course Raskolnikov, the Underground Man, Ippolit and Kirilov.[4]

Ippolit is forced into a direct and violent confrontation with the idea of God. He's a nihilist, and claims, logically, to be an atheist, since God, of course, has to be rejected along with all other metaphysics and abstract ideas. Dostoevsky, we recall, agreed with those who said that true socialism and belief in God were utterly incompatible, for socialism relies entirely on earthly resources for mankind's salvation. As with Ivan, however, Ippolit's spiritual outlook is not actually stark unbelief, but rebellion. In his Confession, he acknowledges the possibility that there is a 'higher power' which created him and which will destroy him, and that his own existence serves to play some infinitesimally small part in a grander scheme of things – a throwback to the romantic ideas of the previous generation. He thinks he's supposed to accept this with humility and play his part, but it's the question of freedom again, and Ippolit desperately wants to

---

[4] Ivan Karamazov himself is not, strictly speaking, a *raznochinets* because his father owns land, but his rootless upbringing, and his intellectual outlook make him, let's say, an honorary member of the class.

resist being a cog in a machine. He's dying of consumption and only has a few weeks to live, and the only way he can see of rebelling against the preordained plan is to shoot himself before he dies of natural causes.

Ippolit's higher power, whatever it is, is not a loving god, but something more akin to the terrible senseless power of nature, red in tooth and claw, and he can't bear the idea of it getting its own way. Talking about the Holbein painting of Christ in the Tomb that looms over the novel, he says:

Here one cannot help but wonder that if death is so terrible and the laws of nature so powerful, how may they be overcome? How may they be overcome now if they hadn't been overcome even by him who during his lifetime had commanded nature and it had obeyed him. ... At the sight of this picture nature appears as a huge, implacable and mute monster, or, more accurately, and strange as it may sound, as some enormous machine of the very latest construction, which had grabbed, crushed and devoured – mindlessly and brutally – an exquisite and priceless Being. ... This picture appears to represent the idea of that dark, menacing, mindlessly timeless force which holds sway over everything and pervades us insidiously.[5]

The suicide attempt is Ippolit's act of resistance against the dumb beast. He defiantly asks whether anyone up there will care if he refuses to wait for a few more weeks to die a natural death, and in any case, should he be judged if he has failed to understand the designs of the eternal? Everything Ippolit says is intensified by his uncontrollable rage that he is dying so young, and by his jealousy of the living. In an exquisite moment of compassion, Myshkin shows that he understands this, and gently chides him not to begrudge the living their happiness. In the end though, Ippolit fails to destroy himself because he forgets to load his gun properly, and he is carried away in hysterical sobs. There

---

[5] *The Idiot* p427 (Part Three, Chapter 6)

is always a chance of a reprieve, says Dostoevsky, and who knew better than he that life is never over until the higher power decrees that it has to be. The reprieve has little effect though, for if Ippolit's survival has any purpose, it is a devilish one, as his vicious gossip and petty troublemaking play their own little part in driving the novel towards its tragic conclusion.

Ippolit's rebellion against God is a juvenile rage, but when we meet Kirilov, in *The Devils,* we find that Dostoevsky's next great spiritual rebel is has calmly thought his way to a chillingly logical conclusion. He pushes the reasoning of the left-Hegelians to absurdity: God is merely an idea onto which humanity projects itself, he says. Therefore, if God is just my human characteristics, I am God. And if I am God, then I can destroy God forever by killing myself. He further refines his argument by explaining that God is constructed from our pain and terror, so therefore suicide can only destroy God if it is undertaken without fear. Kirilov the man-god will, therefore, through his act of self-annihilation, release mankind from the fear of death, time will stop and all will become good. He has moments when he sees this future clearly, visions of eternal harmony that are not unlike the aura that precedes Prince Myshkin's fits (indeed, when Kirilov tells Shatov about these flashes of glory, Shatov warns him that he may be epileptic). The dream of destroying God through self-destruction is a desperate hope though, and deep down, Kirilov knows it, because he eventually admits that Christ the god-man made the same attempt at sacrificing himself for mankind's salvation and failed miserably.

If the laws of nature did not spare even Him, if they did not spare their own miracle, and made even Him live in the midst of lies and die for a lie, then the whole planet is a lie and is based on a lie and stupid mockery. So the very laws of the planet are a lie and a farce of the devil. What, then, is there to live for?[6]

---

[6] *The Devils* p614 (Part Three, Chapter 6, section 2)

And so, when it comes to the final act, Kirilov funks it and his suicide becomes a grotesque farce. In a gesture worthy of any utilitarian, Kirilov has agreed to make his death useful to Peter Verkhovensky's group of conspirators by killing himself whenever it is convenient to them and leaving a note taking sole blame for one of their criminal acts. In the end though, the crime to which Peters decides Kirilov must confess turns out to be the murder of his friend Shatov, and he wavers, overcome by shock and by decent human anger at Verkhovensky's disgusting action, and suddenly alert to the wider implications of his offer. Peter, ever the cynic, has to work Kirilov back up into his exalted philosophical state, letting him talk through his ideas again until he finally signs the letter. At this point of course, Kirilov now has no choice but to kill himself – if he doesn't, then Peter will either shoot him himself, or (more likely) hand him and his incriminating letter over to the police. Thus Kirilov's lofty ideas about killing God end in dismal failure, and his suicide is no longer the great conquest of fear and God, but the despairing act of a cornered animal.

Kirilov has logically argued for his self-destruction, but what makes him something more than just a cruel parody of atheist humanism is his quiet enthusiasm for life. He takes pleasure in playing ball with a little child; he is kind and thoughtful towards others; and throughout the novel retains a decency and integrity that is matched only by Shatov. He has the potential to bring benefits to society in his career as an engineer, for he has apparently come to the town to work on a new bridge. The life he plans to leave is not an empty, pointless existence – he's not an Underground Man, but he tragically fails to see that he could do far more good to humanity by living than he could ever have achieved through his delusions of deicide.

Dostoevsky returns repeatedly to the clashes between faith and reason in his fiction; the Underground Man, Raskolnikov, Ippolit and Kirilov all attempt to live according to rational precepts, whilst Sonya, Prince Myshkin and Makar Dolgoruky follow their faith. These are mere skirmishes though, preparations for the battle that rages through *The Karamazov Brothers*, where everyone is called upon to make leaps of faith, to throw themselves into the unknown, to accept that there isn't always a rational explanation for everything, or to understand that the obvious answer isn't always the correct answer. These struggles affect the actions of Alyosha, Grushenka, Katerina, Dmitry and even silly little Lise. Only the most boorish characters never suffer from a moment of doubt: Rakitin, Mrs Khokhlakova, Smerdyakov and Father Ferapont live in smug certainty. It is in Ivan Karamazov, however, that the struggle reaches its climax.

To begin with, we soon discover that Ivan's outright denial of God over the brandy was just teasing, and when he has the opportunity to sit down quietly with Alyosha and talk properly, the truth emerges. He begins with what is now the familiar proposition that God may exist, or he may have been invented by man, but he marvels over how such a 'savage and vicious animal as man' could possibly have come up with the noble, beautiful idea that is God. Ivan then develops this further by talking about mankind's understanding of the universe; he's living in a time when mathematicians such as Nikolai Lobachevksy and Bernhard Riemann were exploring beyond the bounds of the simple, three-dimensional universe as laid out in Euclid's geometrical theorem, and by doing so, they prepared the ground for the elaborate beauties of twentieth century maths and physics. Showing the same egoism as Ippolit who could not comprehend his impending destruction, Ivan says that if he, Ivan Karamazov cannot understand these mathematical imaginings, then how can he possibly understand the God who created it all. Unlike Ippolit, however, Ivan is led by his incomprehension to admit to the existence and divine purpose of God. It's a position taken by many scientists, particularly physicists, who, when faced with the incredible and beautiful complexities of the universe and of mathematics, find themselves turning to God, and Ivan returns to this again later, in the course of the Grand Inquisitor poem:

Freedom, science and independence of spirit will lead them into such a labyrinth and confront them with such miracles and such insoluble mysteries that some of them, intractable and savage, will destroy themselves, while others, intractable but less strong, will destroy one another; and those who remain, feeble and unhappy, will crawl up to our feet and will cry out to us, "Yes, you were right, you alone held his secret, and we are returning to you: save us from ourselves."[7]

The idea that mankind cannot handle the knowledge and the marvels of science is dangerously attractive. I am married to an astronomer, and he has taught me to see the strange beauty of the universe, but contemplating such wonders whilst also trying to grasp the dazzling science can be too much at times. A big bang? The entire mass of the universe exploding out of one infinitely small particle? What came before that? Oh, time didn't exist, so you can't ask that question. Or, at the other end of the scale, consider the intricate wonders of natural selection, evolution and genetics a system of such perfect elegance and beauty, but how could that happen on its own, apparently arising from nothing? It's all too easy to run away from the beautiful but hard truths of science, and seek refuge in the arms of a god who has the answer to all the tough questions, and this is what Ivan thinks he would like to do.

His problem, however, lies with the world that God has created. As we've seen, Ivan is caught up in the great dilemma of loving humanity so much that its suffering, represented particularly by the suffering of innocent children, is too much for him to bear, and he wraps this despair up into his formula about believing in God but returning his ticket to God's paradise. He wants to stay rooted in the earthly world of Euclidean geometry, because in that world he is not called on to experience a paradise built on suffering, and he does not have to face things that he

---

[7] *The Karamazov Brothers* p324 (Book Five, Chapter 5)

cannot understand. It's an attempt to bundle up faith and reason into a single package, and it doesn't work.

The Grand Inquisitor poem, which ends with the Inquisitor showing Christ out of the door and commanding him never to return, is another response to the difficulties posed by God's world of freedom, a response that leads to the rejection of God. The cruel enslavement of the masses that the Inquisitor proposes is not Ivan's own preferred solution to the problem – as he says immediately afterwards to Alyosha, he's not about to run off with the Jesuits – but the poem has given him a way of working through and analysing his apprehensions about our God-given freedom to create a world of suffering. In writing the Grand Inquisitor, Ivan is trying to find out whether there is a way in which Christ's uncompromising freedom can be tamed, because it is too much for ordinary weak humans to bear, but he comes to the conclusion that the price of freedom is too great, and that you cannot make Christ's message easier and still believe in it. His Inquisitor is a man who professes to love humanity but who has given his soul over to the Devil, a man who, only the day before his meeting with Christ, has burned a hundred heretics at the stake. This is what his love has brought him to do.

Ivan has an ardent desire to make sense of the world, but he analyses everything too much, and quite frankly, gets himself into rather a muddle. He searches for proof, but he doesn't understand that faith has to be irrational and detached from reality, otherwise it isn't faith, it's knowledge. Dostoevsky shows us the real instinctive faith of the Russian peasants when they visit Father Zossima and contrasts their simplicity with Mrs Khokhlakova who prattles meaninglessly and is more interested in parading her doubts like a fashionable hat than actually listening to the elder's advice. Alyosha's faith undergoes its greatest test when it comes up against the hard scientific reality of a rotting corpse, but he is a being who is built for faith, because he has the mental ability to surrender to the unknowable. In the end, it doesn't matter whether this surrender is really to an external higher power or whether its his own subconscious that takes control; for Alyosha it's real and it provides him with comfort and strength. Ivan, on the other hand, is trying to force himself to do something for which his particular psychological make-up isn't suited. He can't simply let go and believe, it's not the way he is, and his devil says as much to him:

What's the good of believing against your will? Anyway, when it comes to believing, no proof is any use, least of all material proof. Thomas believed not because he saw the risen Christ, but because he already wanted to believe.[8]

Dostoevsky's faith, as we have seen, was built on a passionate love of Christ, but his emphasis on Christ's qualities as a perfect human being, and his perceptive and sympathetic treatment of people who are wrestling with doubt suggest to me that maybe, just maybe, Dostoevsky could also have been one of those who wants to believe and is reluctant to admit to himself that in fact God does not exist for him. Alyosha, coming from the view of someone with a living faith, thinks that Ivan is an unbeliever who secretly does believe and that he will only find happiness when he confesses his faith, and he doesn't see that in fact the opposite is true: Ivan is trying too hard to conjure something up from nothing, and what he needs to do is actually stop trying so hard to believe. Ivan, and perhaps Ippolit and Kirilov too, would be much happier if they were to follow the advice given in an advertising campaign in 2009 by the British Humanist Society:

There's probably no God.
Now stop worrying and enjoy your life.

Enjoying life is something that Ivan really should be good at, because before the solemn gloom of the Grand Inquisitor, we're treated to a view of the other side of Ivan: his ability to drop all reason and follow his instinct in a wholehearted love of life. I

---

[8] *The Karamazov Brothers* p798 (Book Eleven, Chapter 9)

cannot help but smile and be swept away by Ivan's seductive hymn of praise, sharing his visceral joy in the beauties and pleasures that surround us – his delight in blue skies, the sticky green leaves of Spring, and a good fish soup. The shared feeling of joy becomes all the more intense on subsequent readings, when you have full knowledge of the darkness that Ivan will soon face. He attributes this love of life to the Karamazov side of his nature, and assumes that this can only be a bad thing, but actually, the 'base Karamazov force' that seems to blight the entire family is really nothing more than a burning enthusiasm for life, and what matters is whether that power is channelled into good, as it is in Alyosha and, eventually Dmitry, or whether it drives a life of sensuality and vice as it does for their father Fyodor. Ivan seems uniquely susceptible to both possibilities; he intends to enjoy the blue skies and sticky green leaves until he is thirty, then he will 'dash the cup to the ground' (a reminder, too, of just how young these boys are). It's easy to infer from this that he intends to kill himself, but what he really means, as Alyosha understands, is that once he reaches thirty, he will surrender to the darker, vicious side of his nature, abandoning the love of good things in favour of nastiness.

This love of life is shared by Dostoevsky himself, and it's always my first line of defence whenever anyone dares to suggest to me that Dostoevsky's novels are depressing. Even in *The Idiot*, which is by far the darkest of the major novels, the spirit of life shines out, in different ways, from Nastasya Filippovna, Kolya, Lizaveta Prokofyevna, General Ivolgin, and of course in Ippolit who so desperately doesn't want to leave the world. Dostoevsky's own biography would put anyone's love of life seriously to the test, but it tells us where he acquired the mental robustness that he needed to survive the horror of Semenovsky Square,[9] then Siberia and the endless woes that beset his later life. On the same

---

[9] At least one of Dostoevsky's companions from the Petrashevsky circle lost his mind completely because of the horror of the mock execution.

day of the mock execution, after he had been taken back to his prison cell, he wrote a gloriously optimistic letter to his brother Mikhail. Reading it, I'm struck by the practical details and arrangements he makes and the messages he asks Mikhail to pass on, all of which give an extraordinary sense of a man renewed, mustering his spiritual resources for the trials ahead, but it is also an outpouring of joy:

Life is life everywhere, life is within ourselves and not in externals. There will be people around me, and to be a man *among men, to remain so forever and not to lose hope and give up, however hard things may be – that is what life is, that is its purpose. I have come to realise this, This idea has now become part of my flesh and blood. Yes, this is the truth! ... They will lacerate and torment me now, it is true! But I have, inside me, the same heart, the same flesh and blood that can still love and suffer and pity and remember – and this, after all, is life. On voit le soleil!*[10]

This last phrase refers to Victor Hugo's short novel *Le Dernier Jour d'un Condamné,* which takes the form of a prisoner's musings on the eve of his execution. The narrator would rather endure any other punishment than death, because at least then he would still be able to see the sun. Knowing about this phrase of Hugo's adds to the pathos of Pokrovsky's death in *Poor People* when the dying man begs Varvara to open the curtains so that he can see the sun, but all he gets is dreary grey cloud. With his last hope of seeing the sun extinguished, he dies. Whilst in prison before his trial, Dmitry Karamazov too echoes Dostoevsky's letter, declaring that he exists and can see the sun, and that even when he can't see the sun, he at least knows that it is there, and what clearer indication could there be that the Karamazov love of life will carry him through. The reverse of this comes when Raskolnikov notes the evening sun in Alyona Ivanovna's flat on his trial run, and shudders as he realises that it will like

---

[10] *Selected Letters*, p51 (22 December 1849, to M.M Dostoevsky)

that when he does the real thing – his horror at the sunlight gives us a brief indication of how far from life Raskolnikov has sunk.

The positive force generated by a blazing love for life can also be found in the theology and iconography of the Orthodox church, and from what we know of Dostoevsky's traditional upbringing in the heart of Orthodox Moscow, the city of golden onion-domes, these images and ideas must have formed part of those vital, happy, childhood memories that he says we all need. This was wonderfully illuminated for me a couple of years ago in a sermon by Canon David Sudron at Durham Cathedral on the subject of the Transfiguration. He had recently visited the wonderful Norman cathedrals of Sicily, which are resplendent with Byzantine mosaics, and he observed that in the Eastern Church, the dominant images of Christ are of his triumph and glory; the crucifixion is there, but does not have such a central role as it does in the Western church. I couldn't believe I had never noticed this before. Images of Christ's radiant face gazing down from great domes in Orthodox churches filled my mind, and contrasted sharply with the sombre Catholic imagery that I'd been seeing in my own holiday in Rome the week before. Father Sudron quoted the great Orthodox saint and Church Father, St John Chrysostom, who pointed out that after the Transfiguration, when Christ appeared in glory to his disciples, he then told them to say nothing until after he was raised from the dead:

For he did not command them never to tell anyone but "to wait until he is raised from the dead." Saying nothing about the painful part, he told them only of the good. [11]

Suddenly, a lot of things made sense. The great services of the Orthodox church are the Christmas and Easter vigils, celebrating the birth and resurrection of Christ, and there just isn't the same focus on the gloom and terror of Good Friday that we have in the Western Church. Throughout the ages, despite its own or-

---

[11] 13 March 2011, Durham Cathedral sermon archive: http://bit.ly/QRaVZ9

ganisational failings, the Orthodox Church has provided hope and light to the people of Russia in the midst of all their sufferings: even Stalin was forced to accept this, allowing the church to operate again during the dark days of World War II, and Frank suggests that the church's great Easter liturgy was a key part of Dostoevsky's own conversion experience in the camp.[12]

Ivan's breakdown is triggered by what he sees as his own role in his father's murder. His conflicting beliefs about the murderer's identity, and the clash of instinct against proof that he has to face when deciding how to give evidence run in parallel with the spiritual crisis of faith against reason that is taking place in his soul. The evidence points so clearly to Dmitry's guilt that those who love him can only have faith in his innocence, but suddenly, Ivan finds himself in sole possession of the absolute truth, and is the only living person who knows what happened. What if you were to come into incontrovertible proof of the existence of God? What would you do? Do you share the knowledge and destroy the beauty of sustaining faith? Or do you fear ridicule and mockery and keep it to yourself? Alyosha sees this connection, likening the proof of the murderer's identity to the truth of God and he hopes fervently that Ivan will give his evidence at the trial, because for Alyosha this will indicate that he has accepted God:

He was beginning to understand Ivan's illness: the torments of a proud decision – and an active conscience. God, in whom he did not believe, and truth were overwhelming his soul, which still did not want to submit. "Yes", the thought occurred to Alyosha as he rested his head on the pillow, "yes, now... no one will believe Ivan's testimony; nevertheless he'll go and testify!" Alyosha smiled gently: "God will win!" he thought. "Either he will arise in the light of truth or... he will perish in hatred, taking revenge on him-

---

[12] Frank p207-211. Frank takes the account of the build-up to Easter described in *Notes from the House of the Dead* and the camp memories that Dostoevsky gives us in *The Peasant Marey* and weaves them together into a single narrative to make his point, but offers no evidence to support this merging of stories.

self and on everyone for having done something he doesn't believe in," ... and again [Alyosha] *prayed for Ivan.*[13]

When Ivan appears in court, the struggle in his soul is still unresolved. He appears 'as if touched by decay' and with 'the face of a dying man', causing Alyosha to cry out in horror. He does give his evidence, but in such a way that it seems completely implausible, then all his thoughts come pouring out in an unstoppable stream, full of references to the Grand Inquisitor and the conversation with the Devil. It makes sense to us, but is meaningless to the court, and all we can do is read on in despair.

Just as Raskolnikov is exposed to the emptiness and folly of his theories, so Ivan's fever reaches its crisis when he is forced to see where his ideas actually lead, when they leap off the page, out of his head and into the real world. Ivan's devil forces him to recall another poem he once wrote, called the *Geological Upheaval*. In this, Ivan has imagined a world without God, where everyone has ceased to believe, and where man will exalt in living only for joy and happiness in the present world. The hopes of joy in heaven will be replaced by a delight in science, and every man will accept the finality of death quite calmly. It's a world we don't have to struggle very hard to imagine, because it's more or less how we live today: the geological upheaval has not been the work of millennia as Ivan imagines, but merely a century. The devil (and remember, this devil comes from Ivan's own mind) reminds him that any man who reaches this conclusion ahead of the others already exists in the new world, and is no longer bound by the laws of the old world that is enslaved to God:

The new man has a right to become a man-god, though he may be the only one in the whole world, and having attained that new rank, he may lightheartedly jump over every barrier of the old moral code of the former man-slave, if he deems it necessary.

---

[13] *The Karamazov Brothers* p821 (Book Eleven, Chapter 10)

There is no law for God! Where God stands, there is his place Where I stand, there will at once be the first place...

And now, here it comes...

"Everything is permitted" and that's all there is to it![14]

Ivan reacts by hurling a glass at his tormentor. And why is this such torment? Because this was precisely the conclusion that Smerdyakov had reached in his conversations with Ivan, and he has used it to justify his own actions. Suddenly, everyone's suffering is Ivan's fault. His father has been murdered, Dmitry has been arrested, Grushenka has lost Dmitry just when they've found happiness, Katerina is going to pieces over her role in it all, and Smerdyakov has destroyed himself. These are the real human consequences of 'everything is permitted', and Ivan, who undergoes so much anguish at the idea of human suffering that he is prepared to reject God suddenly finds that everything has come full circle. Absence of God can cause just as much suffering.

The conclusion that we might draw from the *Geological Upheaval* and the events of *The Karamazov Brothers* is that atheists cannot live a good life and be nice to people – Richard Dawkins leaps rather neurotically to exactly this conclusion in his study of atheism, *The God Delusion,* saying:

It seems to me to require quite a low self-regard to think that, should belief in God suddenly vanish from the world, we would all become callous and selfish hedonists, with no kindness, no charity, no generosity, nothing that would deserve the name of goodness.[15]

Dawkins uses Ivan's words to make the case that this is what Dostoevsky thinks, but in fact, Dostoevsky offers us another version. Lurking in the neglected pages of *The Adolescent*, we find in Versilov's vision a far more positive imagining of a life after

---

[14] *The Brothers Karamazov* Magarshack p764 (Book Eleven, Chapter 9)
[15] *The God Delusion,* Richard Dawkins p227 (Bantam Press, 2006)

God. It's the golden age dream again, Dostoevsky's vision of paradise that was inspired by Claude Lorrain's *Acis and Galatea* painting, but whereas Nikolai Stavrogin and the Ridiculous Man dreamed of an innocent, uncorrupted world, and the dreamers themselves played a role in despoiling paradise, Versilov's dream is of a future in which people have been purified by throwing off the shackles of religion to live simple, harmonious lives, enlightened by science, free of superstition and without fear of death. As this novel is probably unfamiliar to many English readers, this passage is worth quoting in greater length. Referring directly to Lorrain's painting, Versilov says:

I imagine to myself ... that the battle is over and the fighting has subsided ... people are left <u>alone</u>, as they wished: the great former idea has left them; the great source of strength that had nourished and warmed them till then is departing, like that majestic, inviting sun in Claude Lorrain's painting. ... The people would at once begin pressing together more closely and lovingly; they would hold hands, understanding that they alone were now everything for each other. The great idea of immortality would disappear and would have to be replaced; and all the great abundance of the former love for the one who was himself immortality, would be turned in all of them to nature, to the world, to people, to every blade of grass. They would love the earth and life irrepressibly. ...They would wake up and hasten to kiss each other, hurrying to love, conscious that the days were short, and that that was all they had left. They would work for each other, and each would give all he had to everyone, and would be happy in that alone. ..."Tomorrow may be my last day," each of them would think, looking at the setting sun, "but all the same, though I die, they will all remain, and their children after them" – and this thought ... would replace the thought of a meeting beyond the grave.[16]

---

[16] *The Adolescent,* p471 (Part Three, Chapter 7, Section 3)

He rather spoils it on the next page by saying that his vision ends with Christ appearing on the water, asking the people how they could have forgotten him, and the people greet him with an exultant hymn of praise as the scales of delusion fall from their eyes. It's a pity because initially Versilov's vision of a world without God is a good deal more attractive than the nightmares presented by the *Geological Upheaval,* or Raskolnikov's dream.

However we may dress things up with myths and theology, humans can basically figure out what's right and wrong on a 'do unto others' basis. Quite simply, it boils down to don't steal, don't hurt people, don't kill, and think carefully about who you sleep with; and this is what glues human society together. We don't actually need God to tell us this, even though the grand inquisitors over the ages, since time immemorial and across the globe, have feared human freedom so much that they've felt it necessary to impose the fear of God on us in a vain attempt to make us behave.

The paradox of Dostoevsky's fiction is that he actually demonstrates quite powerfully that the absence of God in human lives does not, in fact, lead us to think that everything is permitted, but quite the contrary, because like Ivan and Stavrogin and Raskolnikov, we would quickly feel the consequences if we were to abandon all our moral codes. Kirilov didn't need to try to kill God, and we needn't fear a world without him. Ivan's glorious message is that it is better to embrace the world and love life.

Because Dostoevsky fully intended to write a sequel to *The Karamazov Brothers,* Ivan's story is left unfinished. At the last we hear of him, he is seriously ill, his spirit broken by the mental strains he has endured, but we know that he's a Karamazov, and that he shares Dostoevsky's life-force, so we have to believe that he survives his mental breakdown, and becomes strengthened by the experience. Surely of all his characters, Dostoevsky would not have wanted Ivan to die, for to kill Ivan would be to kill the spirit of life itself.

Epilogue

With the exception of *The Karamazov Brothers,* Dostoevsky ties up the loose ends of his other novels with a neat little epilogue, very much in the nineteenth century tradition, telling us what happened to everyone after the story had finished. The loveliest ending is that of *Crime and Punishment* – a rare moment of lyricism as Dostoevsky describes the vast Siberian countryside and he leaves Raskolnikov on a river bank, a man reborn, with a brighter future awaiting him.

Like Raskolnikov, I'm finding myself, at the end of this book, in a place I didn't expect. When I started writing, I thought that I would learn more about Russia, but instead it turns out that the great humanity of Dostoevsky's Russians transcends national boundaries. Dostoevsky is at his best when he is writing about universal human experiences – love, lust, sin, fear, pride and guilt. As we've seen, he had his own rather daft ideas about Russia's destiny to bring light and salvation to the decaying society of Western Europe, but Dostoevsky's own Russians have done just that, bringing a new clarity to the life of this one Western European woman, although perhaps not in the way he would have expected.

I hope he would approve though, for what Dostoevsky's Russians have given me is a strange new freedom. After half a lifetime of church-going, a life which has been enriched greatly by the liturgy and music of the Anglican Church, I have found freedom from God; freedom from struggling with a faith that was never really there except for the odd fleeting moment. The realisation that I could admit my non-belief came while I was writing about Ivan Karamazov's struggles, but it has behind it the weight of all the other figures who suffer until they either accept what they are, or perish. The survivors, like Raskolnikov, live on because they change. Those who perish, like Stavrogin, do so because they cannot reconcile their divided personalities. For me, the admission that there is no God has been as exciting as any conversion experience, and has brought an exhilarating new intellectual freedom.

The pure, good faith of Alyosha is a beautiful thing, but the message that Dostoevsky's Russians, particularly the Karamazovs, gave me was that if you don't have it, it doesn't matter. Some people, like Alyosha, are born to believe and couldn't do otherwise, but if you aren't an Alyosha, then there is no point enslaving yourself to a non-existent God. At best, you go through life like I did, suffering from a mental itch, an irritation that won't go away, however much you try to ignore it; at worst, you may end up like Ivan Karamazov, with a mind collapsing under the pressure of doubt and confusion.

The overriding importance that Dostoevsky places on individual human freedom is a powerful message. He shows us in vivid practical terms in *Notes from the House of the Dead* how the loss of freedom drives humans into actions against their own best interests, and what is a false faith if not a loss of freedom? The Grand Inquisitor warns us against surrendering our freedom to the rigours of organised religion, but even the Church of England, which is probably the mildest, least demanding church anywhere, held me enthralled, lulling me into a desire to believe with the twin weapons of tradition and beauty, and for too long, I misguidedly thought that trying to believe was easier than admitting the alternative.

You don't have to be a believer to accept that much of Christ's message is extremely powerful, and that much of what he says provides us with a good guide for how to live, so Dostoevsky's passionate adoration of Christ as a perfect man does not actually require any belief in Christ's divinity. Dostoevsky's Christian message of universal brotherhood (and we can safely ignore the hysterical Slavophilia tacked onto it), with everyone taking responsibility for all is a perfectly good humanist case against 'everything is permitted', and its power comes not through the preaching of Father Zossima, but through the terrible ordeals of Raskolnikov and the Karamazovs, who learn the hard way that there are limits to what we can do.

It's been a startling conclusion, and one that has not been accepted without difficulty, but now I find myself, like Raskolnikov, in a new world with a vast open landscape, where my thoughts can range free. On the edge of middle-age, I have a sudden hunger for new knowledge, a desire to re-examine everything I know without trying to fit God into it. And when it all gets too much, I can surrender to Dostoevsky's infectious love of life, remembering the utter pleasures to be gained from contemplating blue skies and spring leaves, eating good fish pie or absorbing myself in the pages of a Dostoevsky novel. Dostoevsky turned my life upside down once when I was seventeen, and now he seems to have done it again. I'll have to keep reading him, and see what happens next.

APPENDIX 1: RUSSIAN NAMES

A full dictionary of Dostoevsky's characters would be beyond the scope of this book, so I have included here those characters who I have discussed, and whose names have potentially confusing variations, particularly among different translators. These variations include interchangeable use of surnames or the first-name and patronymic combination; diminutives and anglicisations.

Patronymics

Russian names consist of a first name, a patronymic and a surname. The patronymic is derived from the first name of the person's father, and will generally end –ovich for a man, and –ovna or –evna for a woman.

A woman will take her husband's surname on marriage, but keeps her own patronymic. Female surnames generally have an –a added.

Thus, Roman Raskolnikov's son will be called Rodion <u>Romanovich</u> Raskolnikov and his daughter Avdotya <u>Romanovna</u> Raskolnikov<u>a</u>

Diminutives

Russians love diminutives (I was known as Janichka by my colleagues in Moscow), but it's not always obvious which names they derive from – Agrafena, for example, becomes Grushenka, Alexey – Alyosha.

Anglicisations

Older translations often use anglicised versions where applicable – so Peter for Pyotr or Nicholas for Nikolai. I have used the original Russian names throughout, unless quoting directly from a translated text.

APPENDIX 2: CHARACTER GLOSSARY

The most commonly used form of each name is underlined.

Humiliated and Insulted

<u>Ivan Petrovich</u> (Vanya) – no surname.
Yelena (<u>Nelly</u>) – surname presumably Smith, but not given.
<u>Natasha</u> Nikolaevna Ikhmeneva
Nikolai Sergeevich <u>Ikhmenev</u>
Alexey Petrovich Valkovsky (<u>Alyosha</u>)
Pyotr Alexandrovich, <u>Prince Valkovsky</u>

Crime and Punishment

Andrei Semeyonovich <u>Lebezyatnikov</u>
Pyotr Petrovich <u>Luzhin</u> (Peter)
Semyon Zakharich <u>Marmeladov</u>
<u>Katerina Ivanovna</u> Marmeladova (Mrs Marmeladov)
Sofia Semyonovna Marmeladovna (<u>Sonya</u>, Sonechka)
Rodion Romanovich <u>Raskolnikov</u> (Rodya, Roddy)
Advotya Romanovna Raskolnikova (<u>Dunya</u>, Dunechka)
<u>Pulkheria Alexandrovna</u> Raskolnikova (Mrs Raskolnikov)
Dmitry Prokofich <u>Razumikhin</u>
Arkady Ivanovich <u>Svidrigaylov</u>

The Idiot

<u>Nastasya Filippovna</u> Barashkova
Gavrila Ardalionovich Ivolgin (<u>Ganya</u>)
Nikolai Ardalionovich Ivolgin (<u>Kolya</u>)
Lev / Lyov Nikolayevich, <u>Prince Myshkin</u> (Leon)
Vavara Ardalionovna Ptitsyna (<u>Varya</u>)
Yevgeny Pavlovich <u>Radomsky</u>
Parfyon Semyonovich <u>Rogozhin</u>
Afanasy Ivanovich <u>Totsky</u>
Ivan Fyodorovich, <u>General Yepanchin</u>
<u>Lizaveta Prokofyevna</u> Yepanchina
<u>Aglaya</u> Ivanovna Yepanchina

APPENDIX 2:

The Devils

Dostoevsky tends to use simple surnames more in *The Devils* than any other book, which is why only a few are included here.

Darya Pavlovna Shatova (<u>Dasha</u>)
Ivan Pavlovich <u>Shatov</u>
<u>Pyotr</u> Stepanovich <u>Verkhovensky</u> (Peter)
<u>Stepan Trofimovich</u> Verkhovensky
Nikolai Vsevolodovich <u>Stavrogin</u> (Nicholas)
<u>Varvara Petrovna</u> Stavrogina

The Karamazov Brothers

Alexey Fyodorovich Karamazov (<u>Alyosha</u>)
<u>Fyodor Pavlovich</u> Karamazov
<u>Ivan</u> Fyodorovich <u>Karamazov</u>
<u>Dmitry</u> Fyodorovich Karamazov (Mitya, Mityenka)
Nikolai (<u>Kolya</u>) Krasotkin - no patronymic given
Pavel Fyodorovich <u>Smerdyakov</u>
Agrafena Alexandrovna Svetlova (<u>Grushenka</u>, Grusha)
Katerina Ivanovna Verkhovtseva (<u>Katya</u>)

APPENDIX 3: READING LIST

The shelf-space dedicated to Dostoevsky in Durham University's library, is intimidating and almost scared me off the idea of adding to such a volume of work, but I think there are as many things to say about Dostoevsky as there are people to say them. I offer below a brief selection of the books I found most helpful in preparing this text:

Biographies

Dostoevsky: A Writer in his Time Joseph Frank,
Princeton University Press, 2010
Dostoevsky: Reminiscences Anna Dostoevsky, translated Beatrice Stillman, Wildwood House, 1975
Dostoevsky: His Life and Work Konstantin Mochulsky
(translated Michael A. Minihan), Princeton University Press, 1967

Criticism

Problems of Dostoevsky's Poetics Mikhail Bakhtin (translated R.W. Ratsel), Ardis 1973
The Religion of Dostoevsky A Boyce Gibson, SCM Press, 1973
Dostoevsky's Unfinished Journey Robin Feuer Miller,
Yale University Press, 2007
The Undiscovered Dostoevsky Ronald Hingley,
Hamish Hamilton, 1962
Dostoevsky: Language, Faith and Fiction Rowan Williams,
Continuum, 2008
Dostoevsky A Collection of Critical Essays edited René Wellek
Prentice-Hall, Inc. 1962

APPENDIX 2:

Works by Dostoevsky

Russian texts

Полное Собрание Сочинений в тридцати томах – Collected Works in 30 Volumes, USSR Academy of Sciences, Leningrad, 1984

Fiction

Poor People Translated by Hugh Aplin, Oneworld Classics 2011
The Gambler, Bobok and A Nasty Story Translated by Jessie Coulson, Penguin Books 1966
Notes from Underground. The Double Translated by Jessie Coulson, Penguin Books 1972
Memoirs from the House of the Dead Translated by Jessie Coulson, Oxford University Press 2008
Crime and Punishment Translated by David Magarshack, Penguin Books 1951
The Idiot Translated by Ignat Avsey, Oneworld Classics 2010
The Idiot Translated by David Magarshack, Penguin Books 1955
The Devils Translated by David Magarshack, Penguin Books 1953
The Adolescent Translated by Richard Pevear and Larissa Volokhonsky, Vintage Books 2004
The Karamazov Brothers Translated by Ignat Avsey, Oxford University Press 1994
The Brothers Karamazov Translated by David Magarshack, Penguin Books 1958

Non-fiction

Winter Notes on Summer Impressions Translated by Kyril Fitzlyon, Oneworld Classics 2008
The Diary of a Writer Translated and annotated by Boris Brasol, Peregrine Smith Books, 1985
Selected Letters of Fyodor Dostoyevsky Edited by Joseph Frank and David I. Goldstein. Rutgers University Press, 1989

Printed in Great Britain
by Amazon